BLACK AMERICA SERIES

AUGUSTA
GEORGIA

BLACK AMERICA SERIES

AUGUSTA
GEORGIA

Sean Joiner and Gerald Smith
foreword by Marva Stewart

ARCADIA

ISBN 0-7385-1668-6

Published by Arcadia Publishing
an imprint of Tempus Publishing Inc.
Charleston SC, Chicago, Portsmouth NH, San Francisco

Printed in Great Britain

Library of Congress Catalog Card Number: 2004104908

For all general information contact Arcadia Publishing at:
Telephone 843-853-2070
Fax 843-853-0044
E-mail sales@arcadiapublishing.com
For customer service and orders:
Toll-Free 1-888-313-2665

Visit us on the internet at http://www.arcadiapublishing.com

FOREWORD

African Americans have played a vital role in the growth and development of Augusta, Georgia, and the Central Savannah River Area. Dr. Gerald J. Smith and Mr. Sean Joiner are commended for researching, collecting, and making available to the general public a photographic record of African-American life and livelihood in Augusta, Georgia, and the surrounding area. This pictorial volume not only provides a glimpse into local African-American history, but also pays tribute to the role African Americans have played in this community.

Life for African Americans up to the 1950s was one of change and flux. This book offers readers and viewers insight into a diverse, vibrant, and challenging life. This engaging collection of photographs documents how African Americans looked, where and how they lived, and what they were doing during this time. Readers are given a panoramic view that records the religious, social, educational, and cultural life of African-Americans in this area. It records them as Americans from all walks of life, coping with changing times, and as a community with a rich heritage that contributed to the overall development of Augusta.

Marva Stewart
Paine College

CONTENTS

ACKNOWLEDGMENTS

The authors wish to thank the following persons and institutions for their contributions to this project: Gordan Blaker (Augusta Museum of History), Augusta State University (Reese Library), Augusta Historical Society, Paine College, Marva Stewart, Milledge G. Murray, the Lucy Laney Museum, and Mildred Davis.

INTRODUCTION

By the year 1790, African Americans were a viable part of life in Augusta. Against the tenets of the Georgia Charter of 1732, which forbade any form of human slavery, slaves were slowly and illegally smuggled into the new colony. When Augusta was established in 1735, African Americans came with the white settlers up the Savannah River to the new frontier town. In bondage, they worked in the forests, clearing land for the houses and stores that sprang up. They cultivated the cleared land or served in the households. The Old Slave Market was busy in the exchange of human chattels.

A small percentage of free African Americans began to establish their own culture. They built their own churches, their own funeral parlors, and developed their own forms of entertainment. Life insurance was a necessity, so they founded a company. Excluded from white cemeteries, they started African-American burial sites—a stark reminder that, even in death, there was no equality. Their schools had exemplary teachers. Restricted from the local medical facilities, they built their own hospital. Freedmen worked for the city fire department in antebellum days, but only in the predominantly German fire station; it seems the Germans had no great qualms about including men of color! They were most likely the first African Americans to work as firemen in Augusta.

The photographs in this volume chronicle much of their lifestyle during the years up to 1955. Denied social equality, the industrious and creative African Americans of the Augusta area nevertheless carved a niche of rich history, often in opposition to the milieu around them. Paine College, established as an experiment in black higher education, has the unique distinction of being founded as a joint venture by the Colored (now Christian) Methodist Episcopal Church and the Methodist Episcopal Church South. In the dark aftermath of Reconstruction, blacks and whites of the Methodist denominations sat down together and established Paine Institute, a beacon of education since then. John Wesley Gilbert, Tobias Channing, George Gomillion, and many others made great strides in public and higher education through Paine College. Their influence impressed the national scene with the famous *Brown vs. Board of Education* case, which profoundly effected public education and helped pioneer the great Civil Rights Movement.

Morehouse College, which continues today as one of the premiere African-American institutions of higher learning, had its humble beginnings in Augusta. Tabernacle Baptist Church, with its nationally known minister C.T. Walker, hosted visits by Dr. Martin Luther King and other prominent men. Butterfly McQueen of *Gone With the Wind* fame, the world-renowned opera diva Jessye Norman, movie actor and director Danny Glover, the

Godfather of Soul James Brown, and Lucius Hosley, the principal founder of Paine College, all had roots in the Augusta area.

Orphanages, community centers for recreation and learning, stores, trade shops, schools, churches, funeral homes, theaters, bowling alleys, pool halls, and many other institutions were established by African Americans of Augusta because other facilities were closed to them. All of this industry, born of a negative social climate, reveals the profound creative spirit that motivated their energy.

Perhaps this spirit may best be revealed in an advertisement that appeared in the *Augusta Chronicle* on January 31, 1866, placed by two African Americans newly freed by the Civil War. "We are prepared to do all manner of wood and iron work—wagon making and repairing included. We have not turned fools because we are free, but know how to work for our living, and are determined to do it. We mean to be sober, industrious, honest, and respectful—William and Jim."

Their determination to make a life for themselves and their families, in spite of many obstacles, epitomizes the history of African Americans and the contributions made to Augusta, the state of Georgia, and our nation.

One
CHURCHES

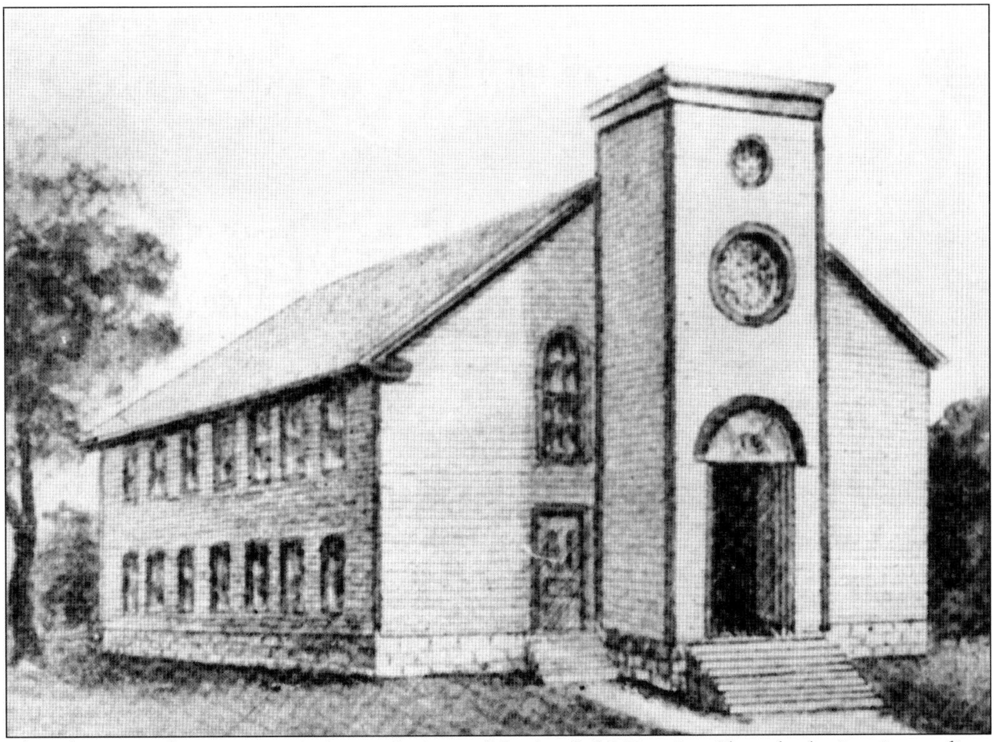

This drawing shows an artist's rendering of Springfield Baptist Church during its earliest years. Founded in the late 18th century, Springfield Baptist is the oldest independent African-American Baptist Church in the United States. (Courtesy of Special Collections, Reese Library, Augusta State University.)

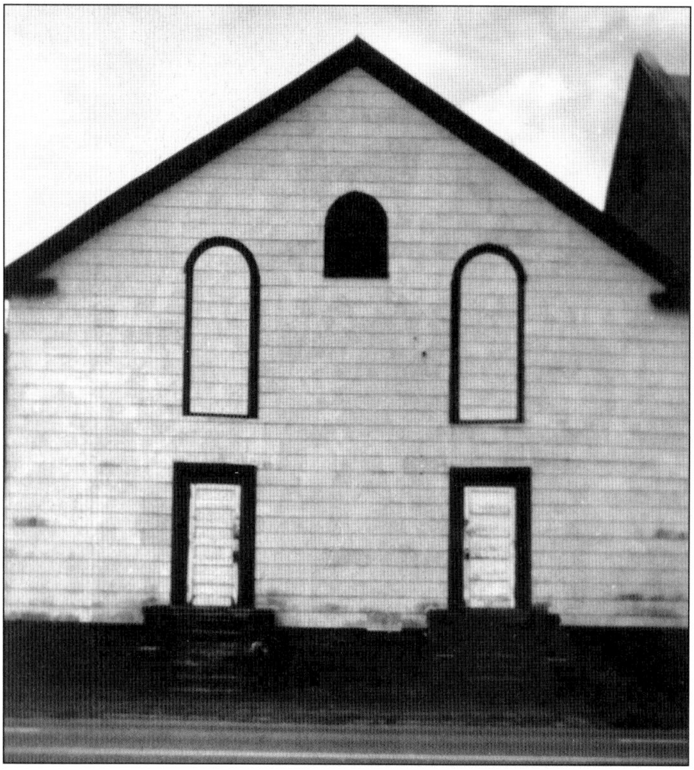

This is Springfield Baptist Church as it looked during the 1950s. The church has not changed much over the years. Across the street, Springfield Park was constructed and is visited by many Augustans and tourists every year. (Courtesy of Special Collections, Reese Library, Augusta State University.)

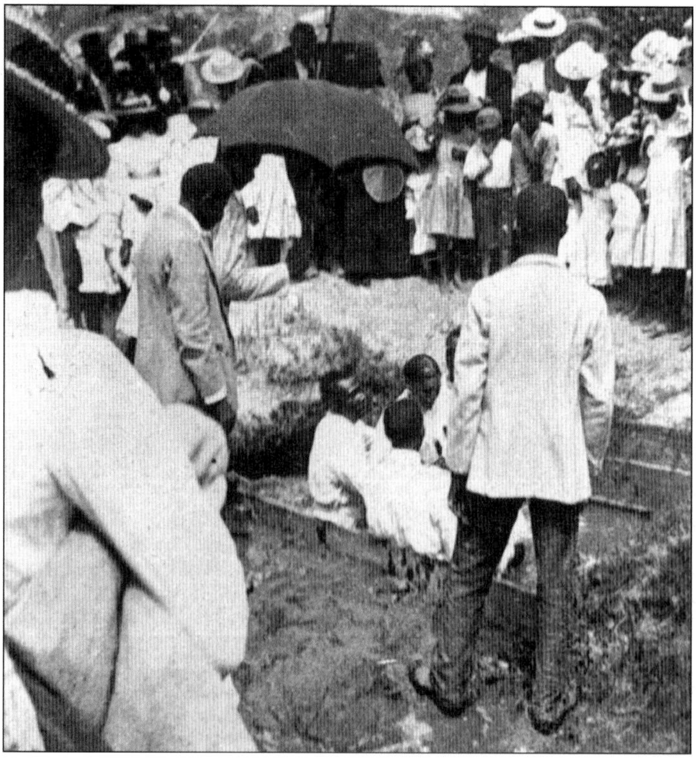

When a church was too far from a river, a baptism pool was dug in the ground, shored with boards and filled with water for the sanctification ritual. This photograph shows a group of unidentified African Americans performing this practice in Augusta. (Courtesy of Special Collections, Reese Library, Augusta State University.)

Baptisms performed off the shores of the Savannah River were not uncommon in the early 1900s. In the distance, a piling can be seen under a bridge that connects Augusta to South Carolina. (Courtesy of Special Collections, Reese Library, Augusta State University.)

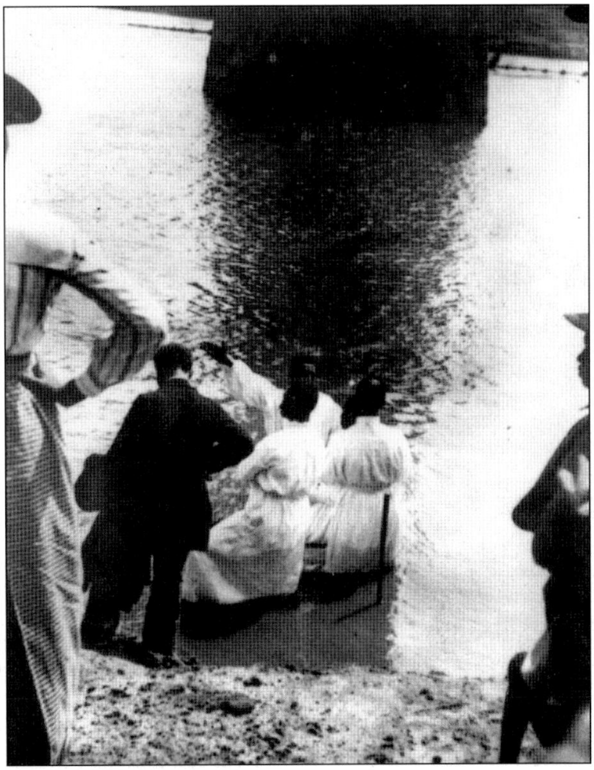

In this photograph, a few members of the Bethel AME Church, along with the pastor in the middle, pose for a group picture. These were important members of the congregation. Notice the ribbons on their jackets and dresses. (Courtesy of Augusta Museum of History.)

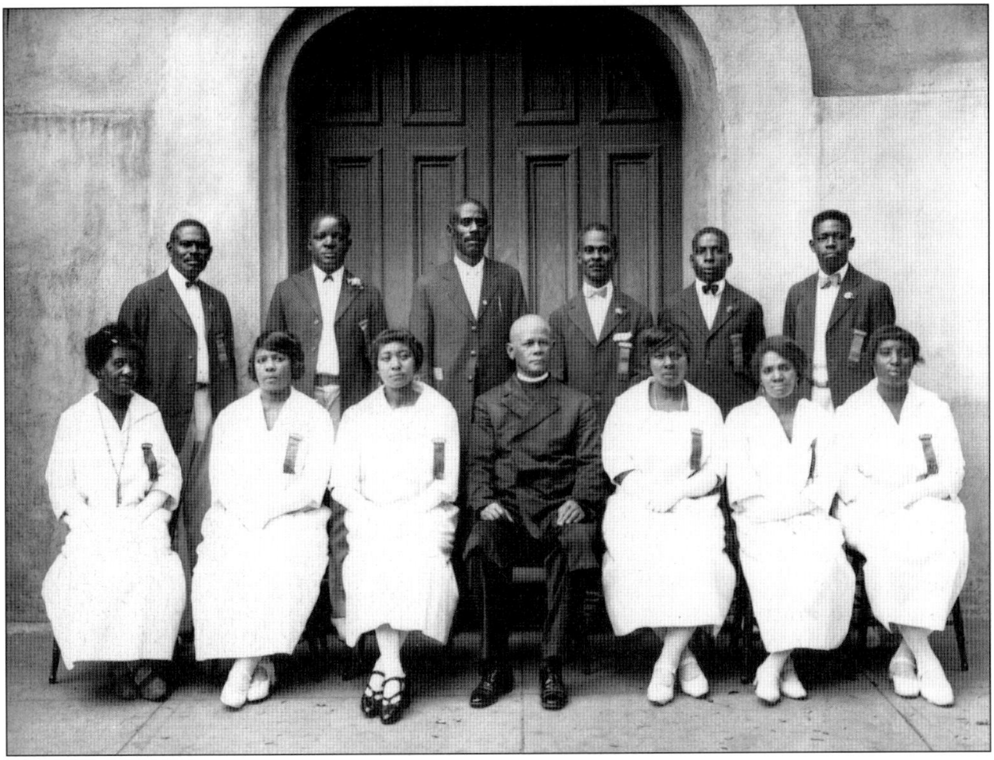

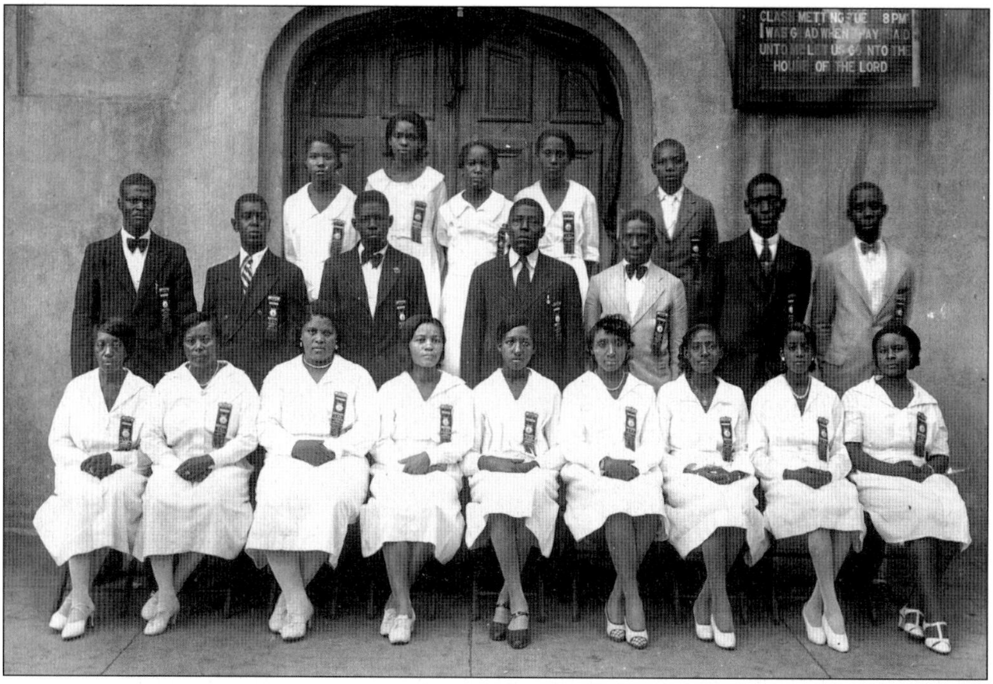

These young men and women pose for a photograph in front of the doors of Bethel AME Church. Behind the group, a sign reads "Sunday morning worship 8 a.m. and 11 a.m., Evening worship 8 p.m., ACE Lecture 6:30 a.m.," and the words "I was glad when they said to me, let us go into the house of the Lord." (Courtesy of Augusta Museum of History.)

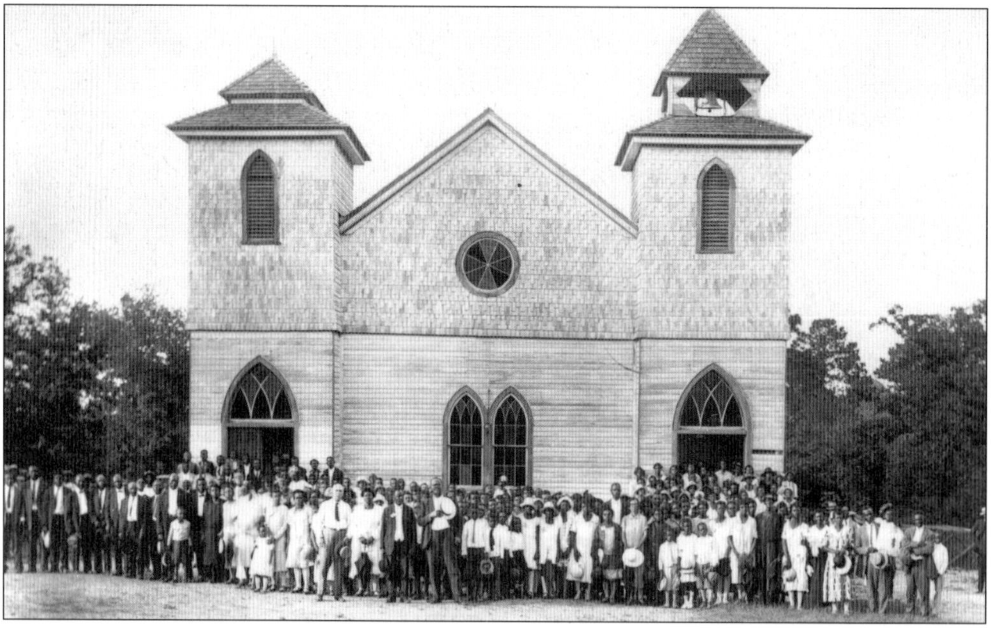

In this early photograph of First Ebenezer Church, the congregation poses for a group picture. The church is located in Hephzibah, Georgia, and shows a beautiful wooden design with two towers and stained glass windows. (Courtesy of Augusta Museum of History.)

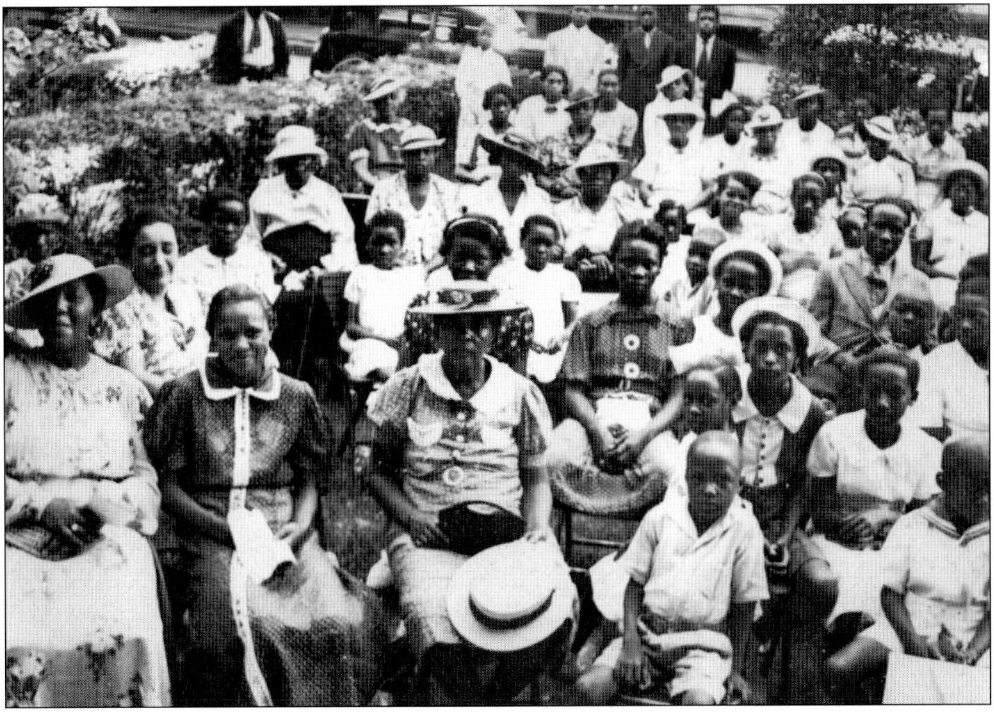

This 1935 photograph shows a Sunday school class posing for a group photo. The group's church of origin and identities are unknown. (Courtesy of Special Collections, Reese Library, Augusta State University.)

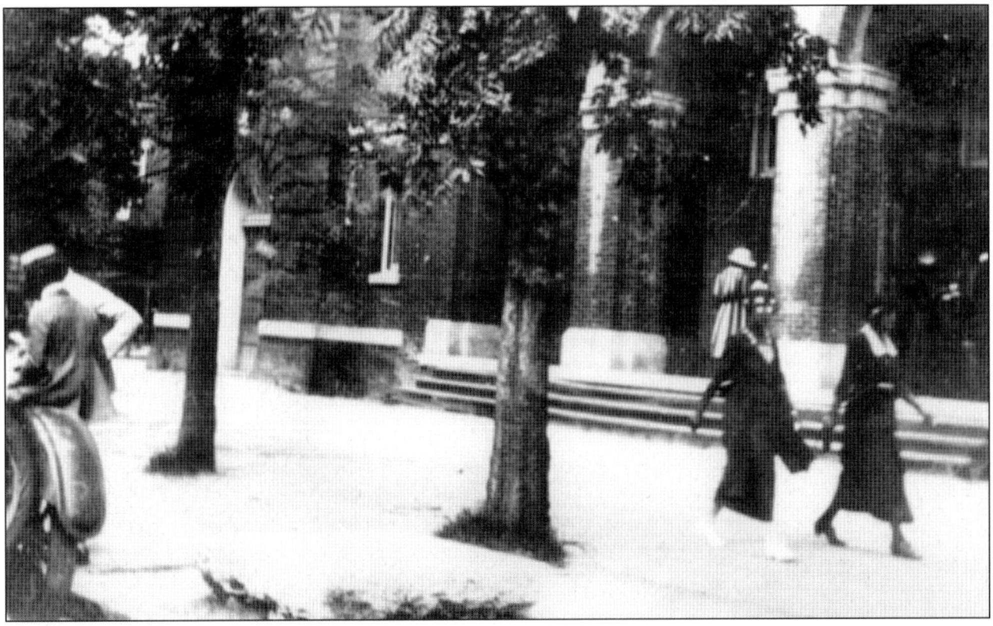

African-American men and women gather in front of a church in Augusta. Notice the vintage car and clothes of the 1920s era. (Courtesy of Special Collections, Reese Library, Augusta State University.)

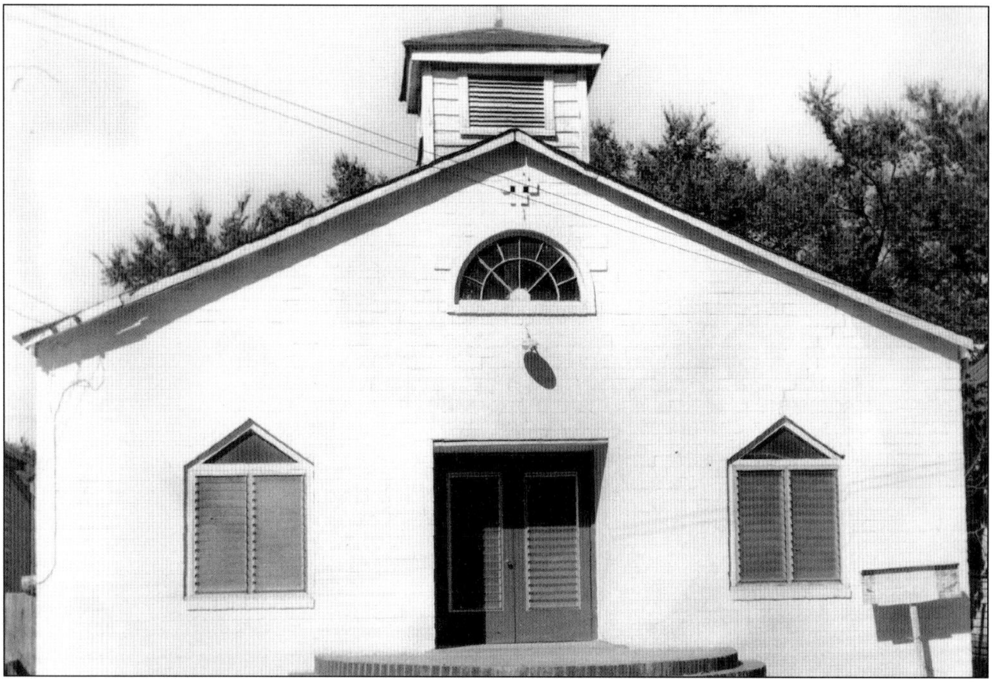

The small and simple African-American church is Unity Baptist Church. (Courtesy of Augusta Museum of History.)

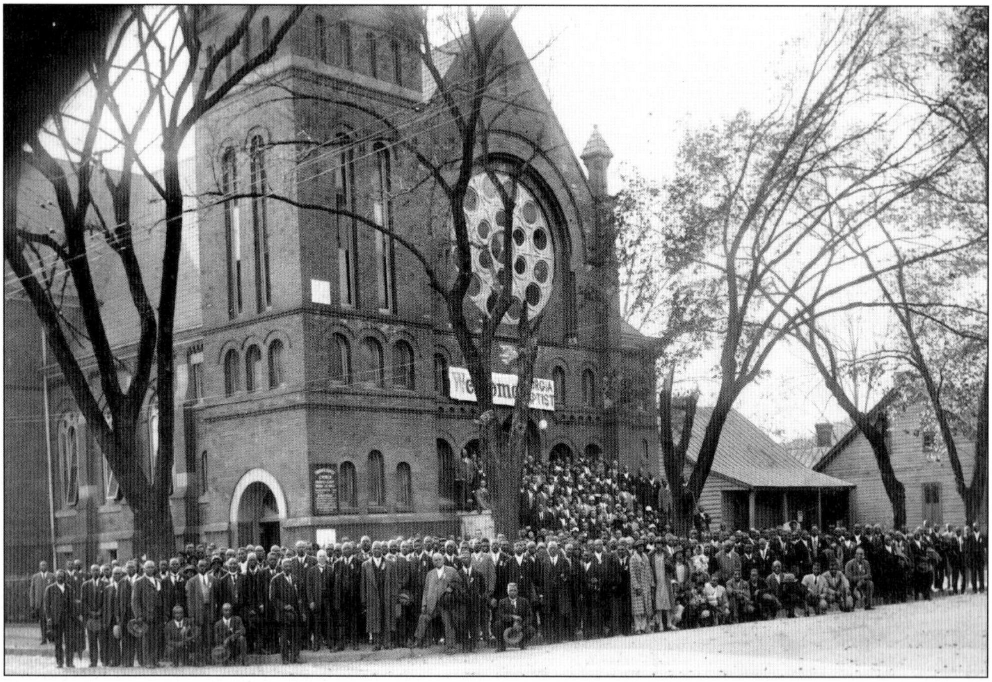

Tabernacle Baptist Church was founded over 100 years ago. It stands on Walker Street and serves the community today just as it has in the past. The Baptist Convention is shown standing outside of the building. (Courtesy of Augusta Museum of History.)

Two
PEOPLE

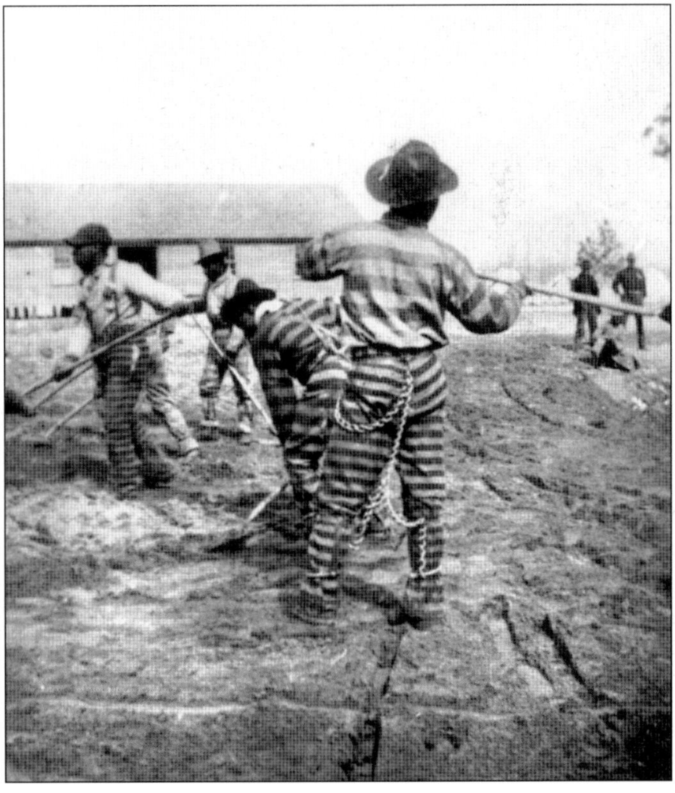

This photograph shows a prison chain gang working with shovels at an unknown location in Augusta. Chain gangs were used as hard labor in Augusta and other locales in Georgia. By 1929, Georgia had 140 prison camps. Prisoners were expected to pay back their debt to society by completing back-breaking work while wearing leg chains. (Courtesy of Special Collections, Reese Library, Augusta State University.)

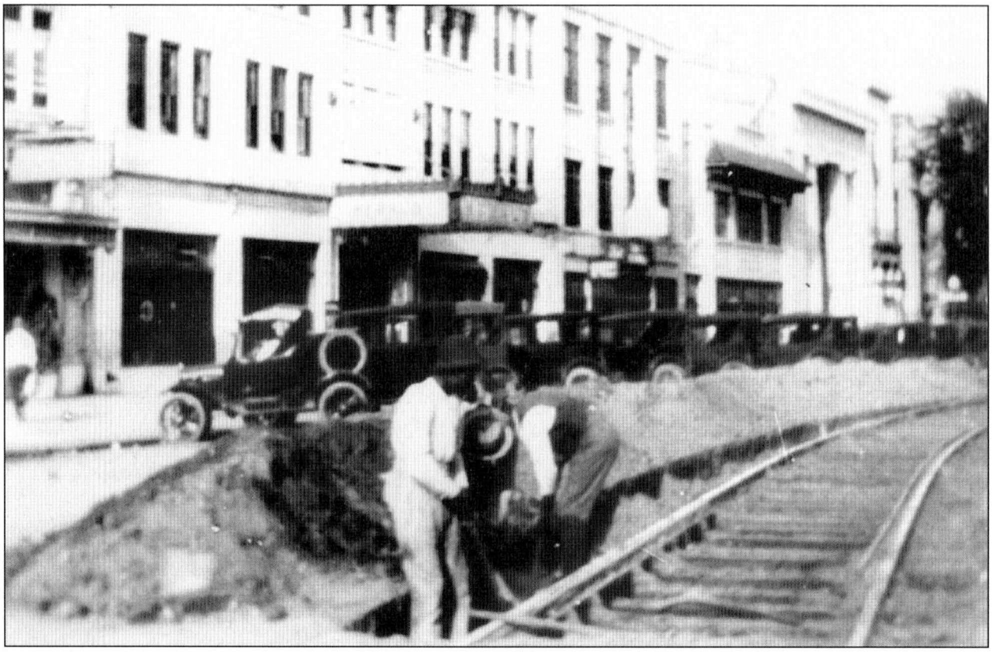

In this 1930s-era photograph, railroad workers conduct maintenance on the railroad tracks on Broad Street. By 1930, railroad maintenance workers made up some 20 percent of all railroad workers. African Americans played an important part in the development of the railroad during this time period. (Courtesy of Special Collections, Reese Library, Augusta State University.)

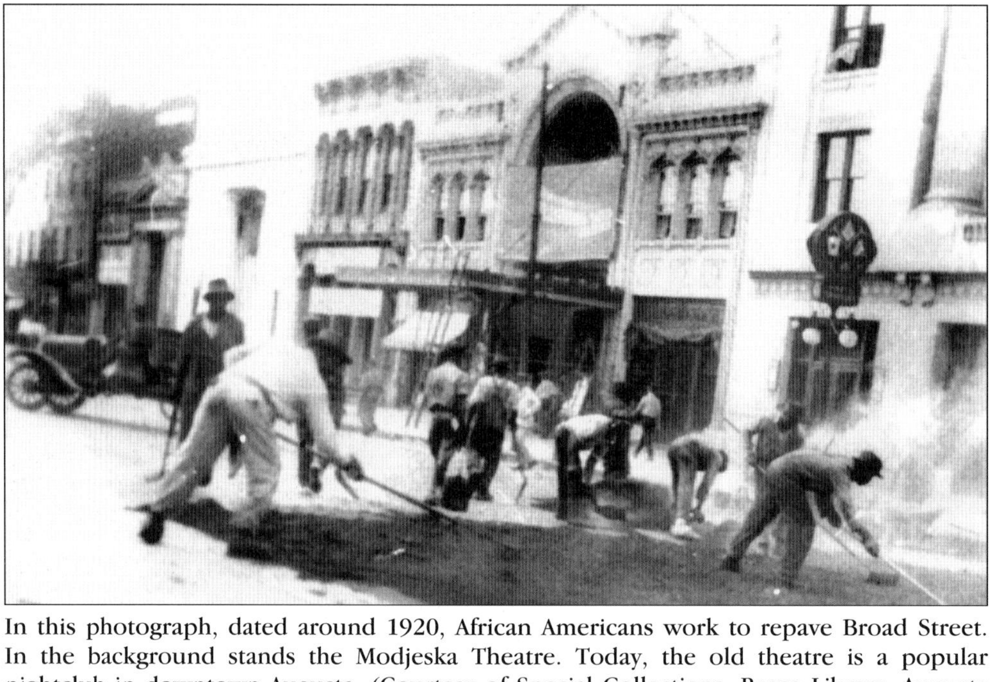

In this photograph, dated around 1920, African Americans work to repave Broad Street. In the background stands the Modjeska Theatre. Today, the old theatre is a popular nightclub in downtown Augusta. (Courtesy of Special Collections, Reese Library, Augusta State University.)

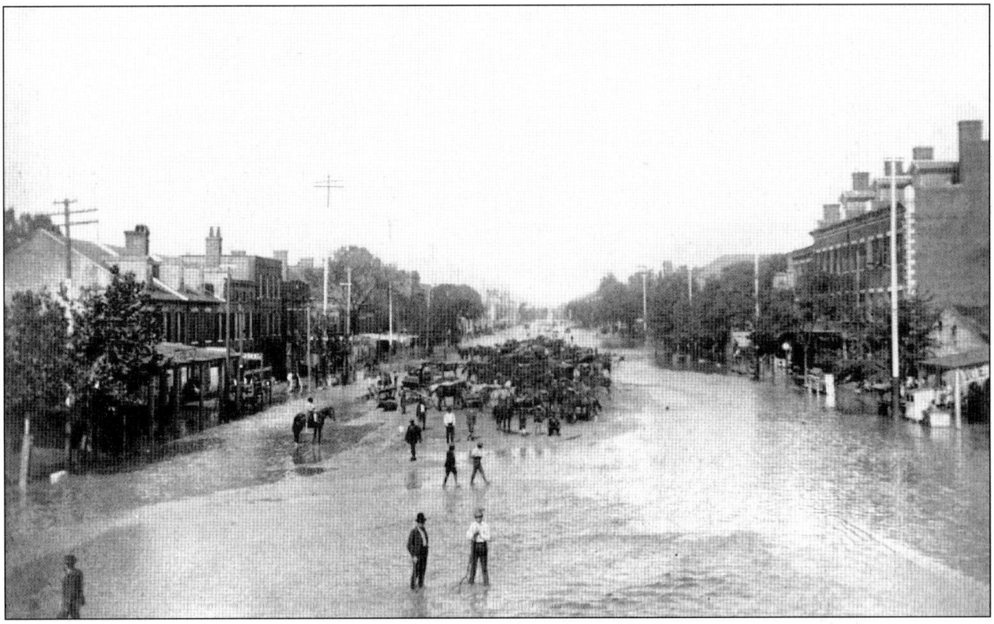

This photograph was taken on September 10, 1888, by the Augusta Photo Company at 702 Broad Street. African-American residents are seen standing in the receding water that flooded Broad Street in one of the worst floods in Augusta's history. Notice in the background that Broad Street is a dirt road. (Courtesy of Special Collections, Reese Library, Augusta State University.)

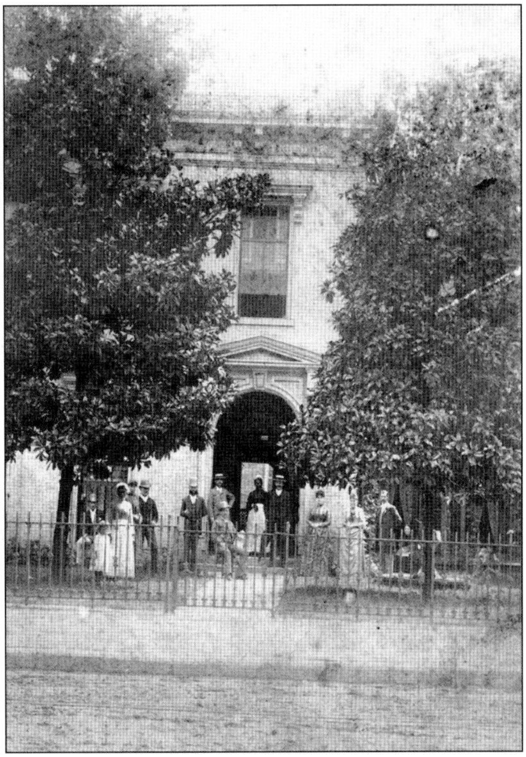

Standing in front of this late 1800s residence, an African-American woman stands next to a small child. She would have been employed as a nanny and would have assisted in daily chores around the house. The nanny is considered an important member of the family, as she poses with them for this group photograph. (Courtesy of Special Collections, Reese Library, Augusta State University.)

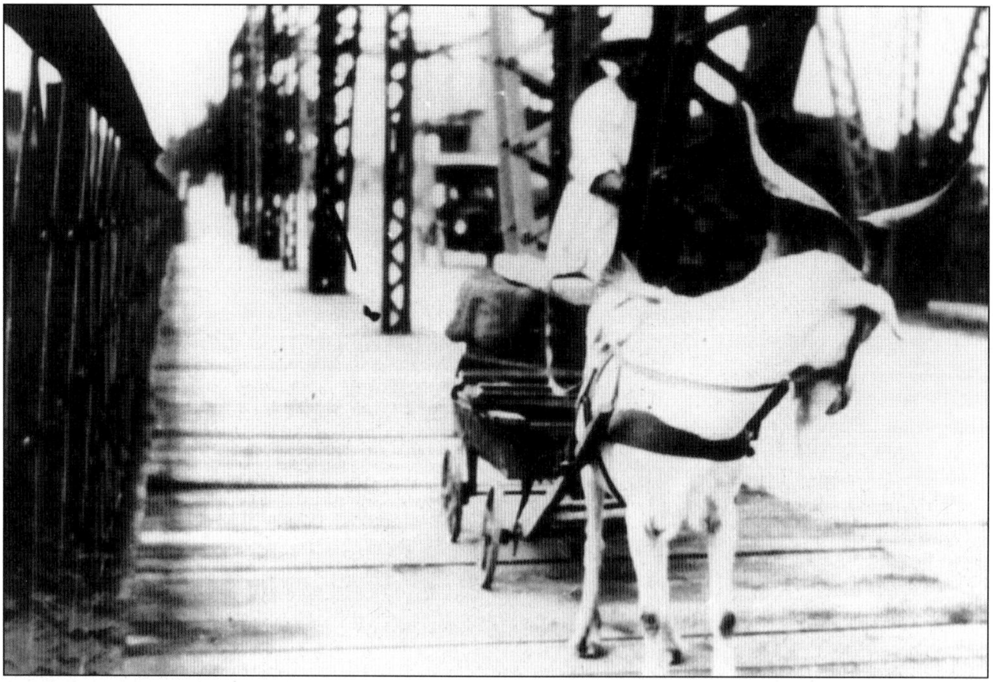

This photograph from the 1930s shows an unidentified African-American woman with a strange cohort—a goat is pulling her small cart across a bridge that stretches over the Savannah River. (Courtesy of Special Collections, Reese Library, Augusta State University.)

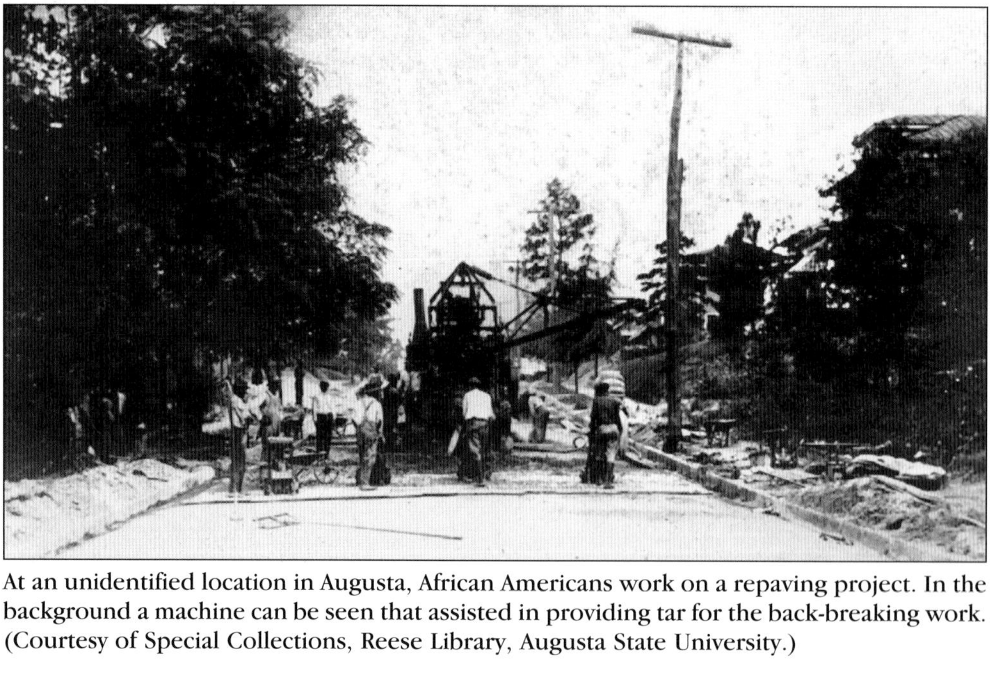

At an unidentified location in Augusta, African Americans work on a repaving project. In the background a machine can be seen that assisted in providing tar for the back-breaking work. (Courtesy of Special Collections, Reese Library, Augusta State University.)

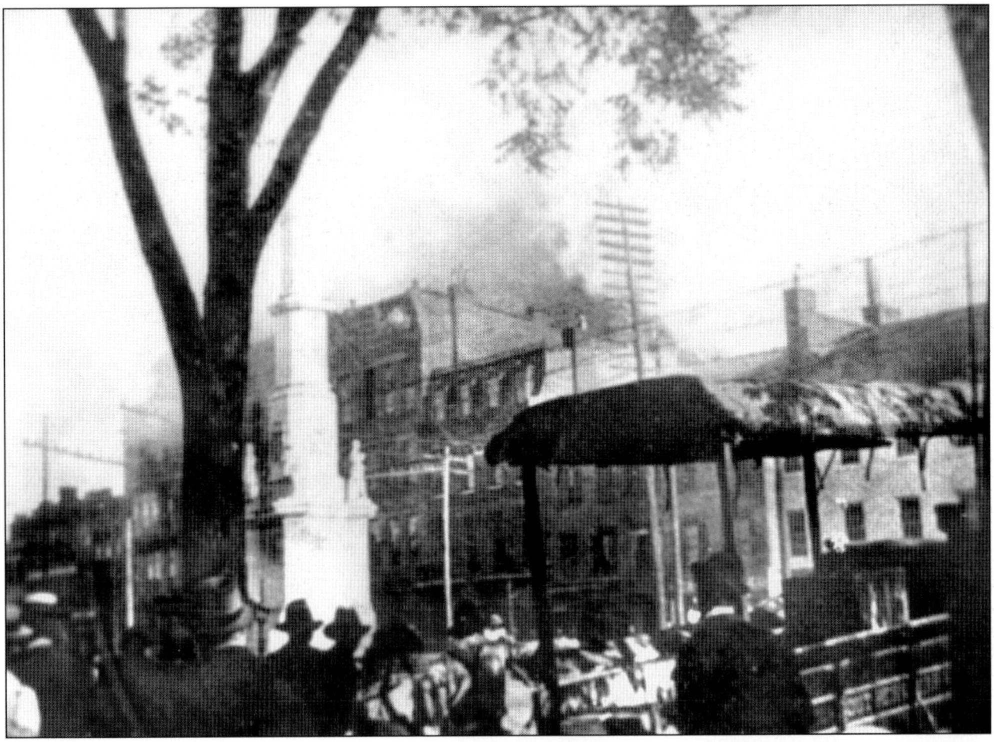

The fire of 1899 destroyed the Montgomery Building. In this photograph, African Americans look on as the flames take over, burning the building into an unrecognizable shell. (Courtesy of Special Collections, Reese Library, Augusta State University.)

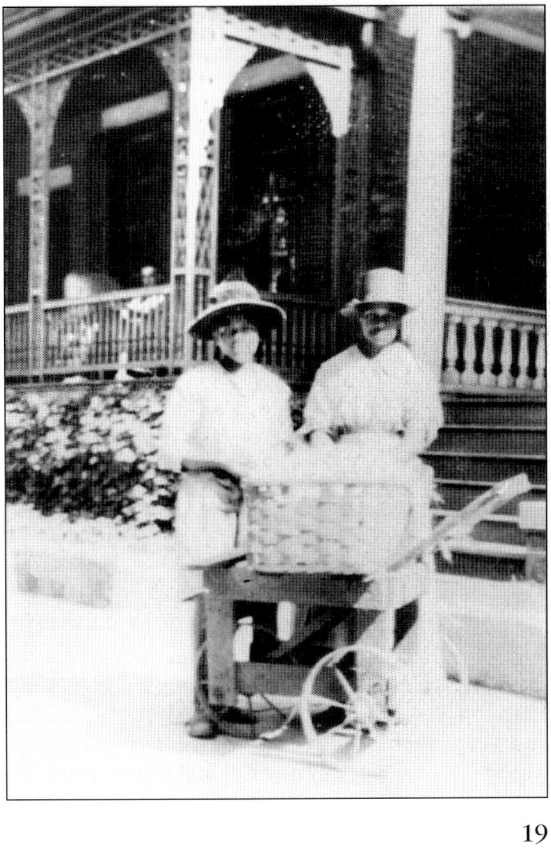

Two unidentified women pose in front of a residence in downtown Augusta. Both women stand next to a wagon carrying their wares. (Courtesy of Augusta Museum of History.)

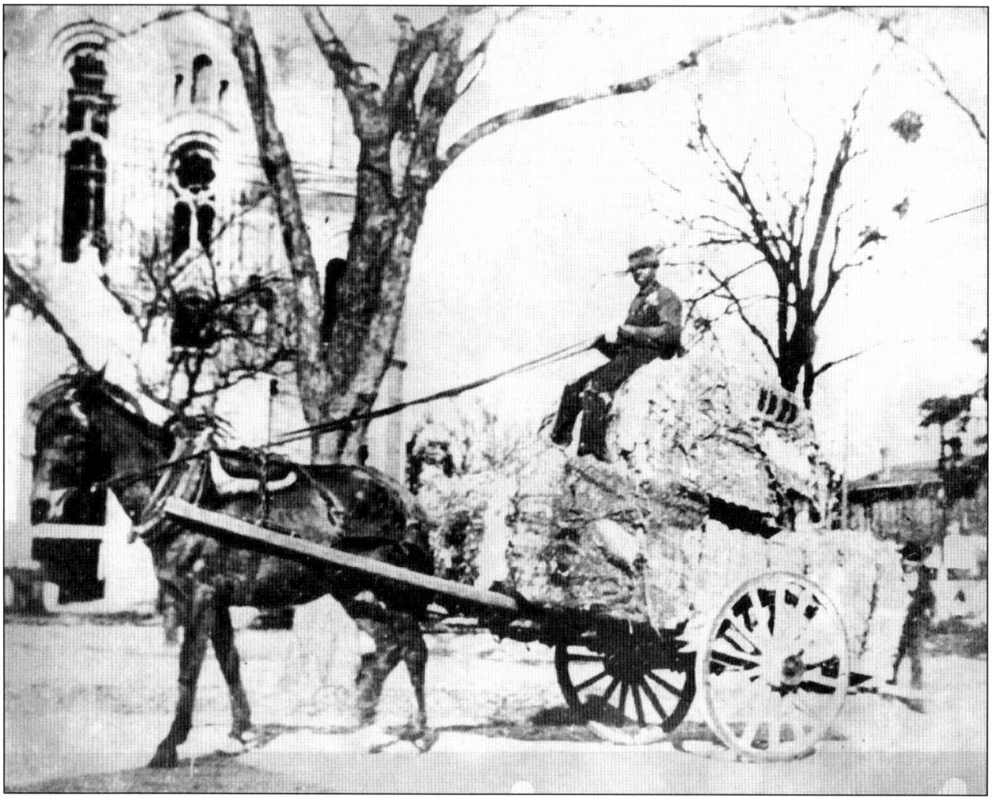

Sitting in front of Scared Heart Church, this African-American man looks south from atop his horse-drawn wagon. Look carefully at the large load of cotton he is hauling: it serves as his seat. (Courtesy of Special Collections, Reese Library, Augusta State University.)

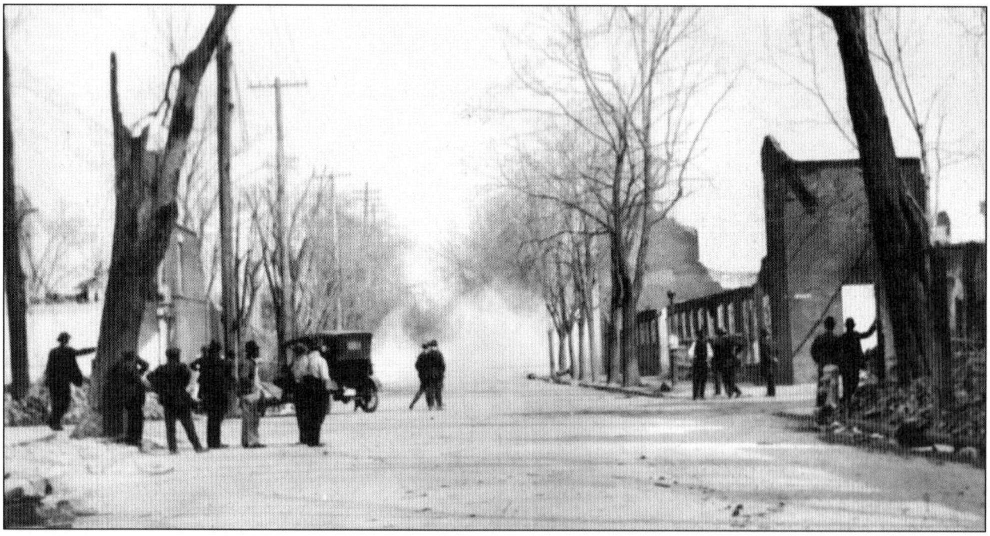

Standing in awe at the sight of the destruction caused by the fire of 1916, a group of African Americans survey the scene. The fire is recorded as one of the greatest disasters in Augusta's history. (Courtesy of Special Collections, Reese Library, Augusta State University.)

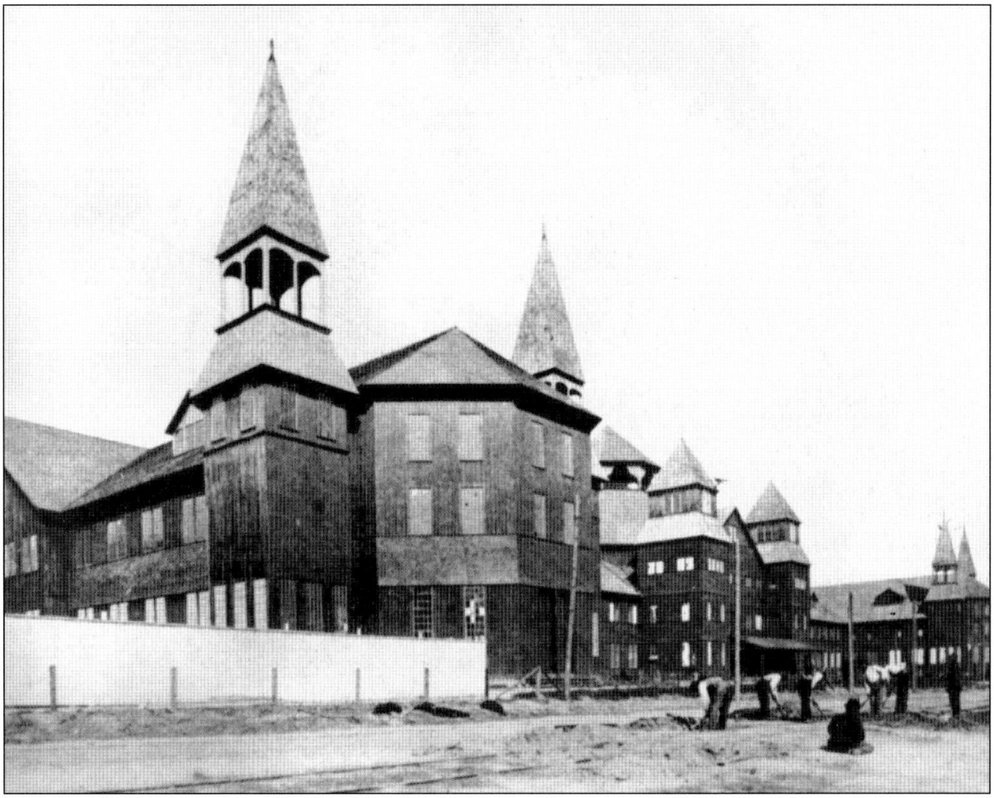

A group or African-American men work next to the Exposition Center. This early glimpse of the center shows its huge size and marvelous architecture. (Courtesy of Special Collections, Reese Library, Augusta State University.)

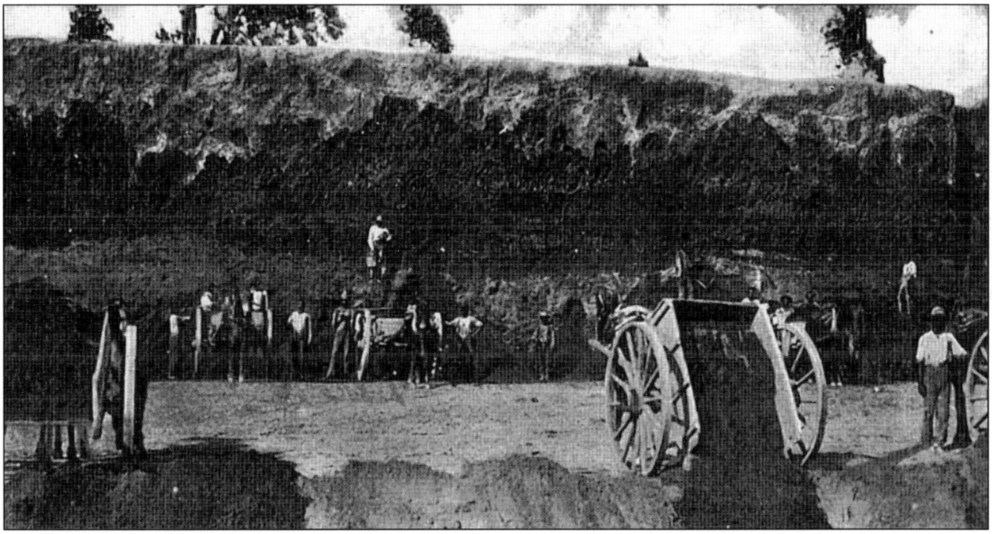

This photograph postcard shows a group of African-American men digging white clay near Augusta. Wooden wagons dump dirt down a manmade hill. (Courtesy of Augusta Museum of History.)

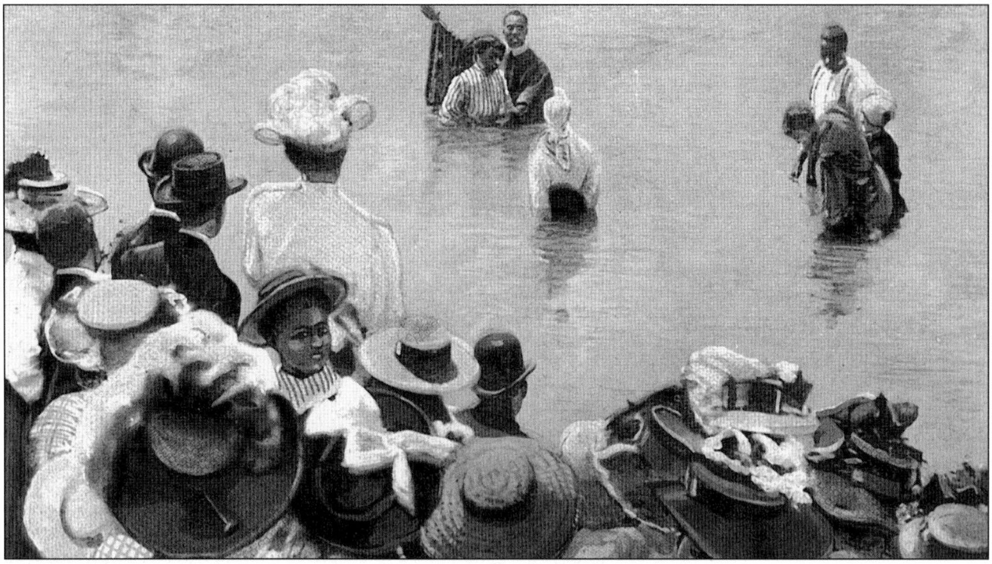

Here is a traditional baptism being conducted. (Courtesy of Sean Joiner, Private Collection.)

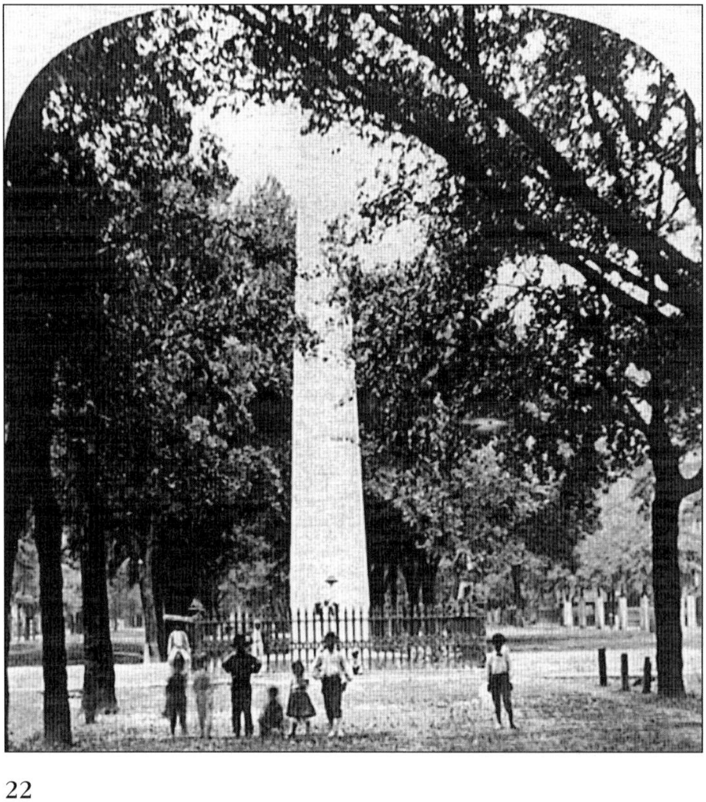

Standing in front of the Revolutionary War Monument, a group of children stop for a photographer for this stereoview. The monument is an important symbol for Augusta. The remains of Revolutionary War heroes Lyman Hall and George Walton are buried underneath the stonework. (Courtesy of Milledge G. Murray, Private Collection.)

An African-American man rests on a bench beside several children. Notice there are trees along both sides of Broad Street, with a wide center for the population to mingle. (Courtesy of Milledge G. Murray, Private Collection.)

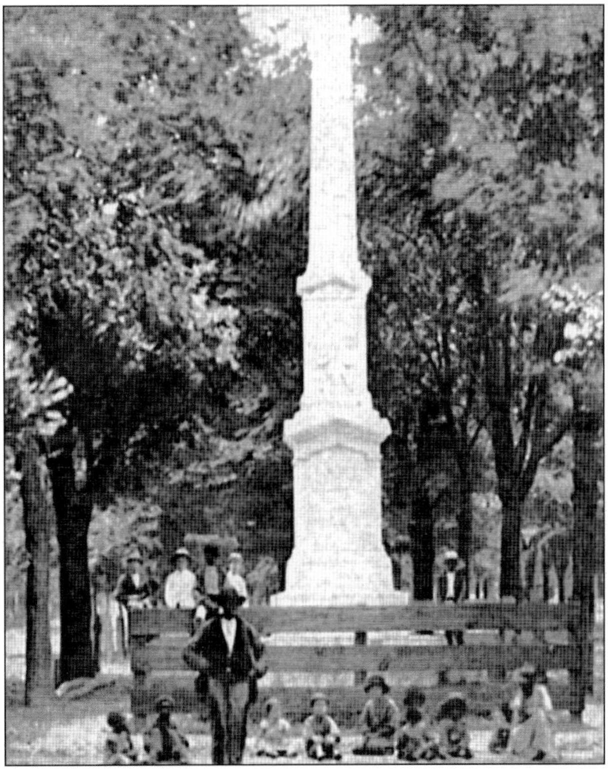

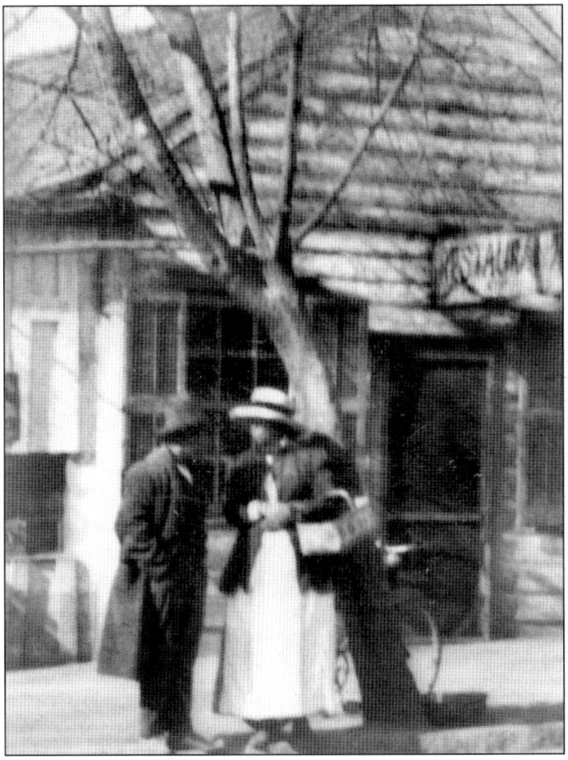

Unaware of the photographer across the street, these two unidentified African Americans are perhaps conversing about their daily chores. The woman can be seen cradling a basket for carrying her goods. Behind her is a bicycle, which was an important mode of transportation in the earlier part of the 20th century. (Courtesy of Augusta Museum of History.)

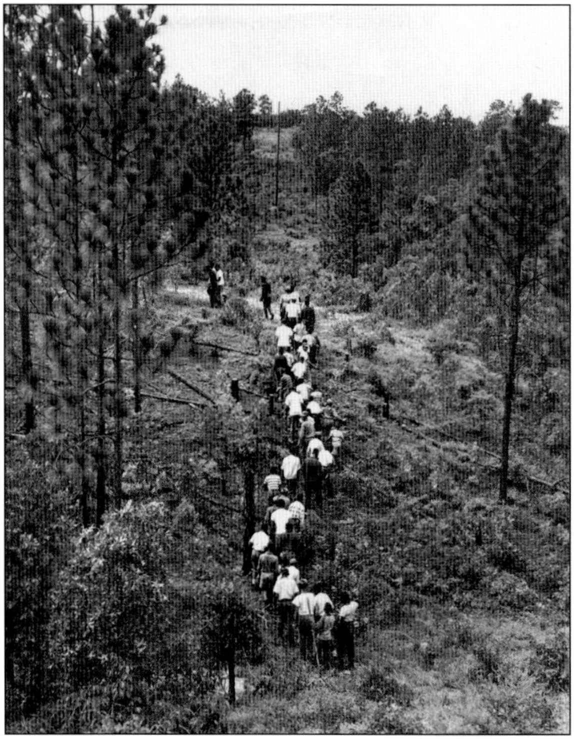

As part of their scouting, African-American youngsters at Camp Josey in Augusta take off on a hike on Augusta 11, 1952. This is a rare picture of young African-American males fulfilling their scouting duties. (Courtesy of Augusta Museum of History.)

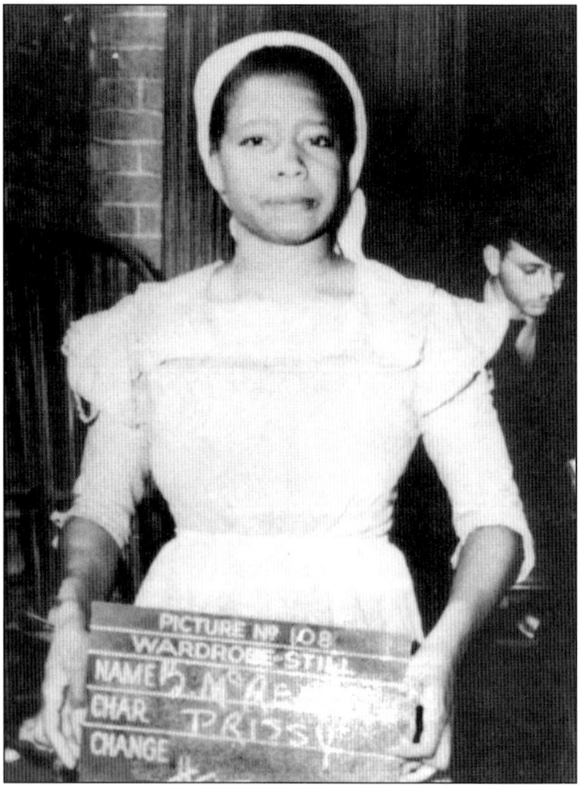

Butterfly McQueen stops to let someone take her picture during the filming of *Gone With the Wind*. She opened the door for many African-American actors and actresses in this world-famous movie. (Courtesy of Augusta Museum of History.)

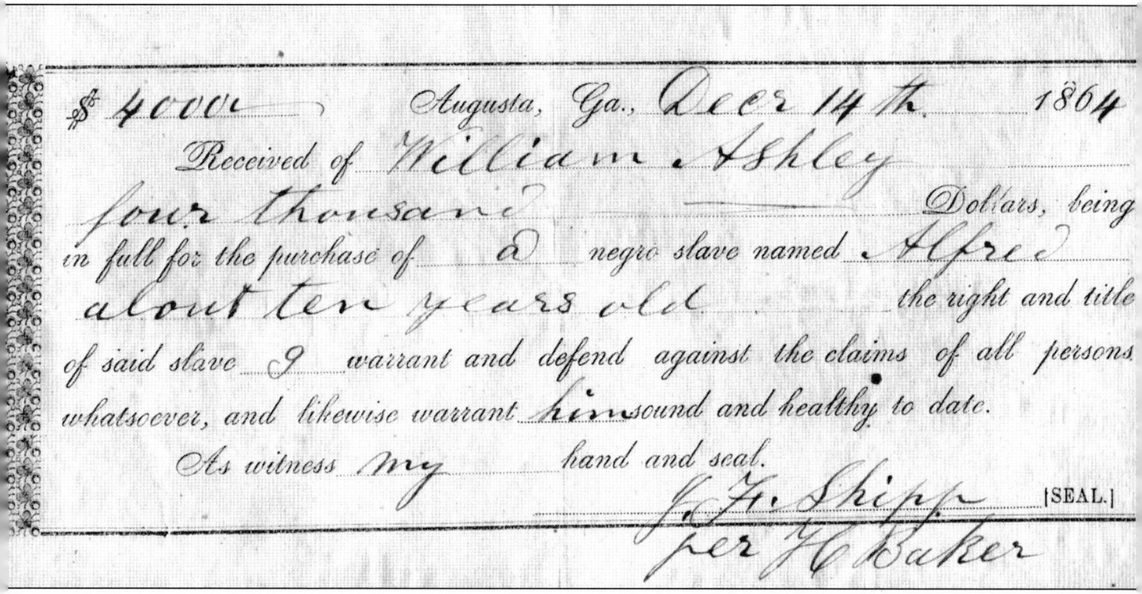

$4000 Augusta, Ga., Decr 14th 1864

Received of William Ashley

four thousand Dollars, being

in full for the purchase of a negro slave named Alfred

about ten years old the right and title

of said slave I warrant and defend against the claims of all persons

whatsoever, and likewise warrant him sound and healthy to date.

As witness my hand and seal.

J. F. Shipp [SEAL.]

per H. Baker

This slave receipt references a date of December 14, 1864, in Augusta, Georgia, for $4,000. Also shown on the receipt is the name Alfred; he is listed as being 10 years old. (Courtesy of Augusta Museum of History.)

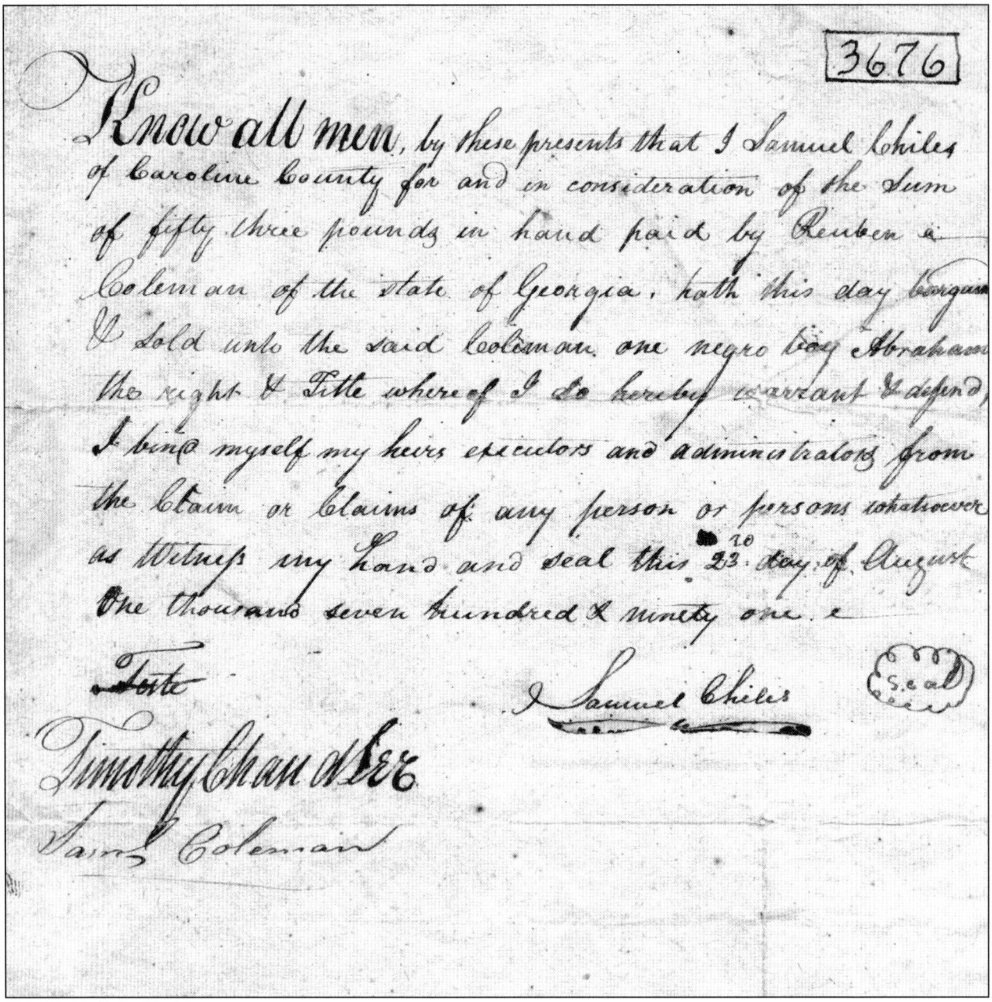
3676

Know all men, by these presents that I Samuel Chiles
of Caroline County for and in consideration of the Sum
of fifty three pounds in hand paid by Reuben a
Coleman of the state of Georgia, hath this day bargain[ed]
& Sold unto the said Coleman one negro boy Abraham
the right & Title whereof I do hereby warrant & defend,
I bind myself my heirs executors and administrators from
the Claim or Claims of any person or persons whatsoever
as Witness my hand and seal this 23 day of August
One thousand seven hundred & ninety one.

Teste

Samuel Chiles (Seal)

Timothy Chandler

Saml Coleman

This document, dated August 23, 1791, states "Know all ye men by these presents that I Samuel Chiles of Caroline County for and in the consideration of the sum of fifty-three pounds in hand paid by Ruben Coleman of the State of Georgia, hath this day bargained and sold unto the said bondsman one Negro boy Abraham the right and title where I do hereby warrant and defend. I bind myself, my heirs executors and administration from the claim or claims of any person or persons whatsoever as witnessing my hands and seal." (Courtesy of Augusta Museum of History.)

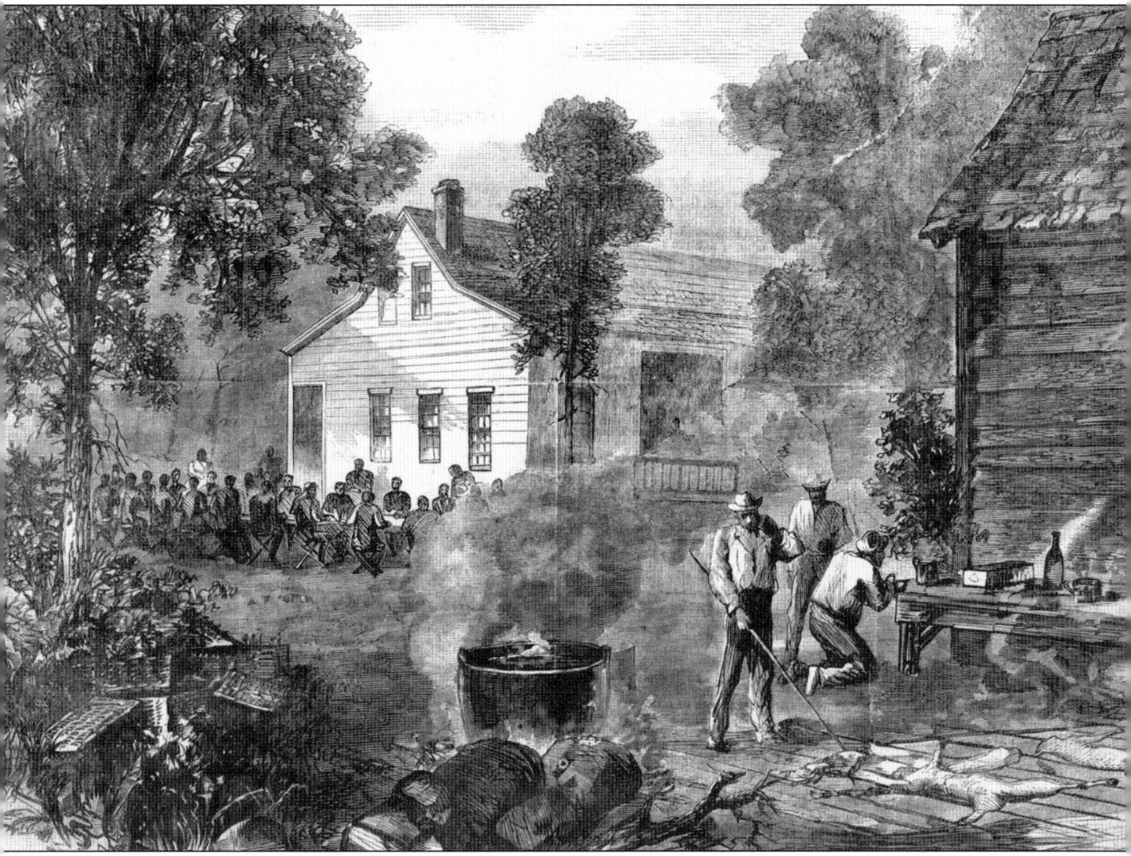

Scenes of back alleys and areas behind residences from the earlier part of the 20th century are rare. In this photograph, African Americans can be seen talking in a group and congregating behind the home. (Courtesy of Augusta Museum of History.)

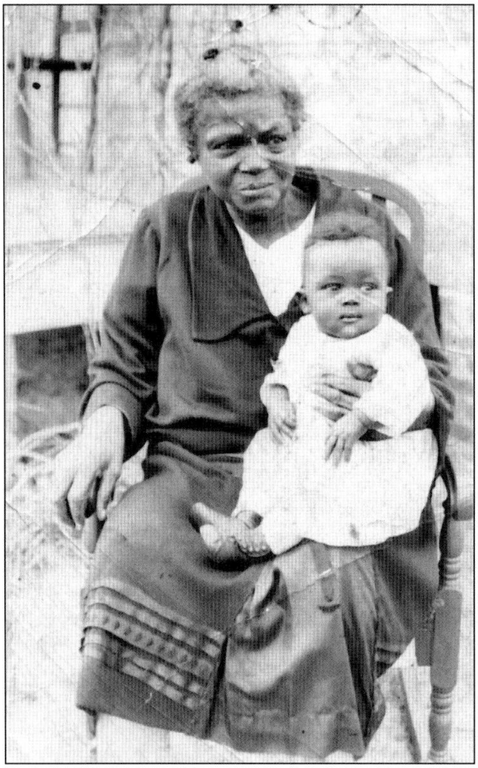

In this photograph, an unidentified woman holds a small child in her arms. (Courtesy of Augusta Museum of History.)

In this early photograph, a group of men pose with a vintage automobile and boat. They are preparing for a day of fishing around Phinizy Swamp. Today, much of the swamp has been bought and turned into a nature reserve for environmental study and education. (Courtesy of Augusta Museum of History.)

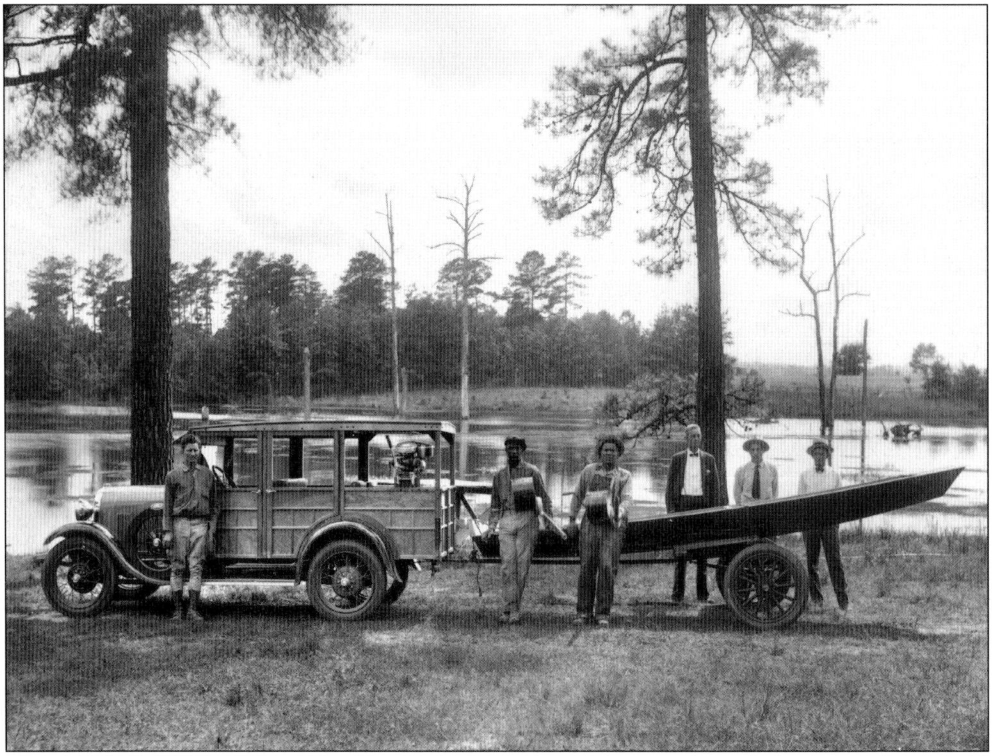

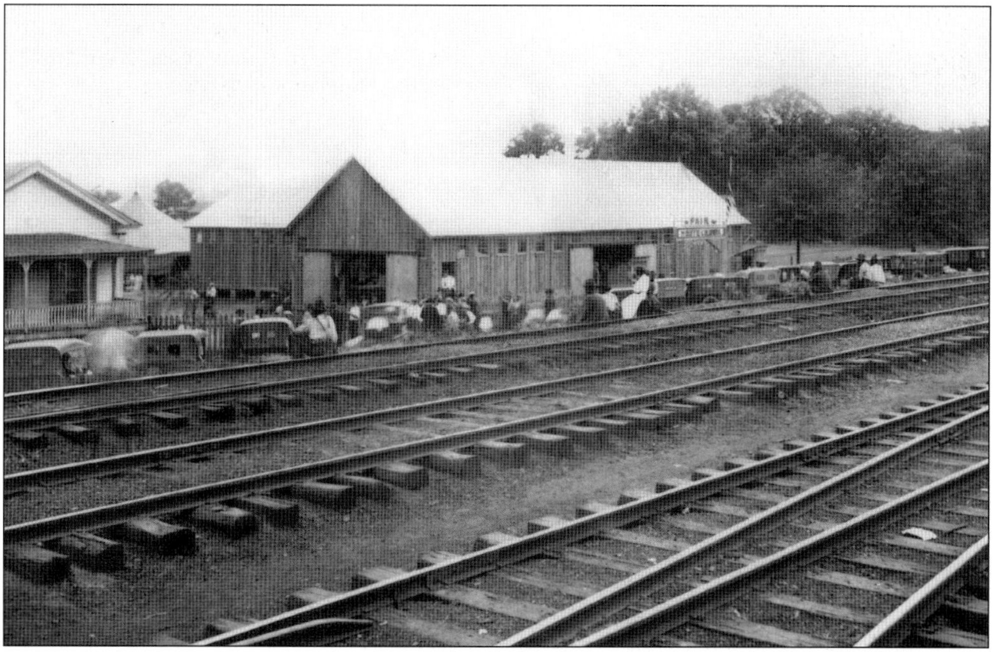

In the forefront, railroad tracks pass by fairgrounds at an unidentified location near Augusta. Near the tracks, a group of African-American men and women can be seen. Another aspect featured is a sign reading the "McDuffie-Columbia County Fair." (Courtesy of Augusta Museum of History.)

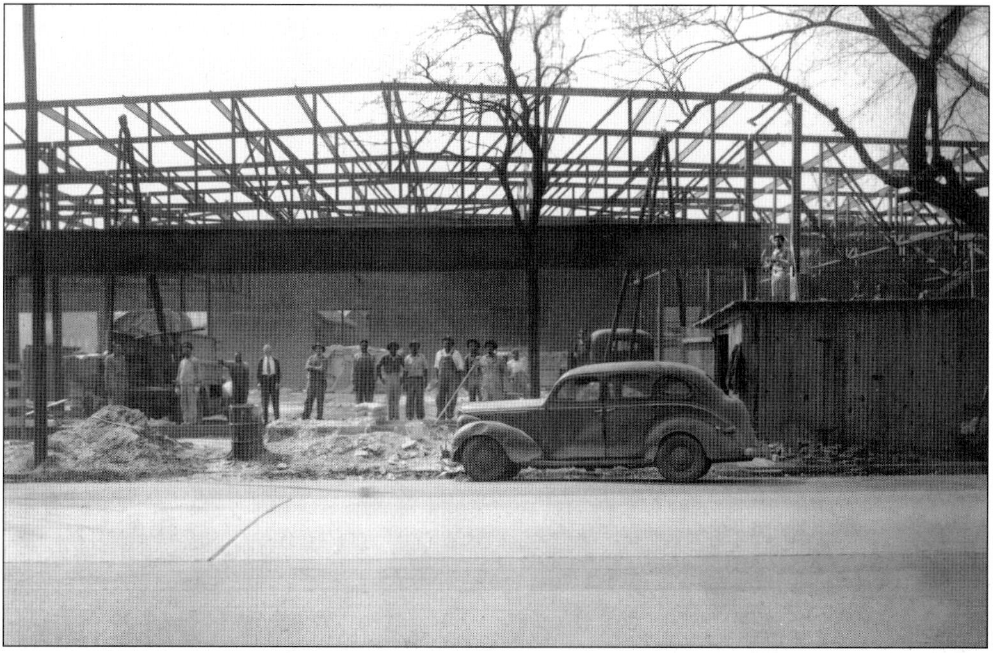

This photograph shows African-American workers constructing the frame to a building in downtown Augusta. In the background, vintage cars and wooden buildings can be seen. (Courtesy of Augusta Museum of History.)

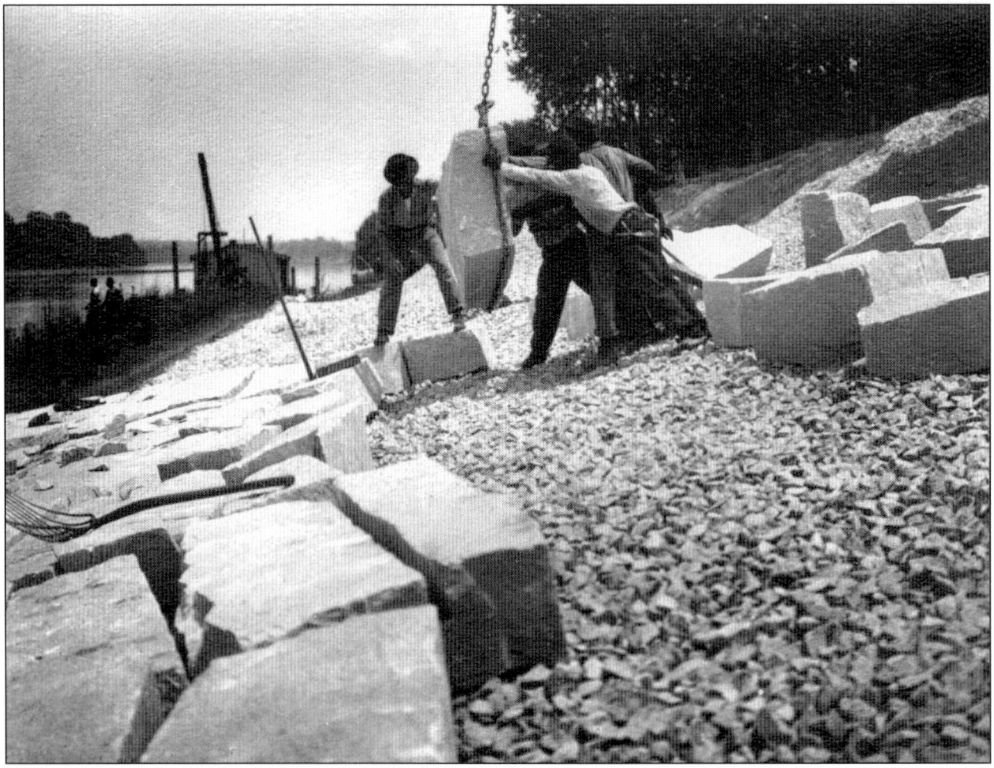

African-American workers labor diligently to build the levee in downtown Augusta near the Savannah River. This was back-breaking work and these men are commended for their efforts in helping to protect Augusta from flooding. (Courtesy of Augusta Museum of History.)

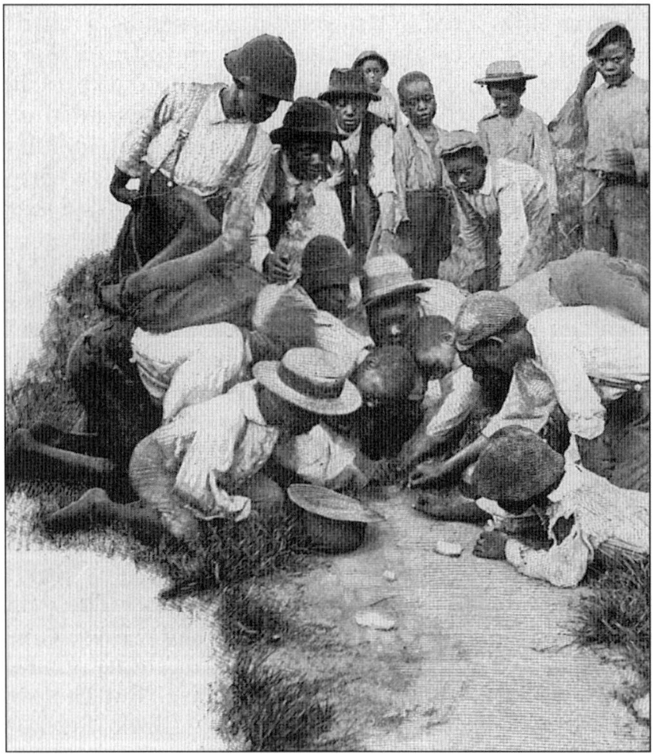

These children play an exciting game of marbles. This early-20th-century photograph shows the common dress of the period. (Courtesy of Sean Joiner, Private Collection.)

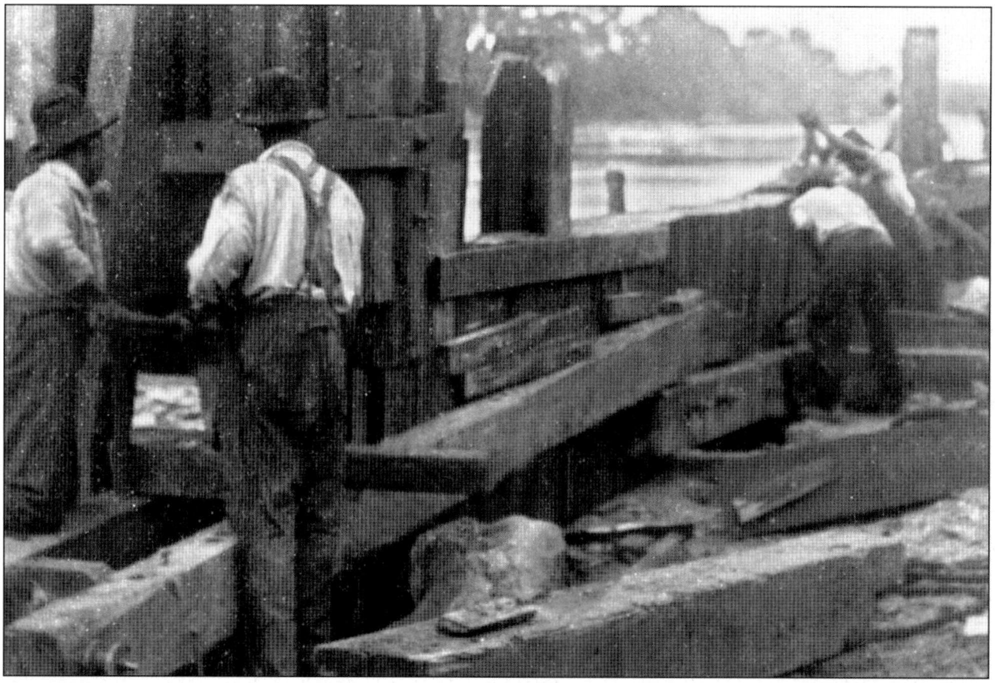

African-American workers build the bulkhead at the city wharf. The wharf was located at Center Street Landing and was built during the 1940s. It was used for docking boats and unloading goods. (Courtesy of Augusta Museum of History.)

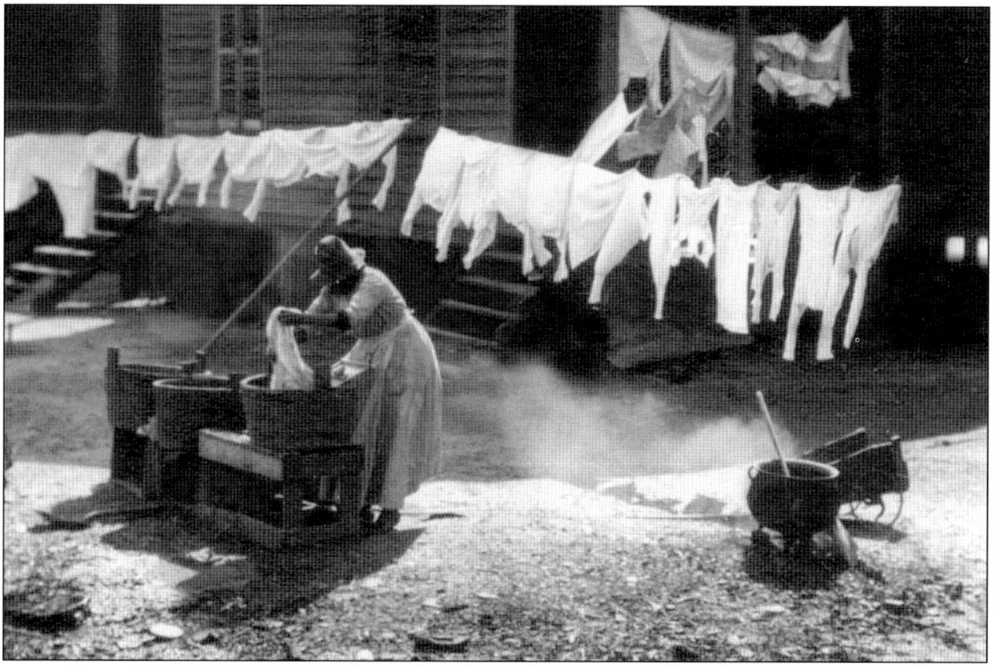

A woman washes her laundry and hangs it on a line outside of her residence in downtown Augusta. This photograph is dated February 10, 1901. In the corner, a wash pot can be seen resting over a fire. (Courtesy of Augusta Museum of History.)

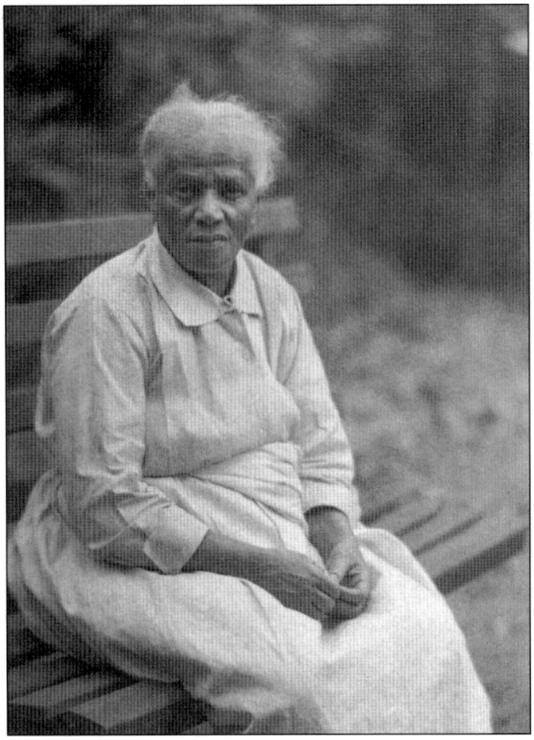

This woman—identified only as Maria—rests on a park bench. The photograph was taken at an unidentified location in Augusta on October 24, 1924. (Courtesy of Augusta Museum of History.)

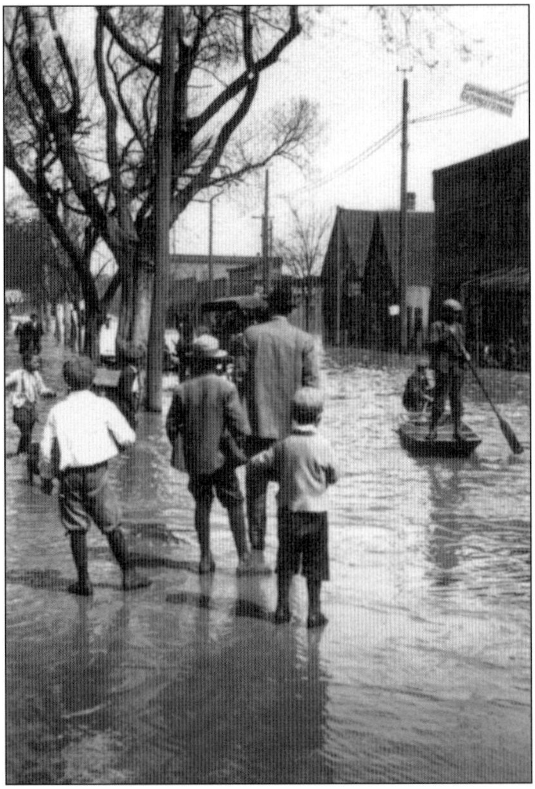

The flood of March 16, 1913, was a devastating one for the Augusta community. African Americans stand in the flood's aftermath and paddle a boat down what was a busy dirt street. Above the street, hanging on wires, a sign reads "Cars do not stop here go to next street." (Courtesy of Augusta Museum of History.)

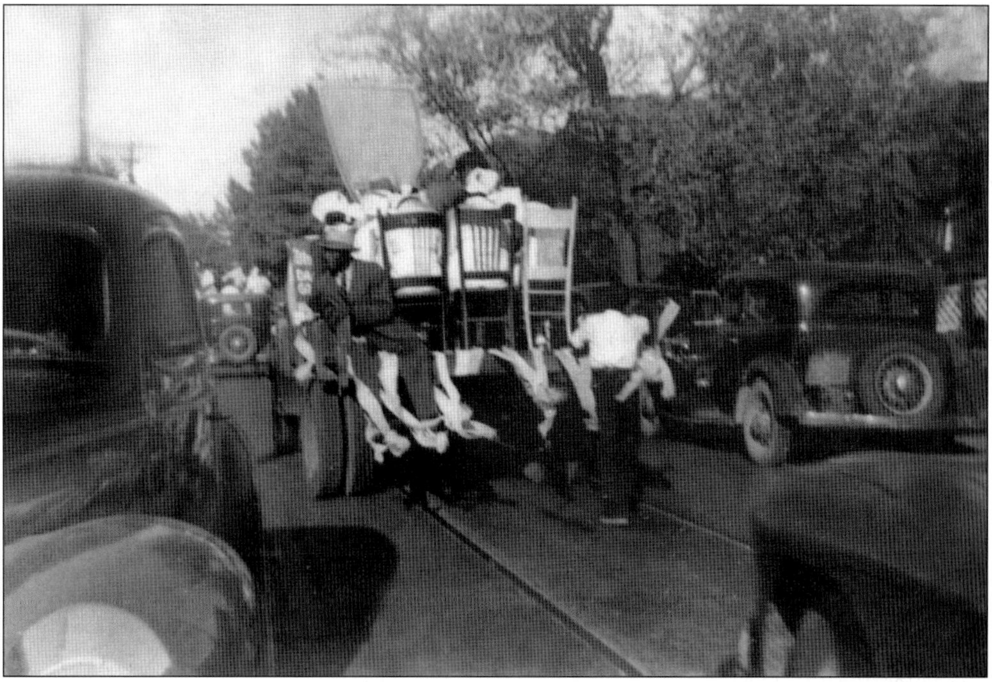

This man sits on the back of a truck, waving to the crowd during the Daddy Grace parade. The back of the vehicle also carries a group of women. (Courtesy of Augusta Museum of History.)

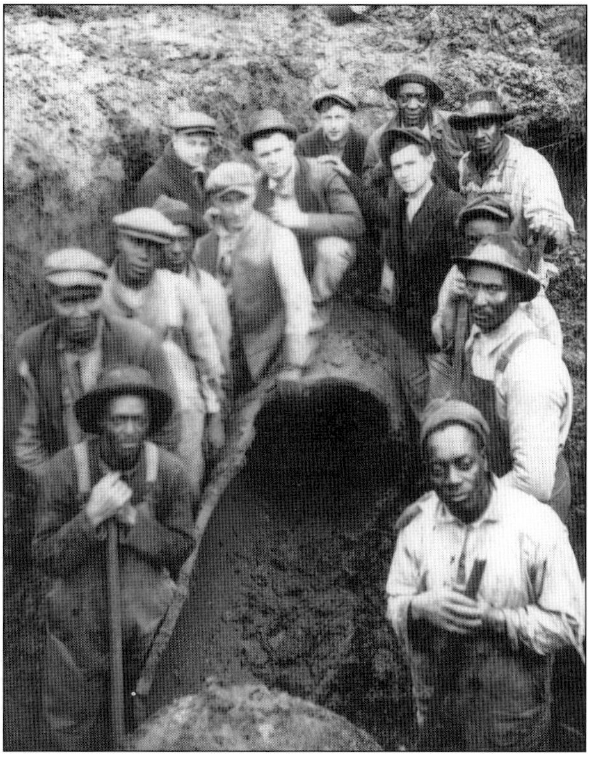

Repair work on a pipe stops as these men turn and pose for a photograph. (Courtesy of Augusta Museum of History.)

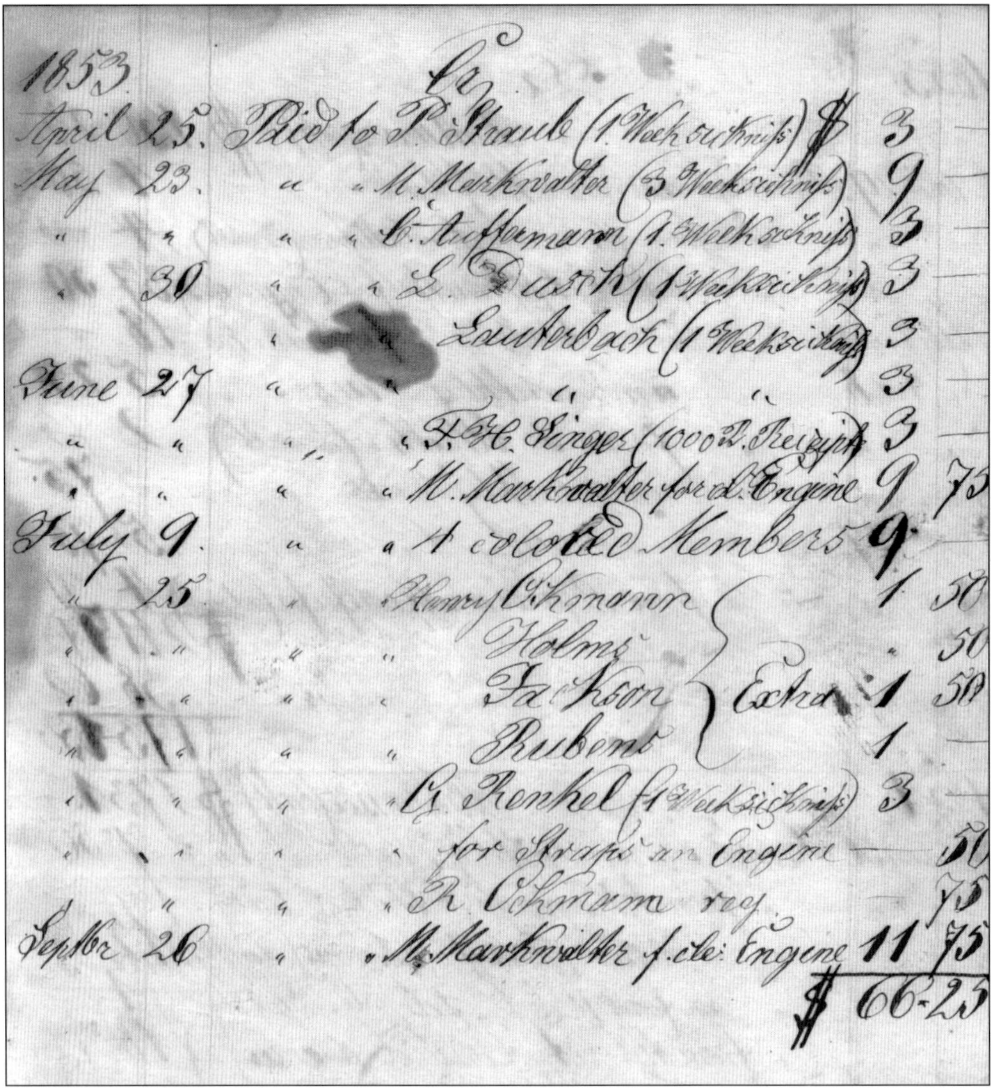

1853 Cr

April 25.	Paid to P. Straub (1 Week [illegible])	$	3	
May 23.	" " M. Markwalter (3 Weeks [illegible])		9	
" "	" " C. Aufermann (1 Week [illegible])		3	
" 30	" " L. Dusch (1 Week [illegible])		3	
	" Lauterbach (1 Week [illegible])		3	
June 27	" " "		3	
" "	" " F. H. Singer (1000 ft. Receipt)		3	
" "	" " M. Markwalter for [illegible] Engine		9	75
July 9.	" " 4 colored Members		9	
" 25	" Henry Ochmann		1	50
" "	" " Holmes	Extra		50
" "	" " Jackson		1	50
" "	" " Ruben		1	
" "	" " G. Renkel (1 Week [illegible])		3	
" "	" for Straps an Engine			50
" "	" " R. Ochmann [illegible]			75
Septbr 26	" " M. Markwalter f. [illegible] Engine		11	75
		$	66	25

A page from an old Augusta Fire Department roster and manual dated 1853 shows the names of African Americans who were free blacks and employed by the fire department. The names listed are "Colored Members: Henry Akman, last names of Holmes and Ruben." The men were listed as colored members and were paid a total of $9 for their services. Other pay listed is a $1 to $1.50. (Courtesy of Augusta Museum of History.)

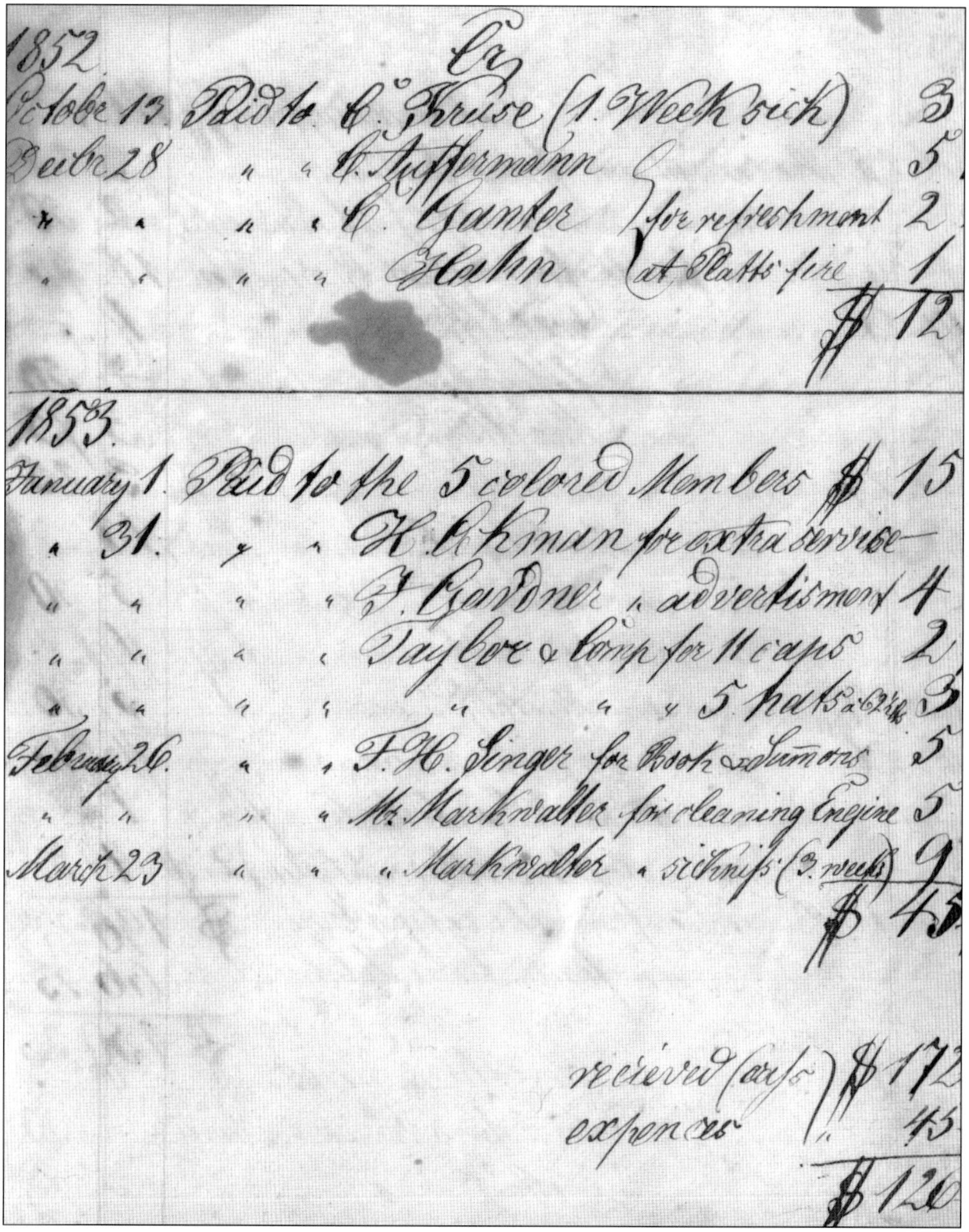

1852 Cr

October 13. Paid to C. Kruse (1 Week sick) 3

Decbr 28 " " C. Aufferman } 5

" " " " C. Ganter } for refreshment 2

" " " " Hahn } at Platt's fire 1

$ 12

1853.

January 1. Paid to the 5 colored Members $ 15

" 31. " " H. Akman for extra service

" " " " F. Gardner " advertisment 4

" " " " Taylor & Comp for 11 caps 2

" " " " " " " 5 hats 3

February 26. " " F. H. Singer for Book & Summons 5

" " " " Mr. Markwalter for cleaning Engine 5

March 23 " " " Markwalter " sickness (3 weeks) 9

$ 45

recieved (cash) $ 172

expences " 45

$ 120

A page dated February 1, 1853, from an old Augusta Fire Department roster shows five black members being paid a total of $15 for their services. Henry Akman is listed, along with F. Gardner and the last name Taylor. Five fire hats are listed at a $1 apiece. This book shows that it is probable that these men were the first African Americans to work for the Augusta fire department. (Courtesy of Augusta Museum of History.)

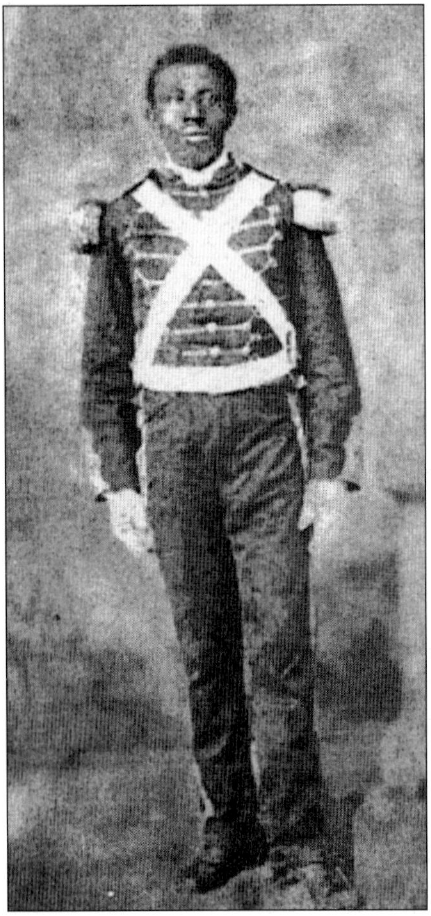

Augusta had an African-American militia shortly after the Civil War. This photograph, taken around 1880, shows a young man in military garb. (Courtesy of Augusta Museum of History.)

The Medical College of Georgia purchased a Gullah slave, Henry Gradison, in 1852. He attended classes on writing, reading, and physical anatomy. He was then sent into Cedar Grove Cemetery to dig up fresh corpses. He returned with the bodies, which were used for medical research. The bodies were discovered in the basement of the old college and reburied in Cedar Grove Cemetery. (Courtesy of Sean Joiner, Private Collection.)

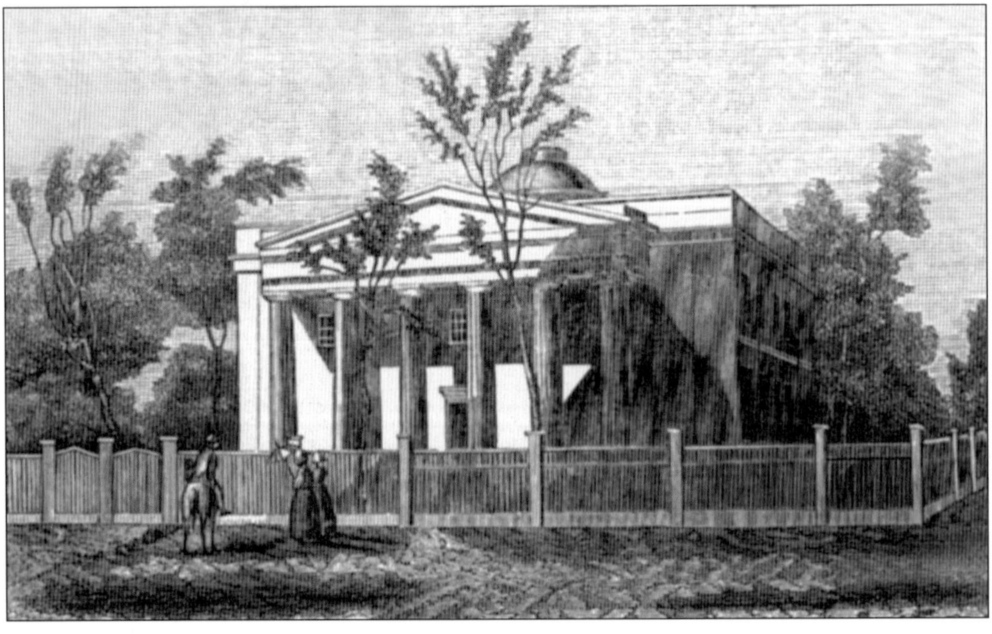

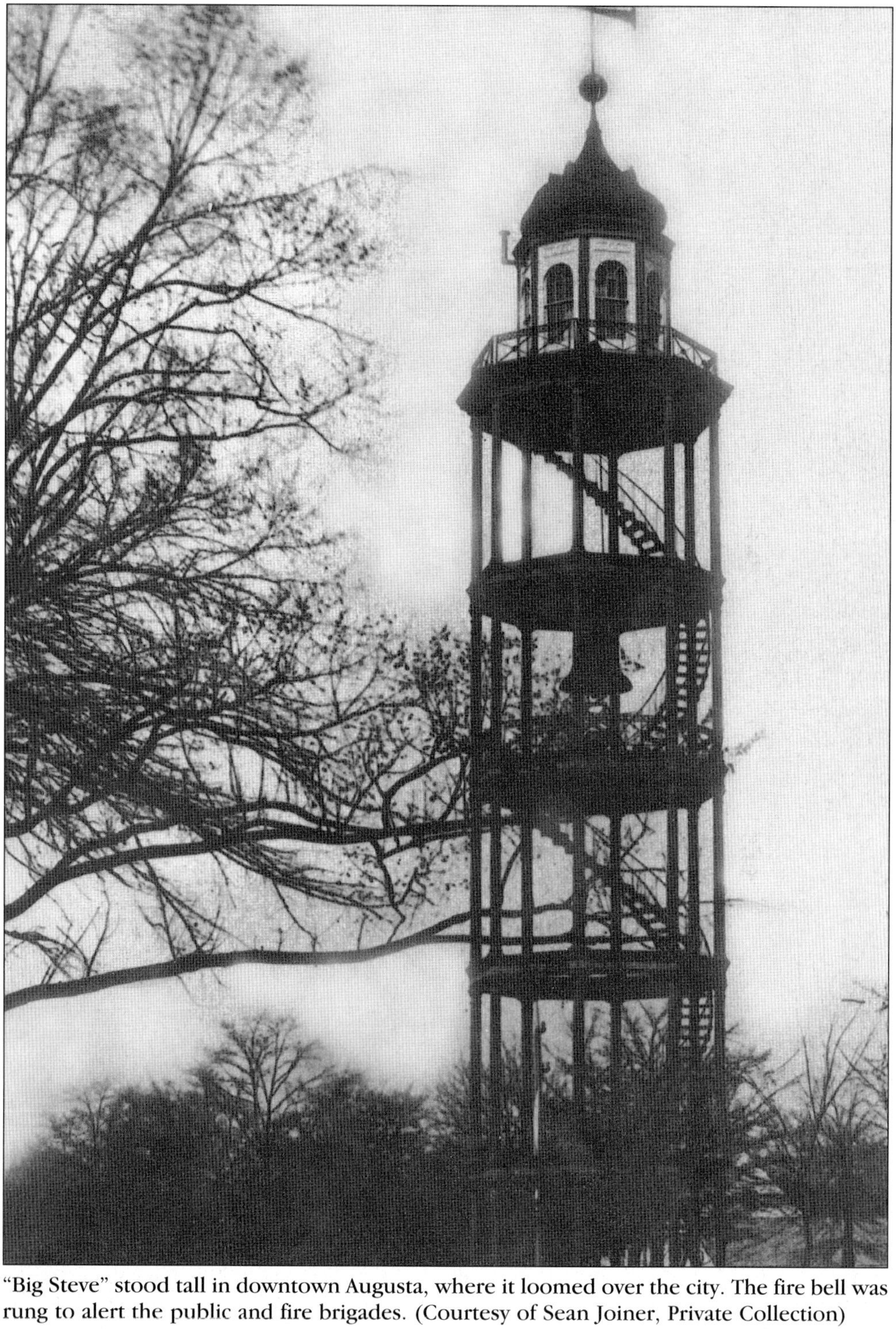

"Big Steve" stood tall in downtown Augusta, where it loomed over the city. The fire bell was rung to alert the public and fire brigades. (Courtesy of Sean Joiner, Private Collection)

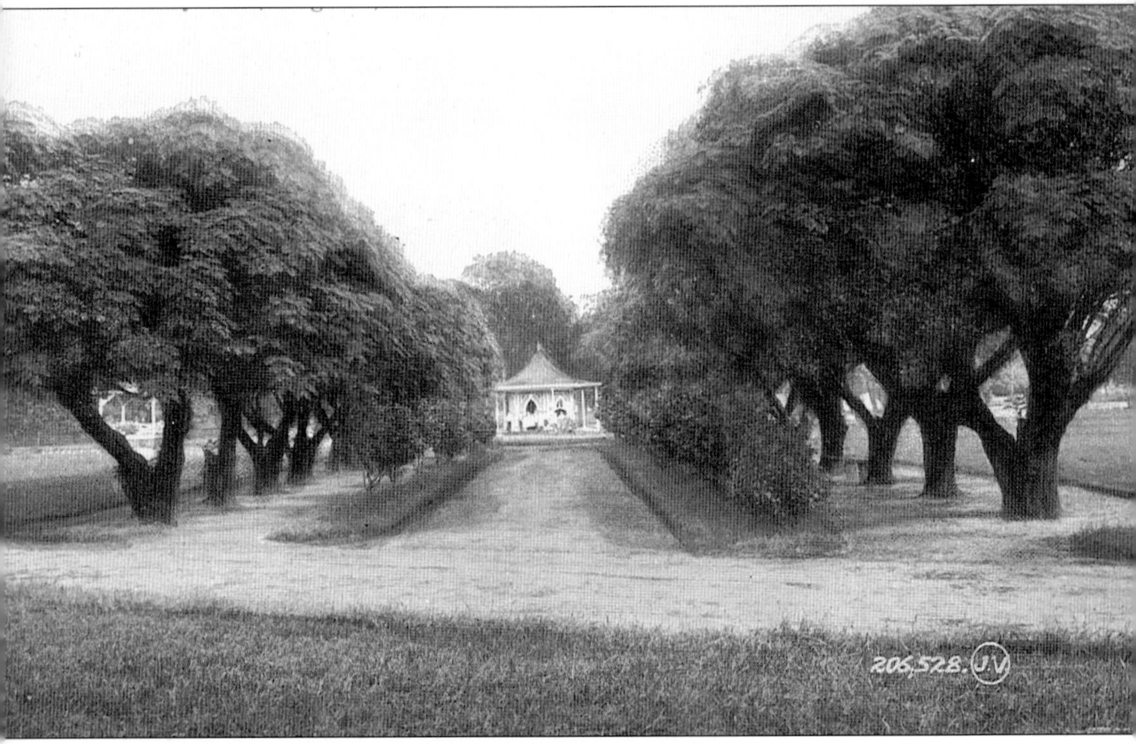

This early postcard shows May Park. The park has entertained Augustans for over a century. Today, May Park hosts many African-American events and continues to benefit those who live in the area. The park includes a baseball field and community center. (Courtesy Sean Joiner, Private Collection)

Three
EDUCATION

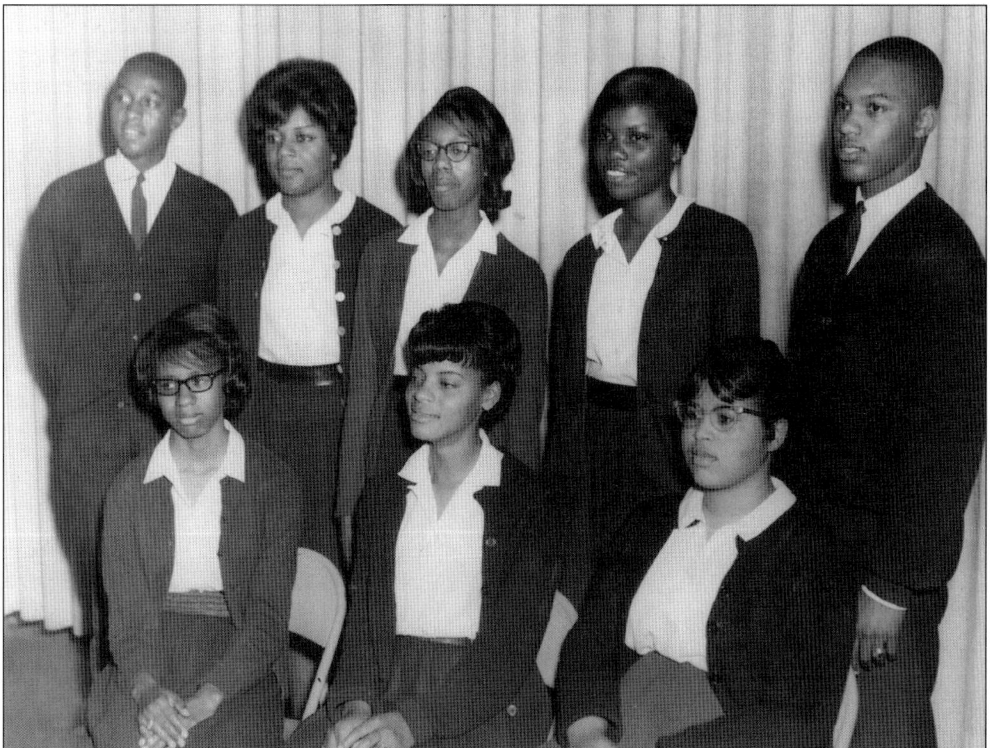

These young men and women pose for a group photograph at The Immaculate Conception High School at 1016 Gwinnett Street. (Courtesy of Augusta Museum of History.)

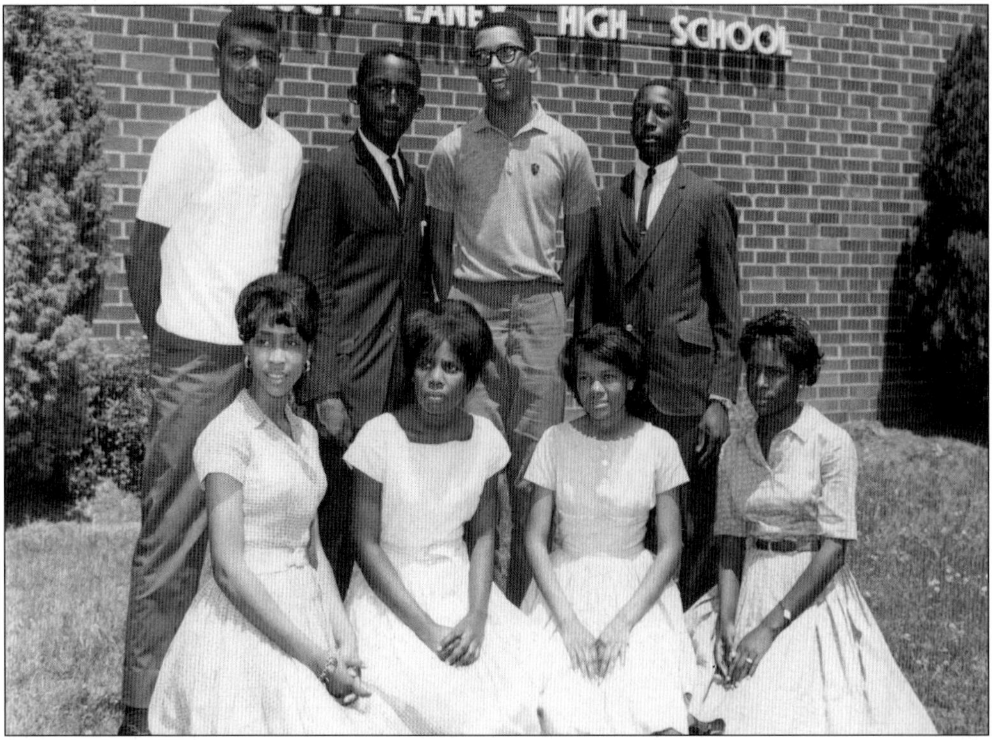

These teenagers stand outside Lucy Laney High School for a group photograph. Lucy Craft Laney High School was named after the famous African-American educator. (Courtesy of Augusta Museum of History.)

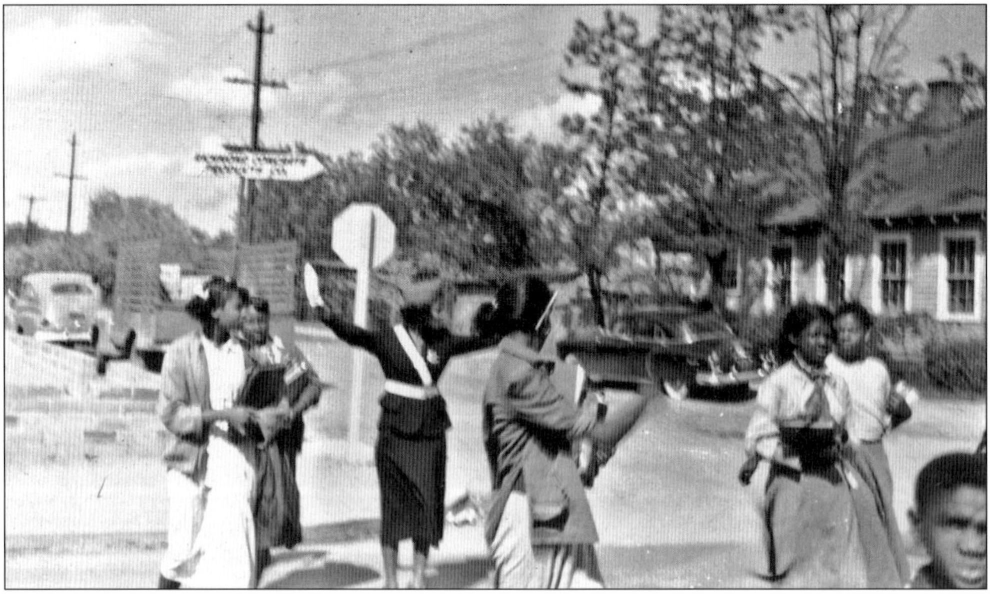

This 1950s-era photograph shows an African-American school crossing guard stopping traffic so students can pass though an intersection unharmed. (Courtesy of Augusta Museum of History.)

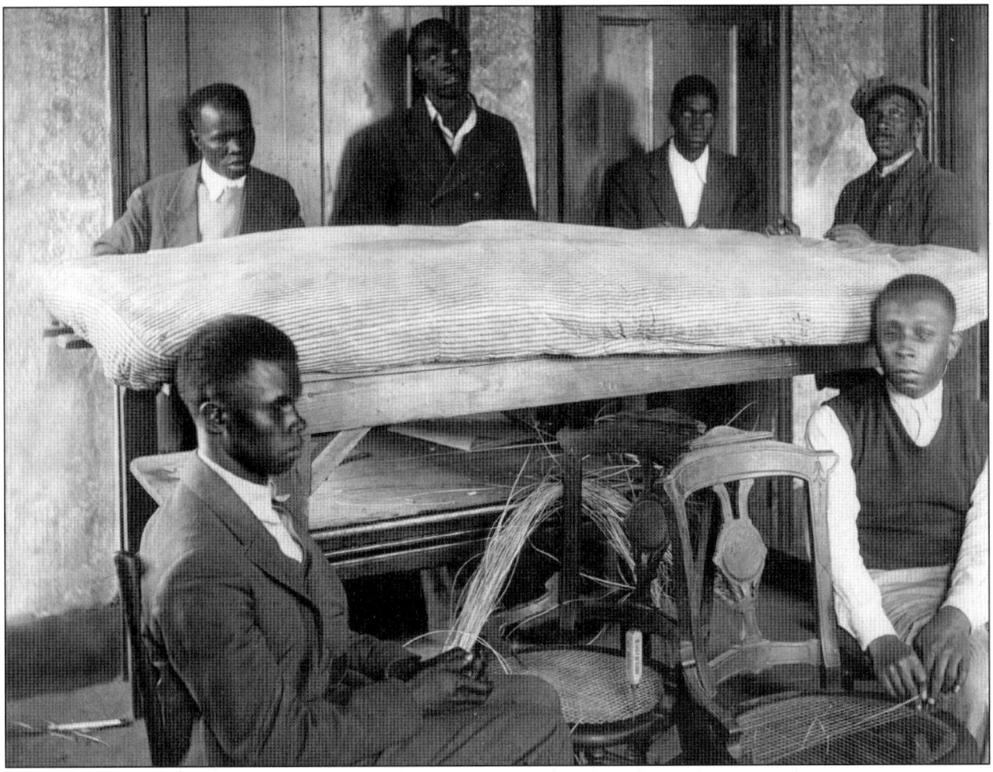

Weaving is a skilled art. This photograph of blind African-American boys was taken at an unidentified school in Augusta. (Courtesy of Augusta Museum of History.)

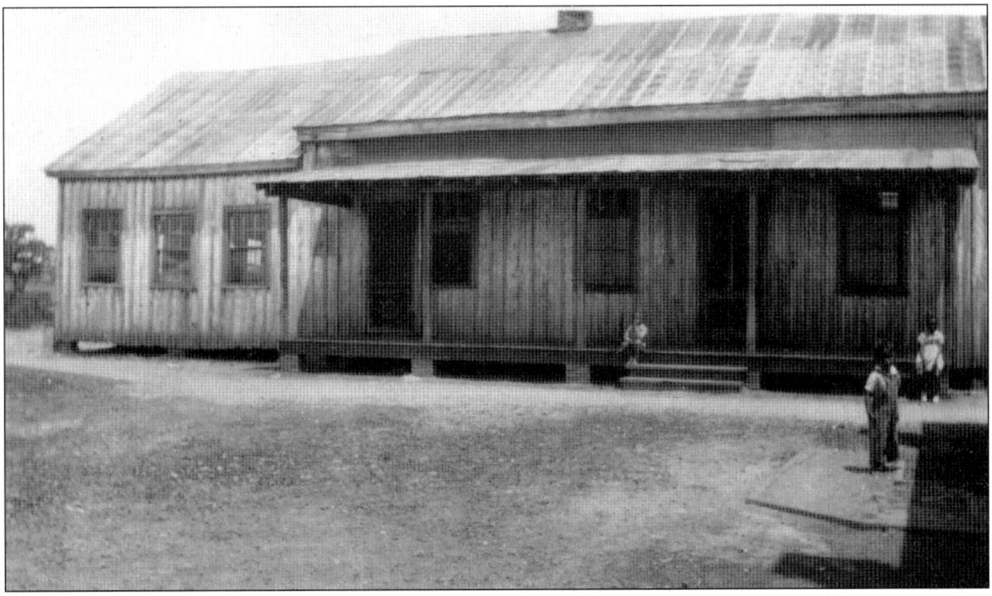

Children stand near an old laundry building that was an annex of the Shiloh Orphanage in Augusta. The photograph was taken in 1943, several years before the orphanage was closed. (Courtesy of Augusta Museum of History.)

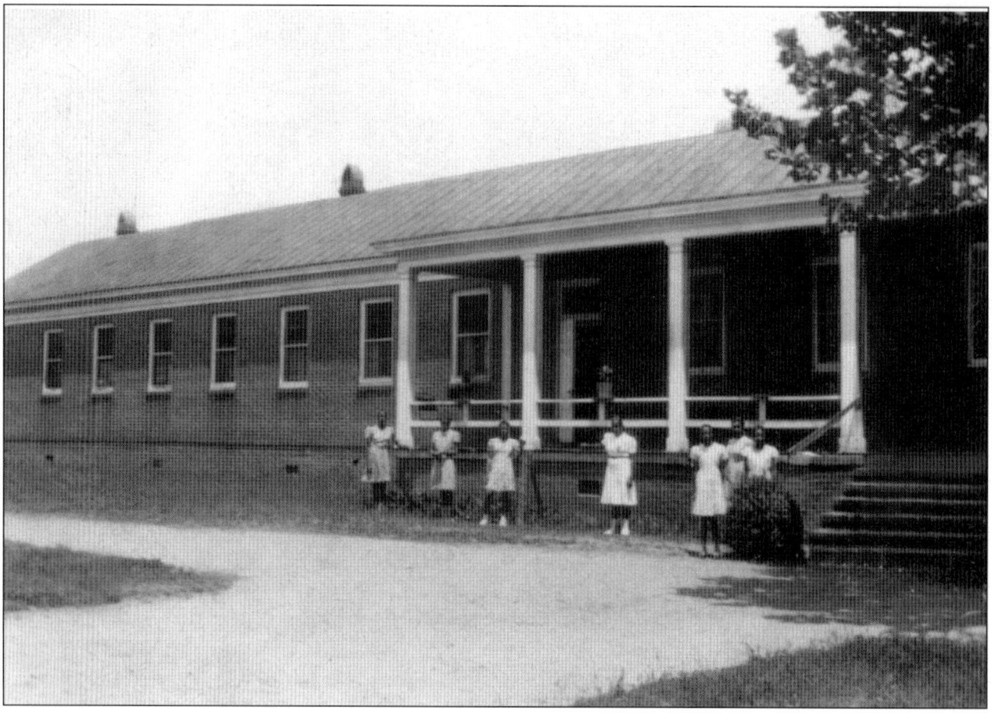

Standing in front of the Shiloh Orphanage, several little girls in their dresses wait to be called for lunch. Other daily activities included going to school and their usual chores. (Courtesy of Augusta Museum of History.)

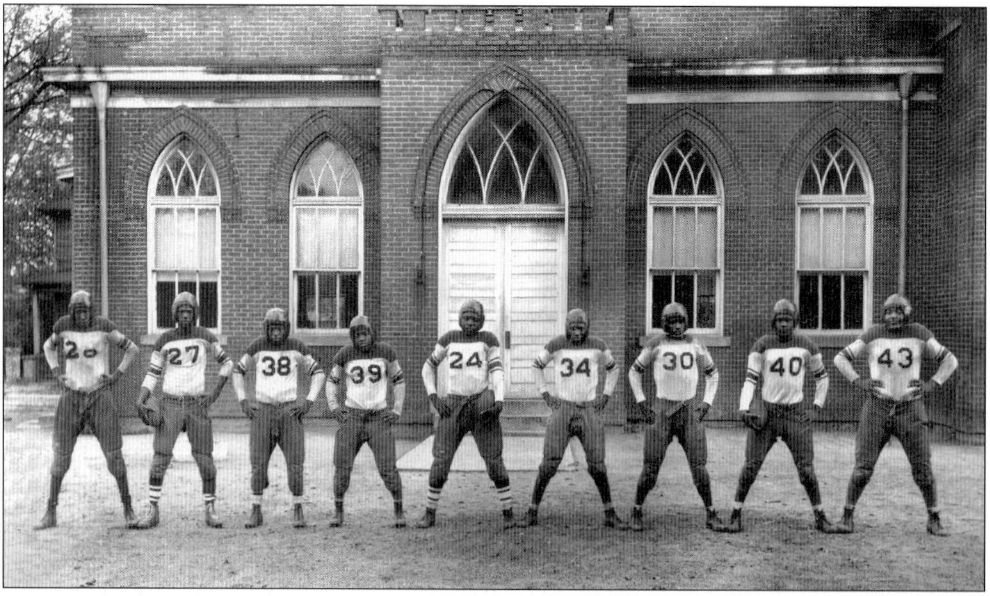

The football team of Haines School stands with their hands on their hips for an imposing photograph, showing what an opponent should fear on the gridiron. The school was an African-American college prep and vocational school. (Courtesy of Augusta Museum of History.)

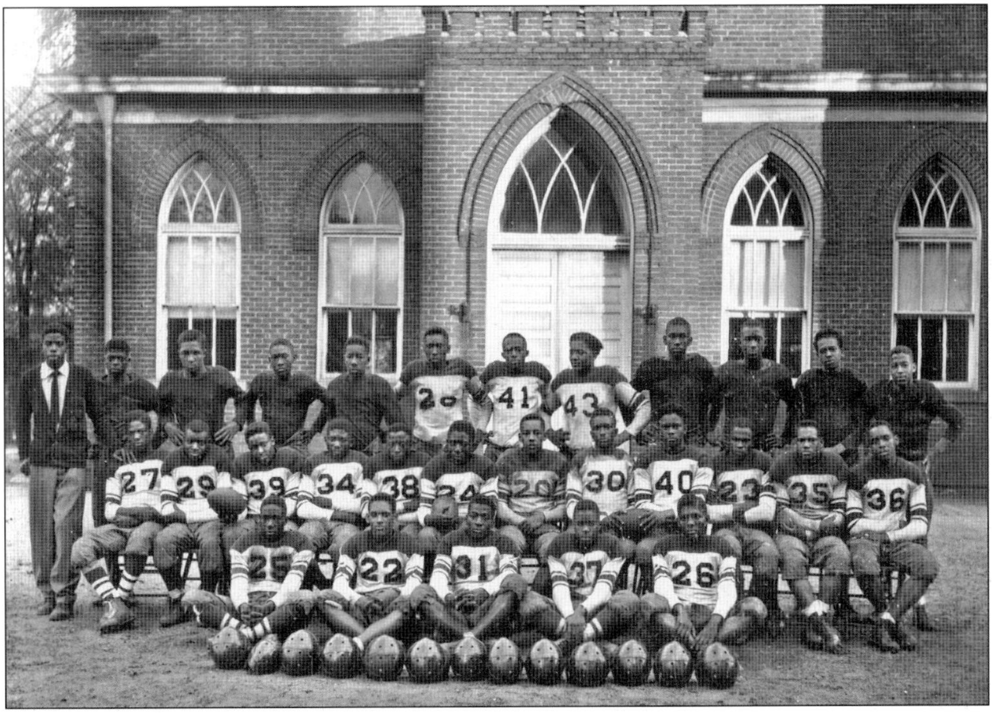

Another group photograph shows the Haines School football team. The group was a dominant team in the Augusta area for many years. (Courtesy of Augusta Museum of History.)

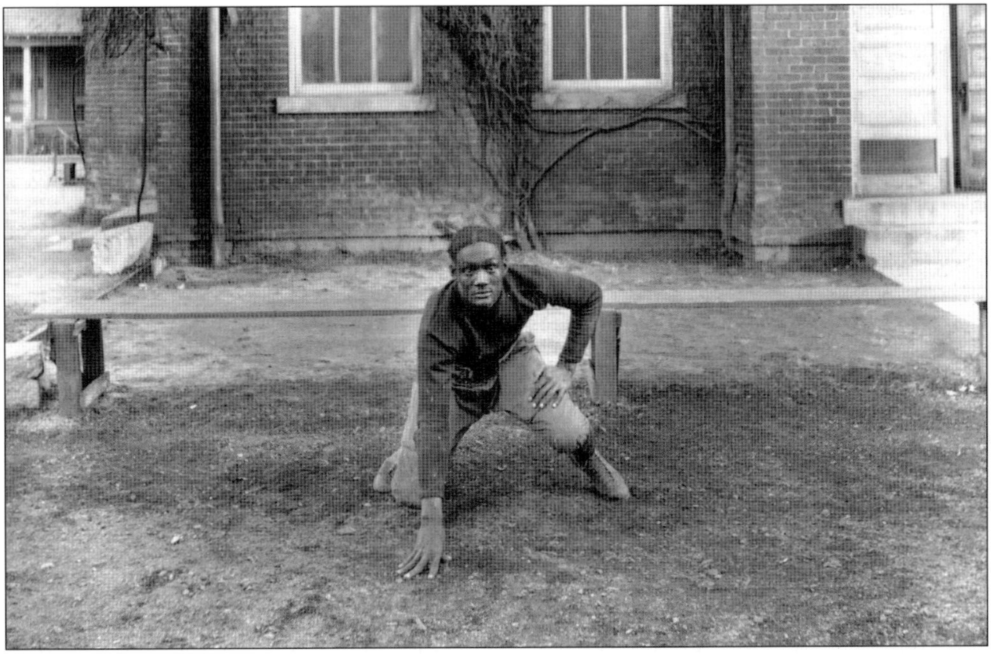

A player poses in a football stance to show his skills. The school assisted African Americans whose parents were slaves only decades before. (Courtesy of Augusta Museum of History.)

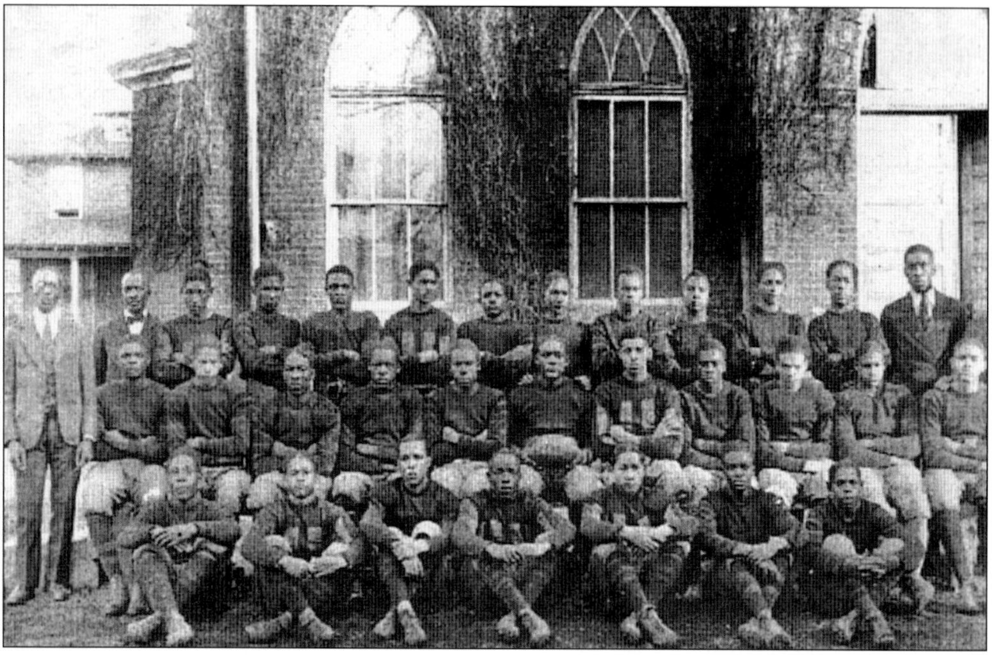

This is the Haines Institute football team shortly after a 26-19 victory in 1929. The captain is in the middle, holding the game ball as a trophy. (Courtesy of Augusta Museum of History.)

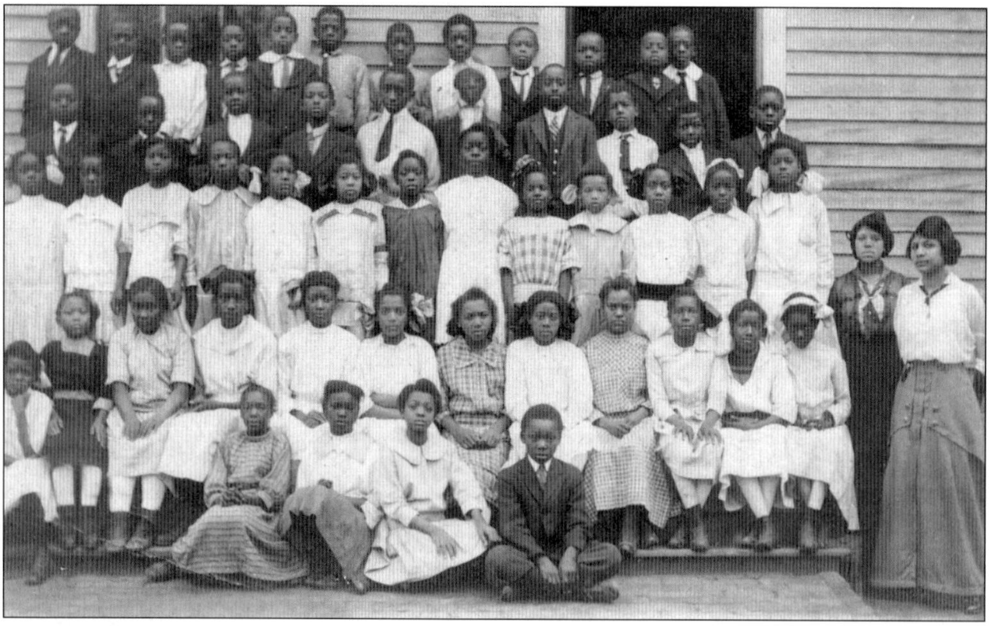

This photograph shows a group of African-American schoolchildren and their teachers. (Courtesy of Augusta Museum of History.)

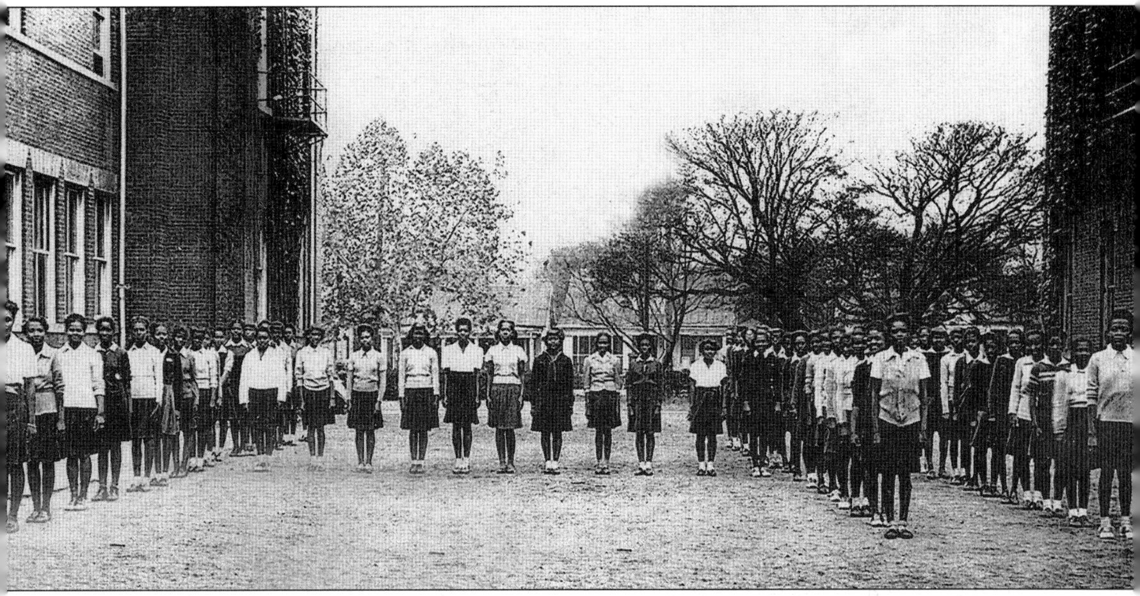

The young ladies that attended Haines Institute were an important factor in the school's success. In this 1925 photograph, these young ladies pose for a group picture. (Courtesy of Augusta Museum of History.)

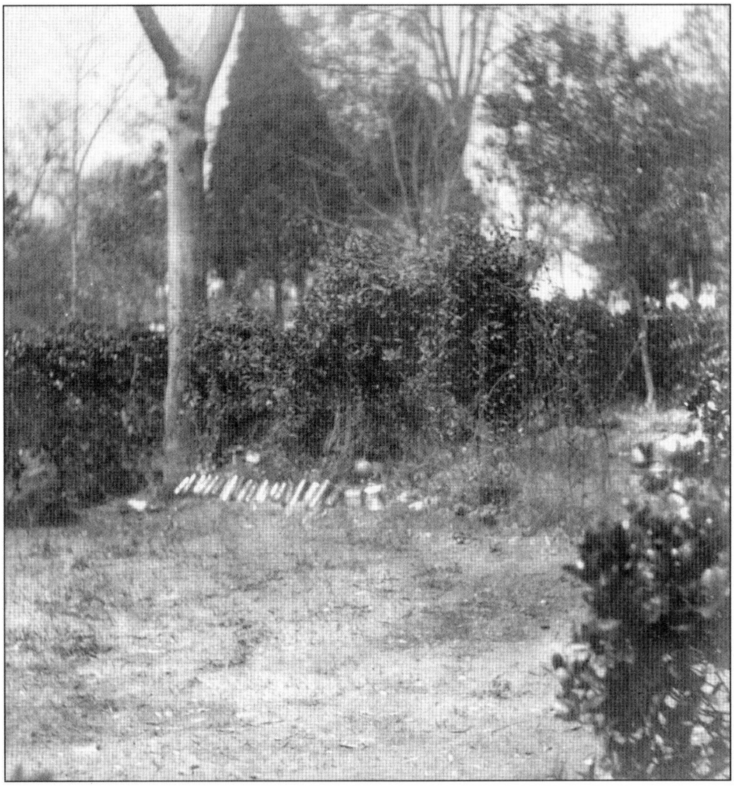

Empty bottles surround this African-American grave. Early burials used colored glass to catch any evil spirits that may come to the site. (Courtesy of Joe Lee, Private Collection.)

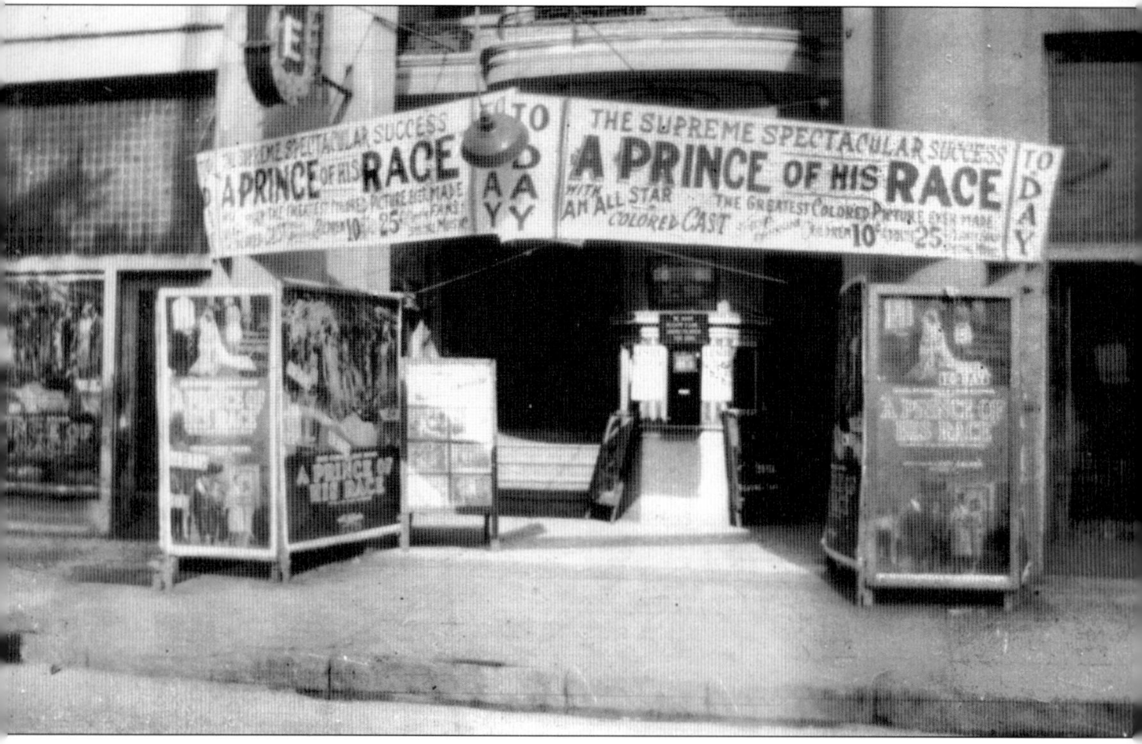

Shown here is the Lenox Theatre, showcasing the movie *A Prince of His Race* in 1927. Cost of admission was 10¢ to 25¢, depending on where the patron was seated. (Courtesy of Augusta Museum of History.)

Four
ENTERTAINMENT

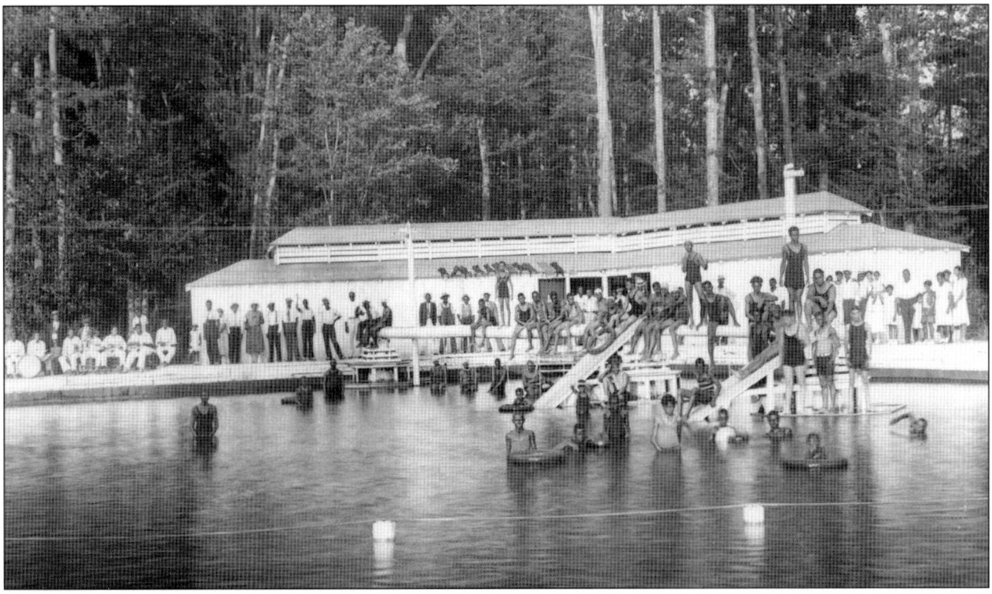

Augusta Sea Beach is shown here as an African-American recreation area. Several groups of people can be seen enjoying the cool water. The swimming pool was owned by John Stroer and located near the Creosote Plant down Long Dirt Road, south of Augusta off Highway 56, near Phinizy Swamp. (Courtesy of Augusta Museum of History.)

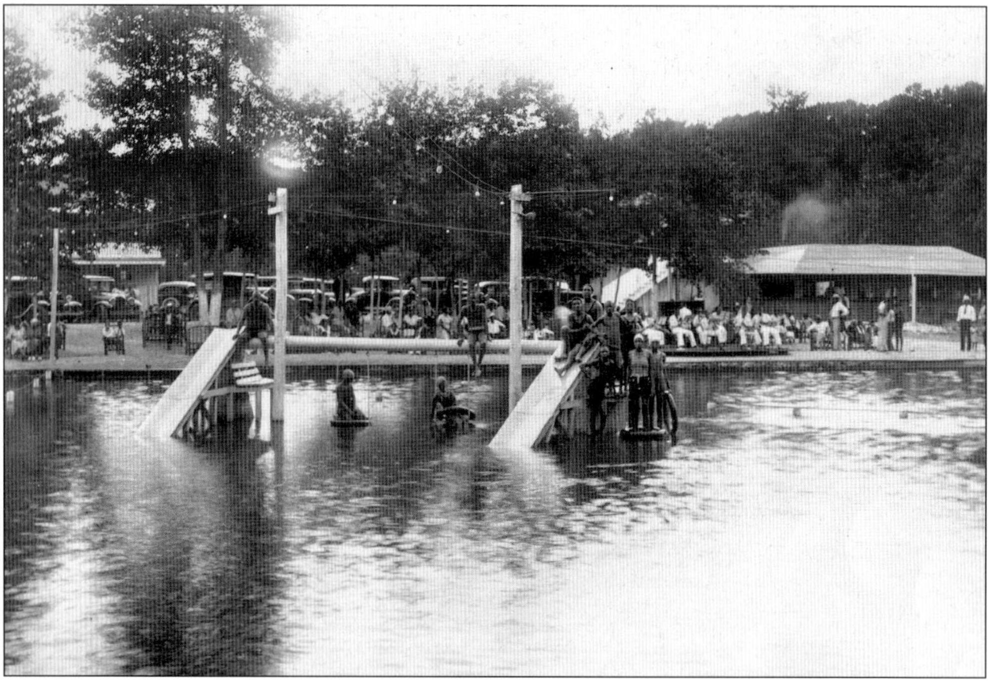

Palmetto Pond was a gathering spot for African-American recreation during the 1920s. The site was located in North Augusta across the Fifth Street bridge. (Courtesy of Augusta Museum of History.)

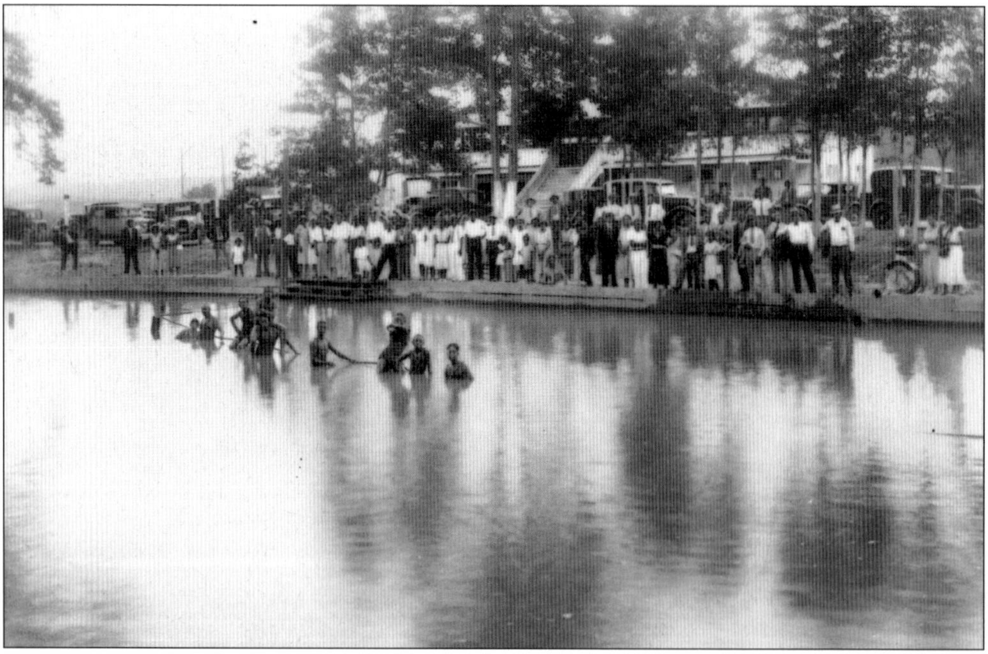

Palmetto Pond offered swimming activities and a chance to get away from the summer heat and humidity that plagues Augusta in July and August. (Courtesy of Augusta Museum of History.)

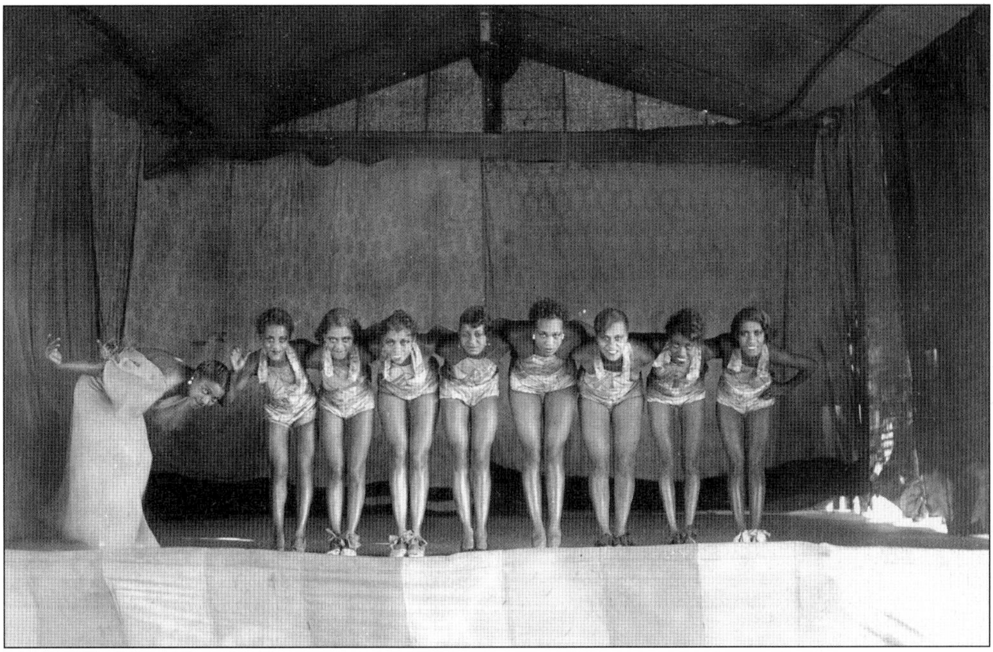

“What an outstanding performance!” bellowed a man seated in the audience when this photograph was taken. Nine young African-American women bow to the audience at the conclusion of a show. (Courtesy of Augusta Museum of History.)

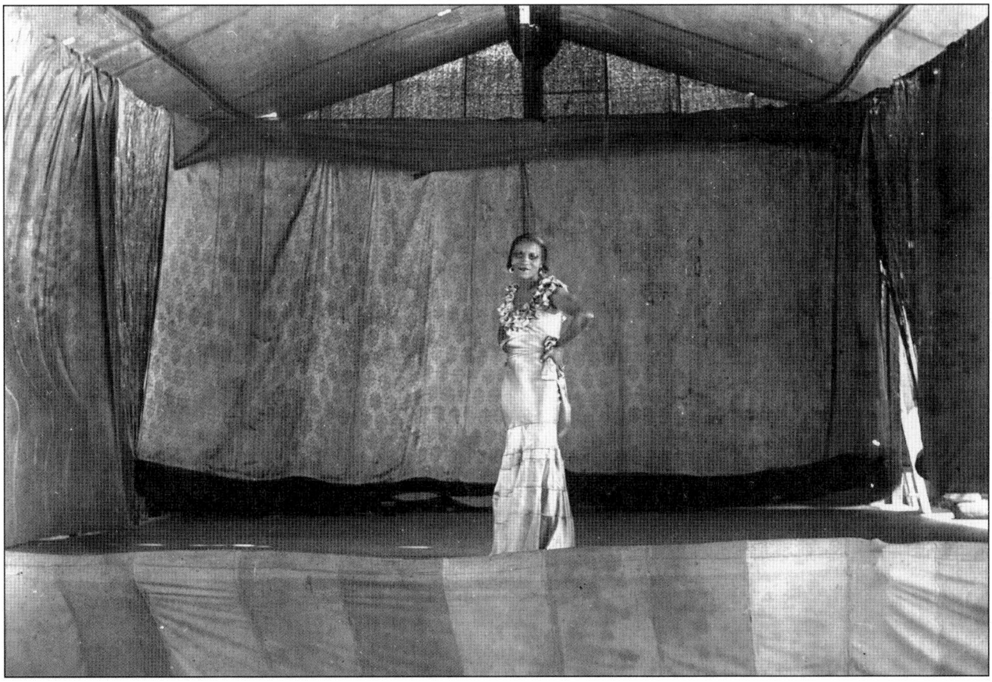

This woman stands with her hands on her hips, smiling at the end of a solo. Notice the simple tattered curtain backdrop she poses against. Most of the time, the performers had to use what was available because of minimal funds. (Courtesy of Augusta Museum of History.)

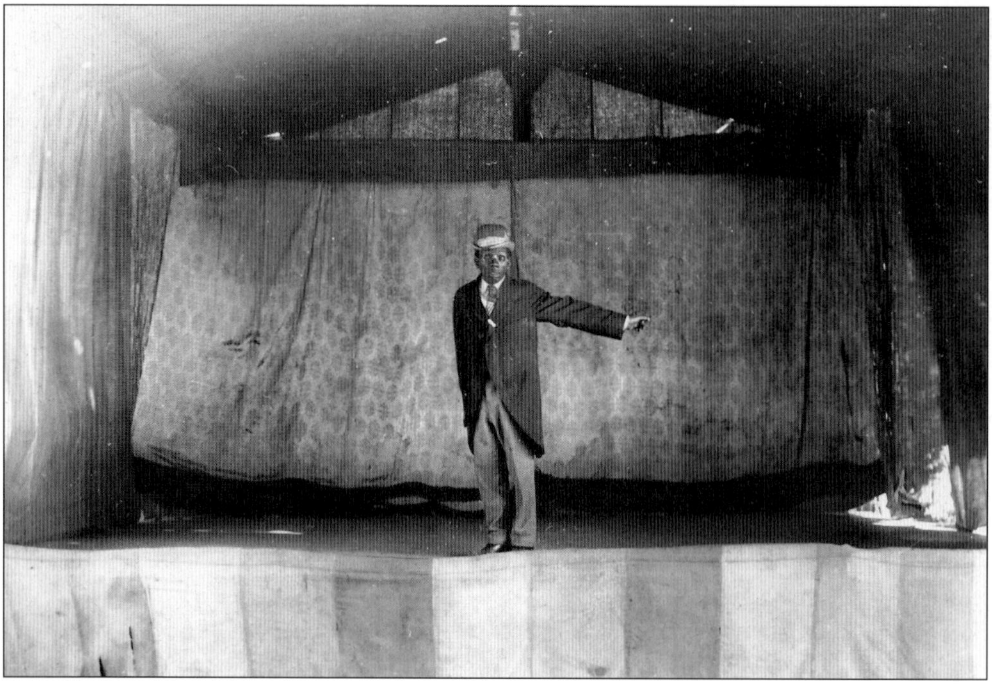

This aspiring actor stands and points to his left during what is probably a comedy skit. His costume resembles the comic fundamentals used during this period for the public's entertainment. (Courtesy of Augusta Museum of History.)

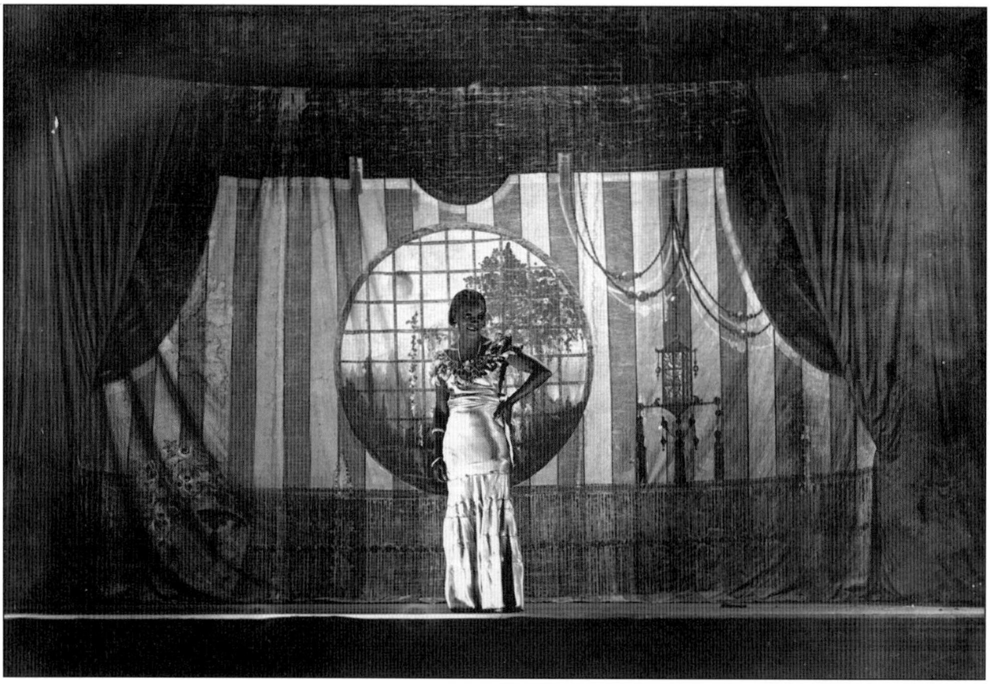

A single actress stands before an elaborate backdrop at the end of a performance. The window shows trees, sky, and the sun. (Courtesy of Augusta Museum of History.)

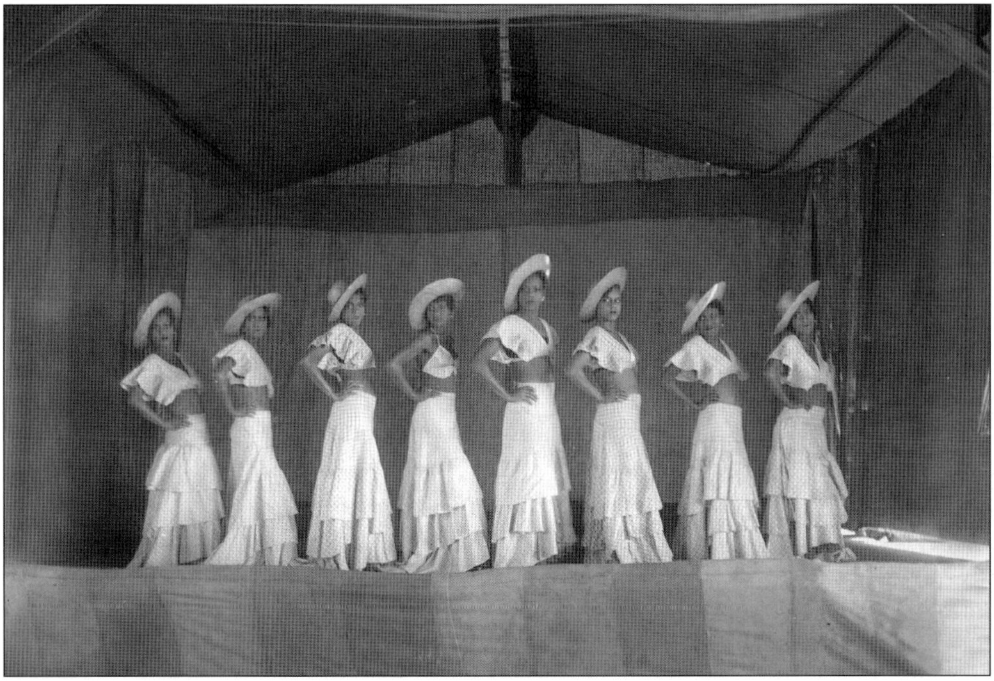

A group of eight actresses stand in a row, probably performing a musical. Their dress reflects the styles of the 1930s. The theatre company spent a large sum of their budget on costumes. (Courtesy of Augusta Museum of History.)

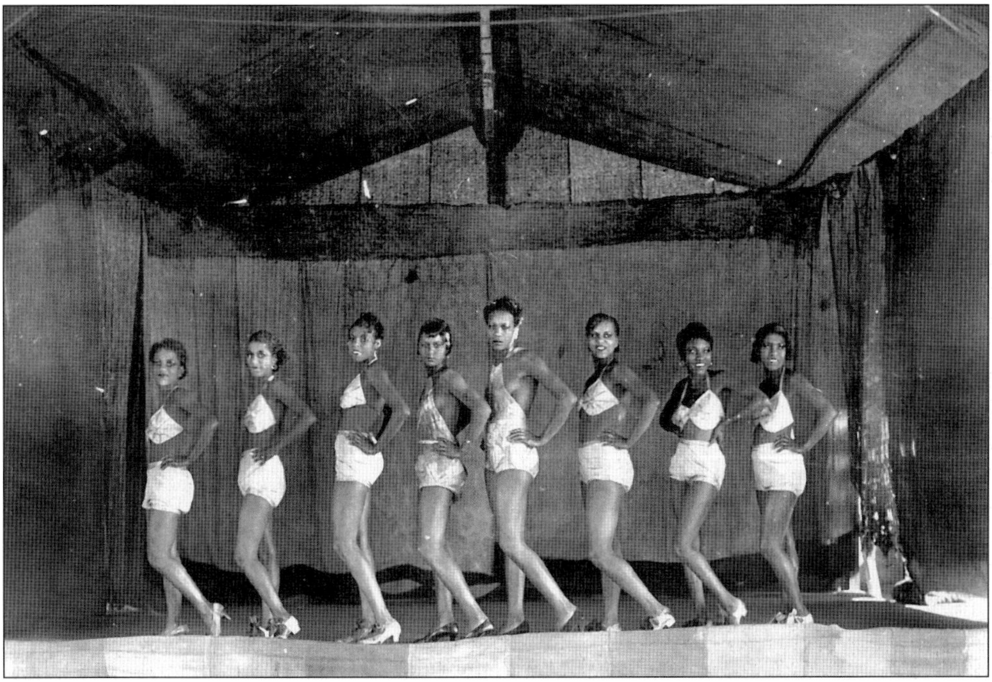

These young women are dressed scantily for their performance. The shorts and tops were pushing the cultural limits of the time. (Courtesy of Augusta Museum of History.)

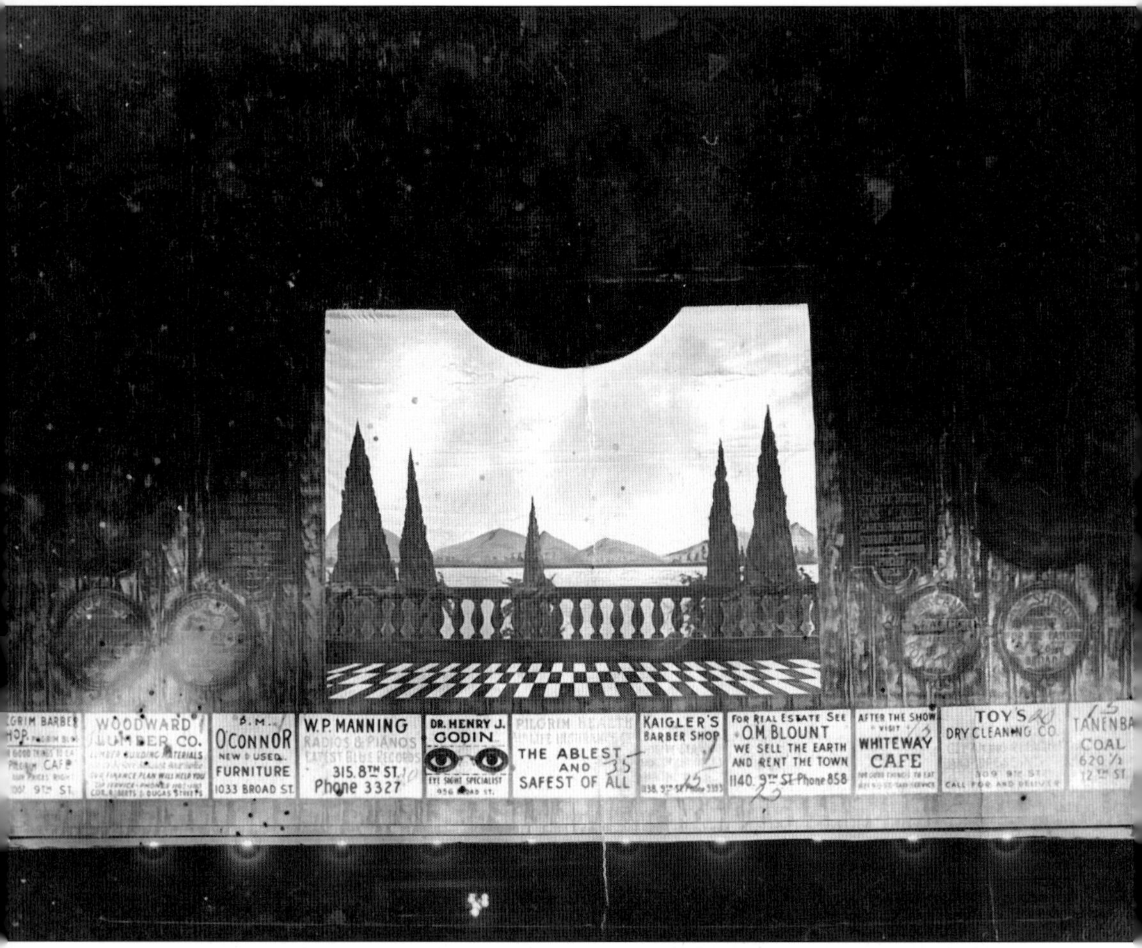

This is the interior of the Lenox Theatre during the 1930s. Many signs for advertisement were mounted on the front of the stage. Dr. Henry J. Godin, O'Connor Furniture, Woodward Lumber Company, and Toy's Dry Cleaning Company are some of the advertisements posted. (Courtesy of Augusta Museum of History.)

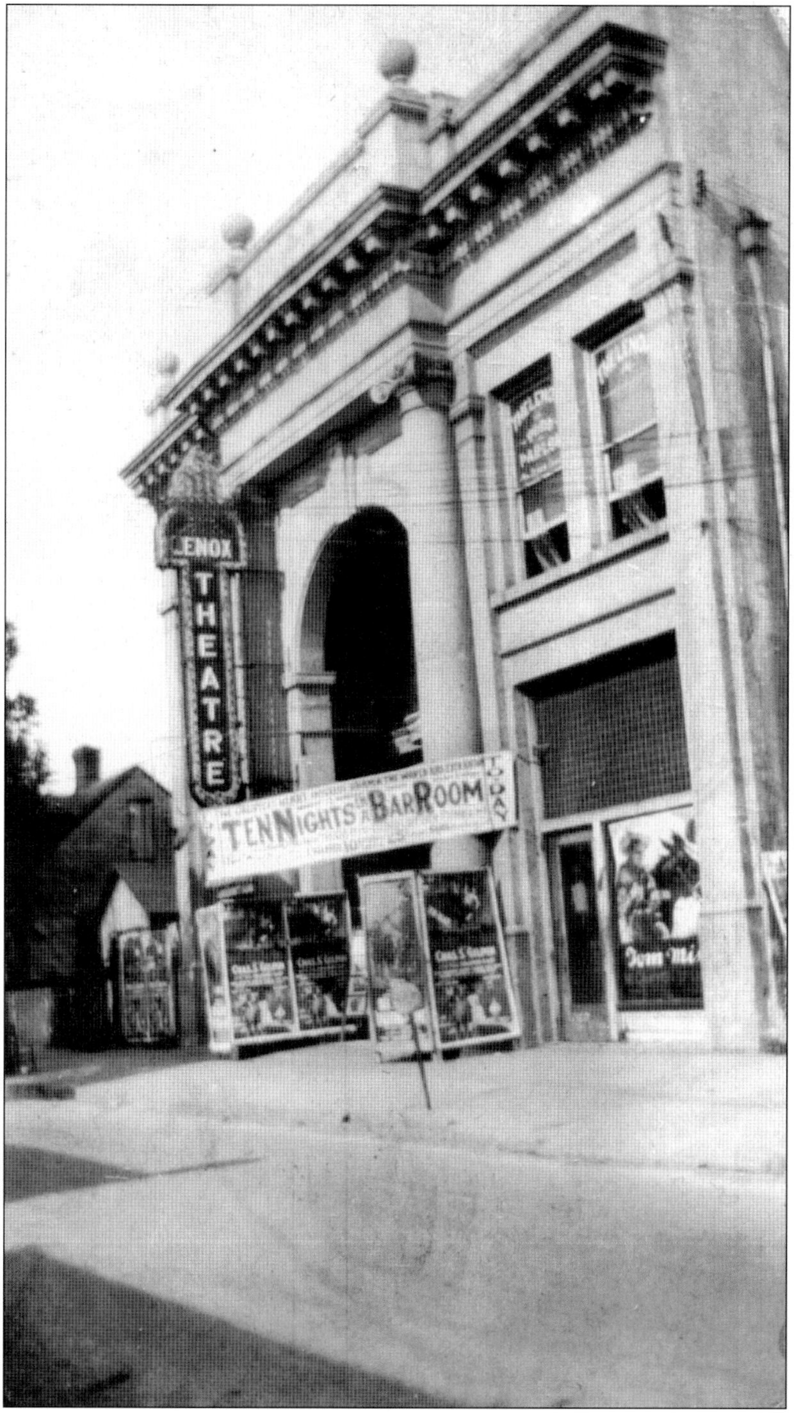

Ten Nights in a Bar Room, starring Chas S. Galen, was the feature movie slated for the day this photograph was taken of the Lenox Theatre. African Americans of the period enjoyed the cinema produced by Hollywood in a time of theatrical growth. (Courtesy of Augusta Museum of History.)

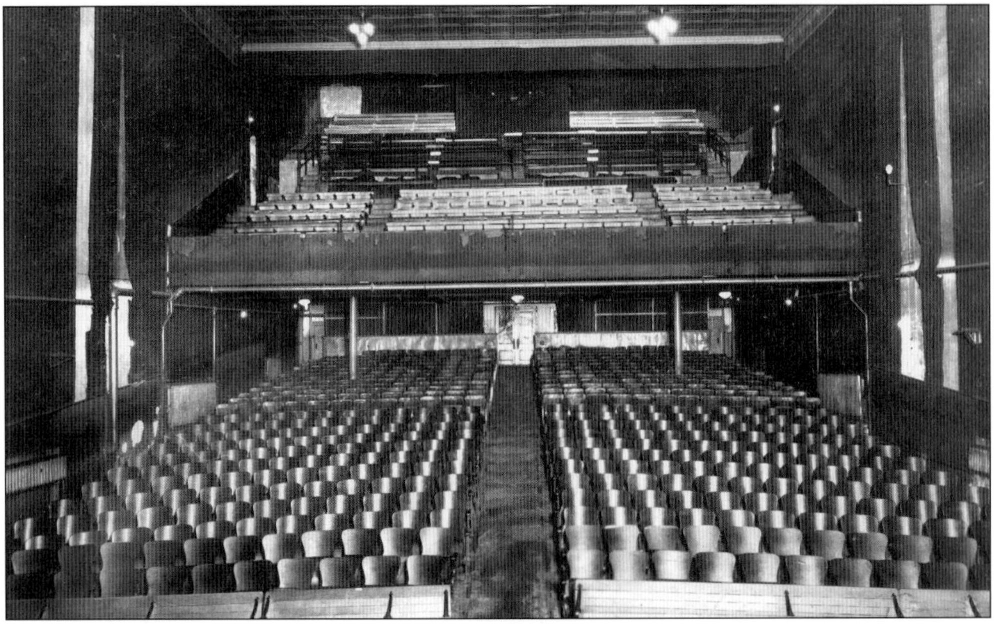

The interior of the Lenox Theatre remained much the same, from its humble beginnings in the late 1920s until 1966. (Courtesy of Augusta Museum of History.)

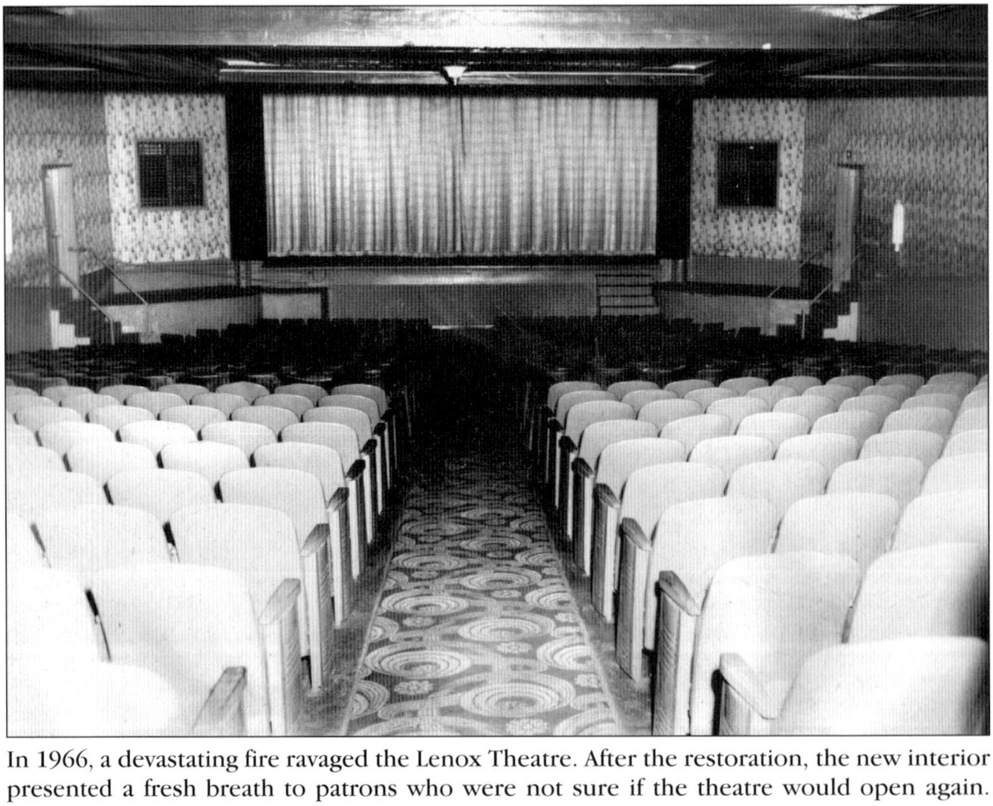

In 1966, a devastating fire ravaged the Lenox Theatre. After the restoration, the new interior presented a fresh breath to patrons who were not sure if the theatre would open again. (Courtesy of Augusta Museum of History.)

Five
BUSINESS

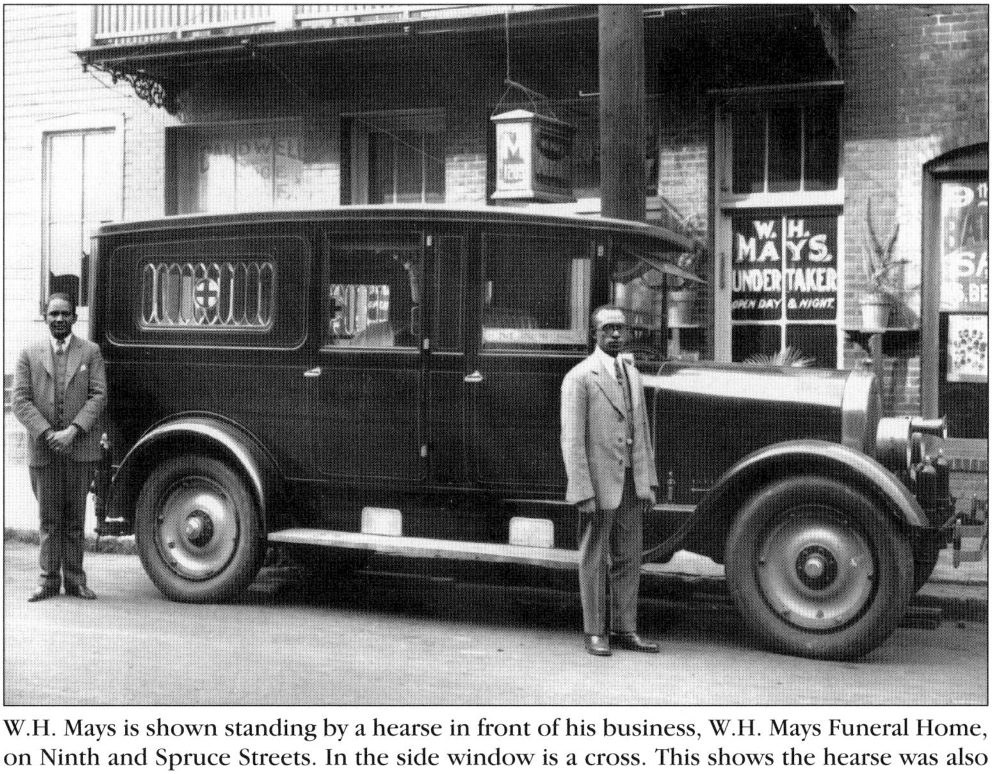

W.H. Mays is shown standing by a hearse in front of his business, W.H. Mays Funeral Home, on Ninth and Spruce Streets. In the side window is a cross. This shows the hearse was also used as an ambulance, which was not an uncommon practice during the earlier part of the 20th century. (Courtesy of Augusta Museum of History.)

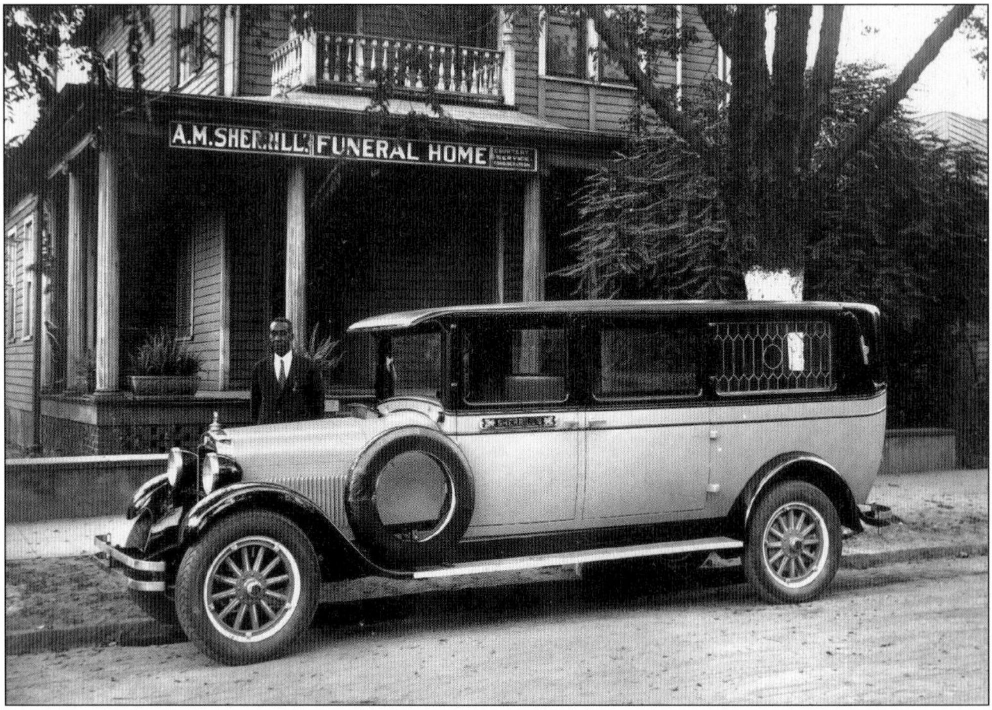

A.M. Sherill Funeral Home boasts "Courtesy, Service, and Consideration" as its motto. The funeral home rose to the occasion as one of the most professional in the area. (Courtesy of Augusta Museum of History.)

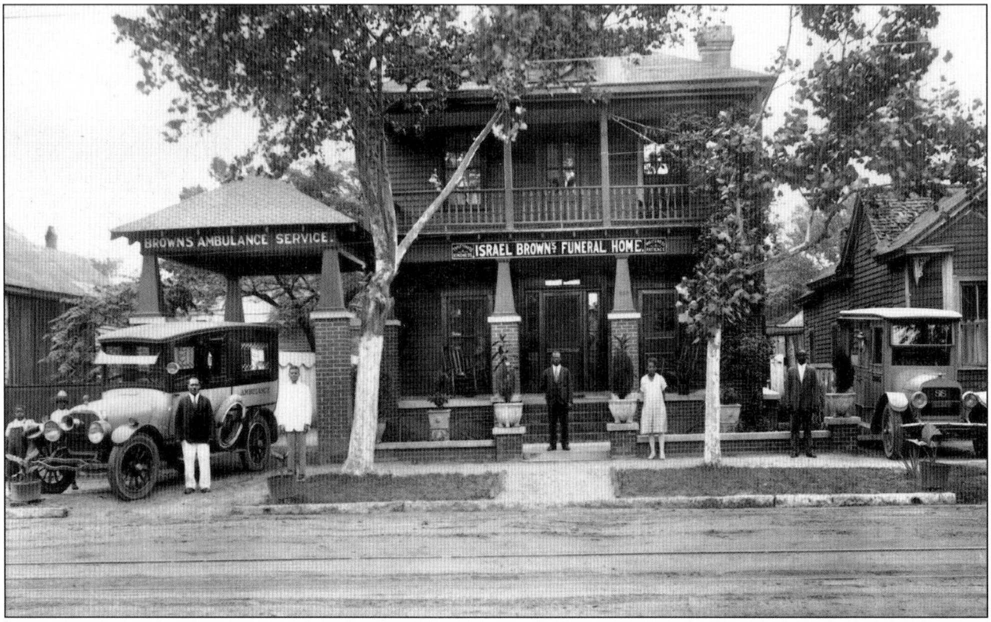

Israel Brown's Funeral Home was located in downtown Augusta and served the community for many years. On the side of the funeral home is a covered driveway. Above the vehicle, a sign reads "Brown's Ambulance Service." (Courtesy of Augusta Museum of History.)

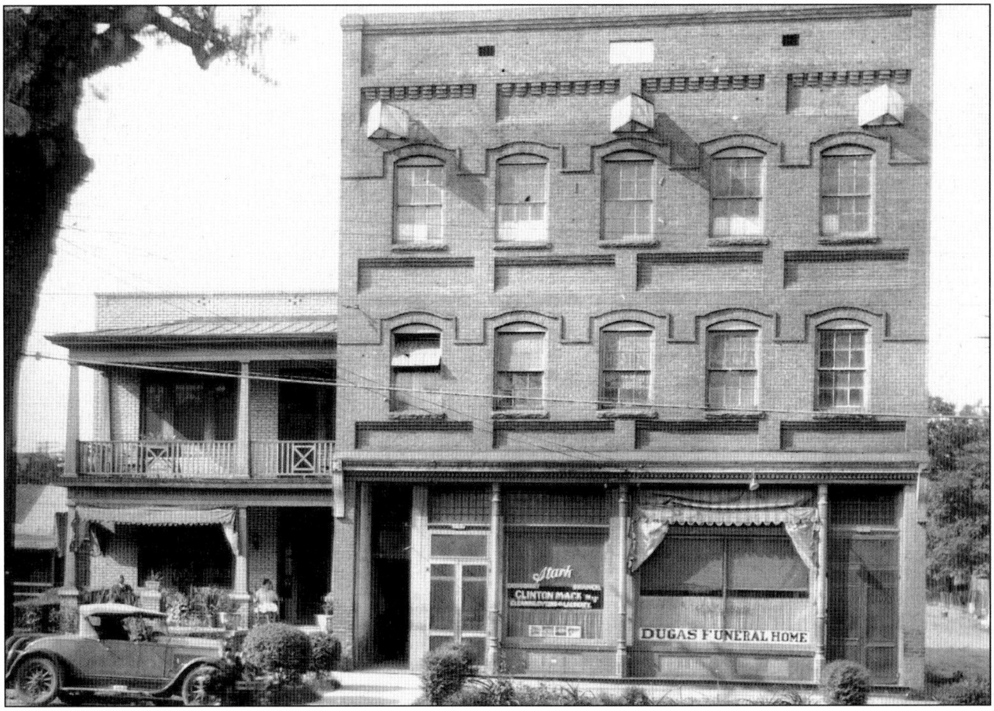

The Dugas Funeral Home was one of many parlors for African Americans in the early 1900s. Clinton Mack Cleaning, Dyeing, and Laundry was next door to the funeral home. (Courtesy of Augusta Museum of History.)

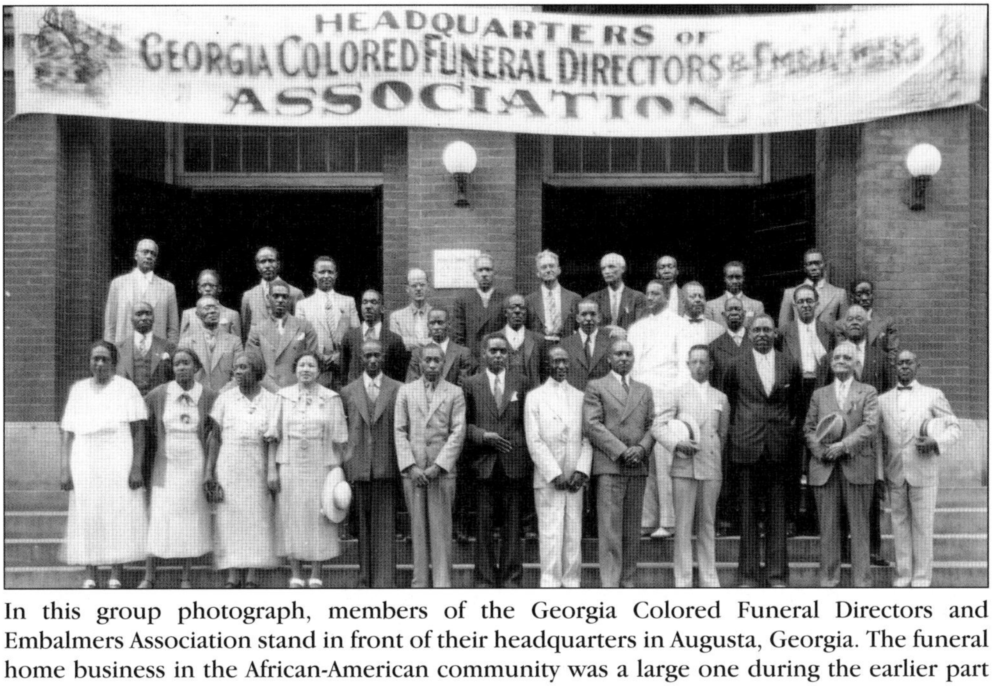

In this group photograph, members of the Georgia Colored Funeral Directors and Embalmers Association stand in front of their headquarters in Augusta, Georgia. The funeral home business in the African-American community was a large one during the earlier part of the 20th century. (Courtesy of Augusta Museum of History.)

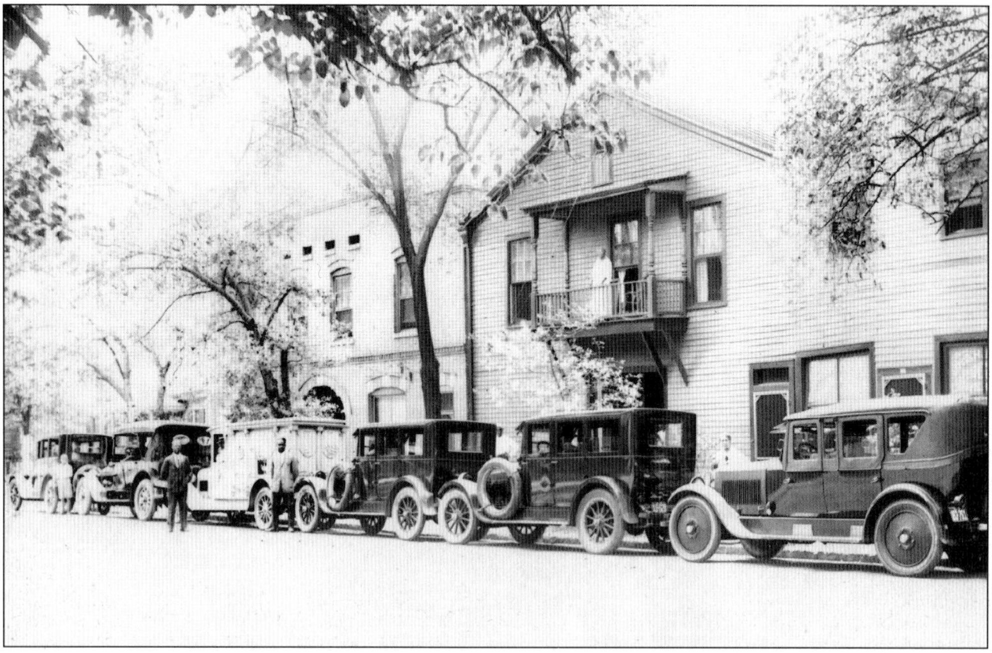

Shown here is an unidentified Augusta funeral home. (Courtesy of Augusta Museum of History.)

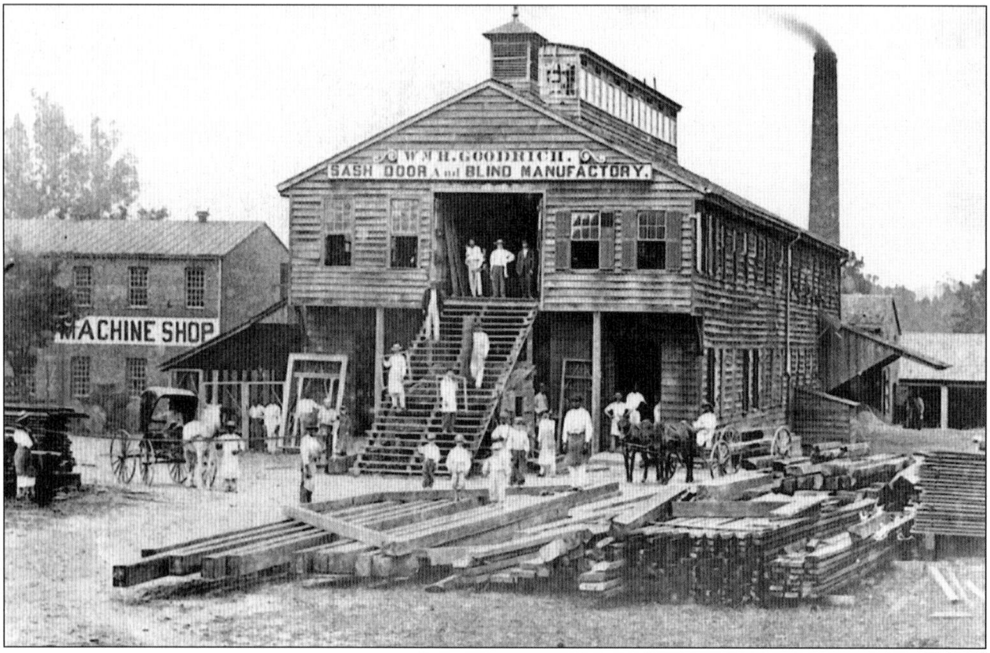

In this picture, dated from the late 1880s, African-American workers stop to pose for a photographer. The business seen in the photograph is W.M.H. Goodrich Sash and Blind Manufactory. Behind the horse-drawn buggy is the machine shop. (Courtesy of Special Collections, Reese Library, Augusta State University.)

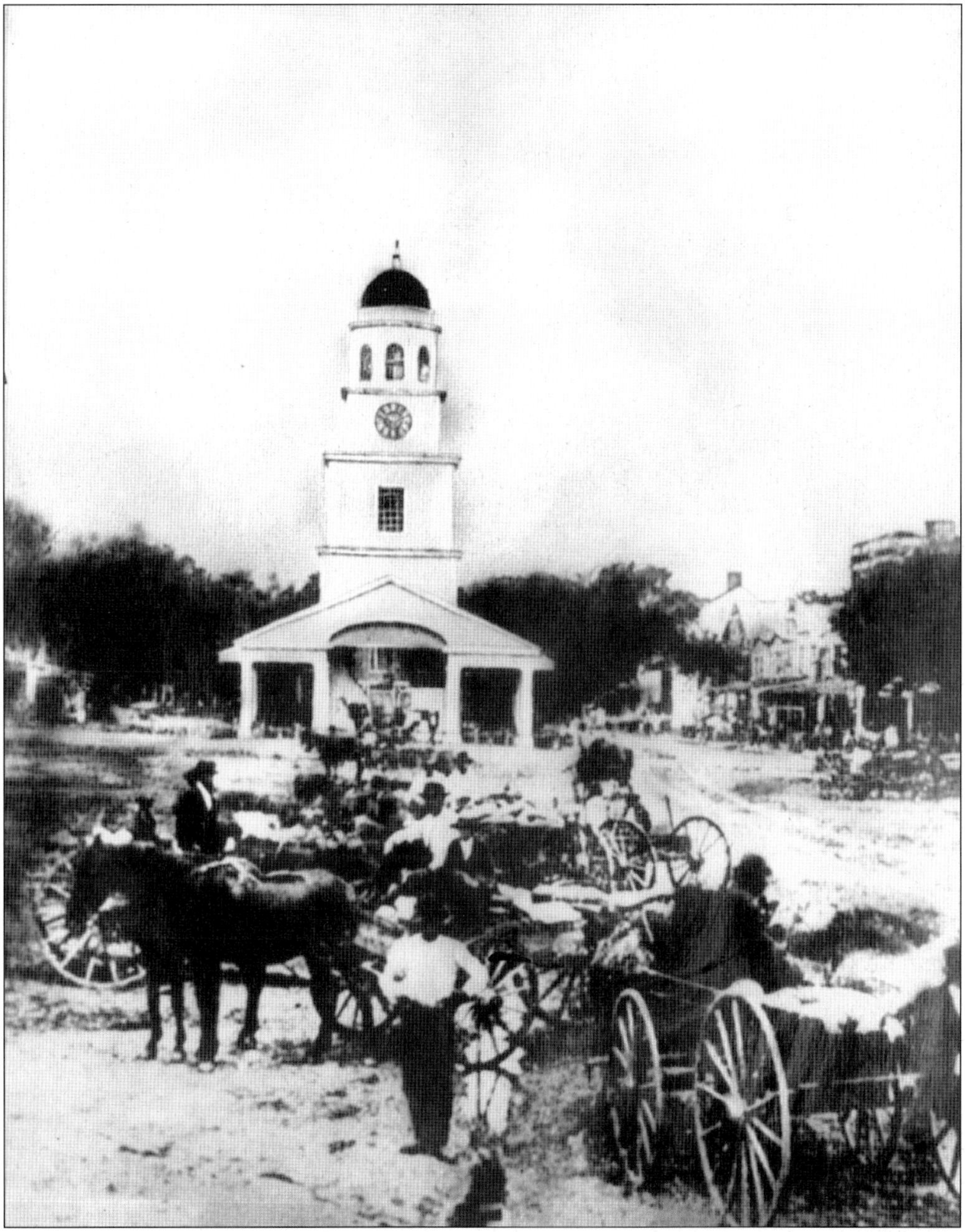

This early picture of the Lower Market on Broad Street shows several African Americans with horse-drawn wagons gathered in the street. The market was a place for trading goods and was used as an antebellum auction site for the marketing of slaves. Today, the only remnant of the market is a pillar that stands on the corner of Broad and Fifth Streets. Legend has it that the pillar is haunted and should not be touched. (Courtesy of Augusta Museum of History.)

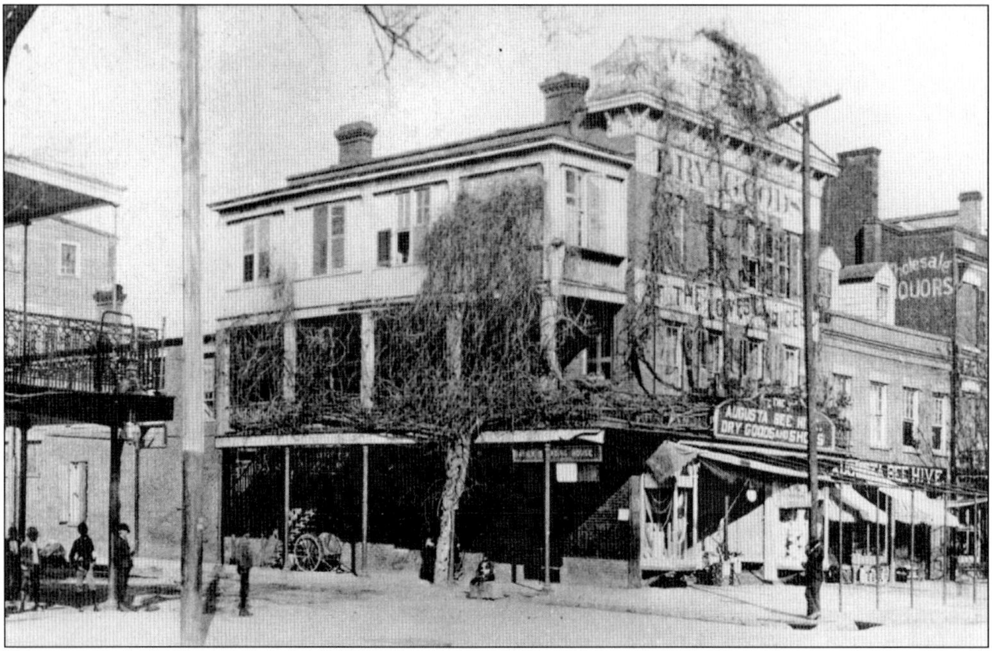

In the background of this photograph, signs read Bee Hive Dry Goods, Boarding House, and Whole Sale Liquors. (Courtesy of Special Collections, Reese Library, Augusta State University.)

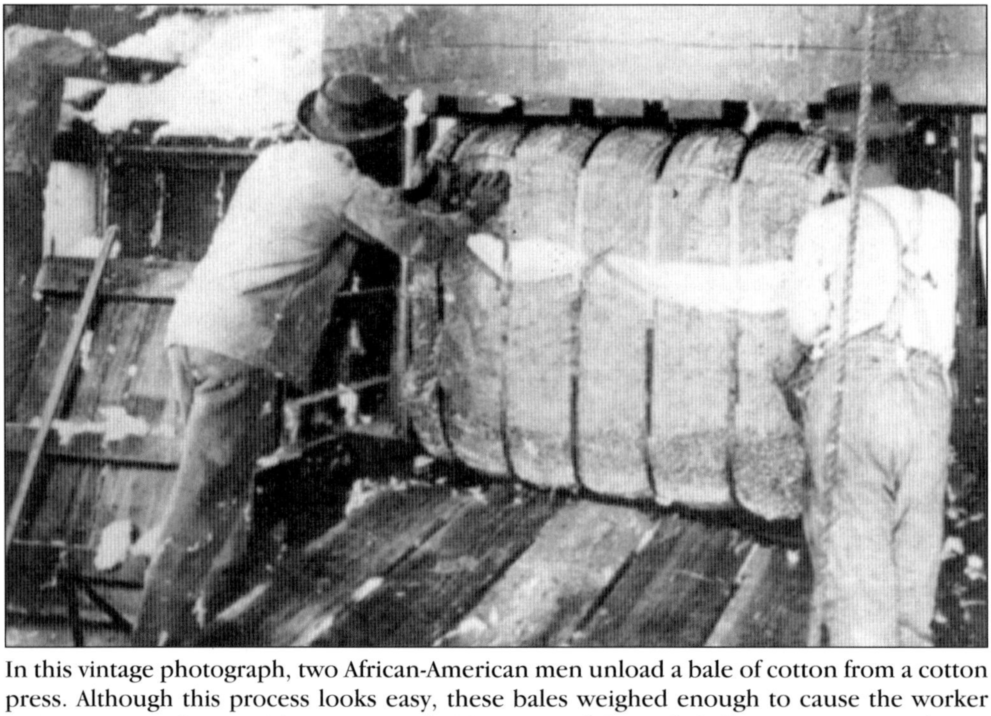

In this vintage photograph, two African-American men unload a bale of cotton from a cotton press. Although this process looks easy, these bales weighed enough to cause the worker serious injury if an accident occurred. (Courtesy of Special Collections, Reese Library, Augusta State University.)

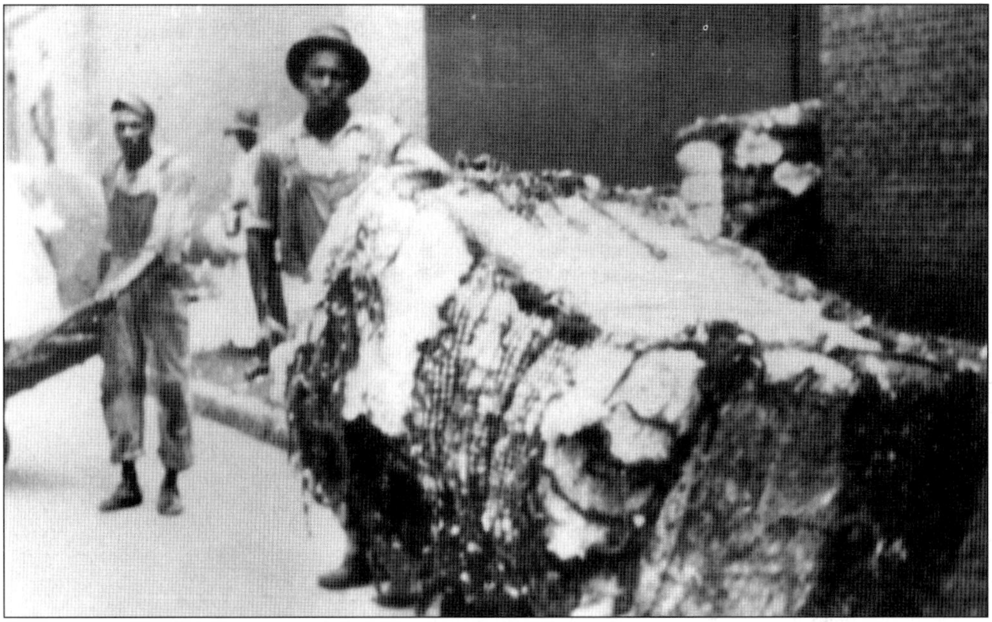

Several African-American men are shown moving bales of cotton on carts. Before the Civil War, Augusta was the second largest center for cotton in the world. The Cotton Exchange was on Reynolds Street and gave updates on cotton prices throughout the day. (Courtesy of Special Collections, Reese Library, Augusta State University.)

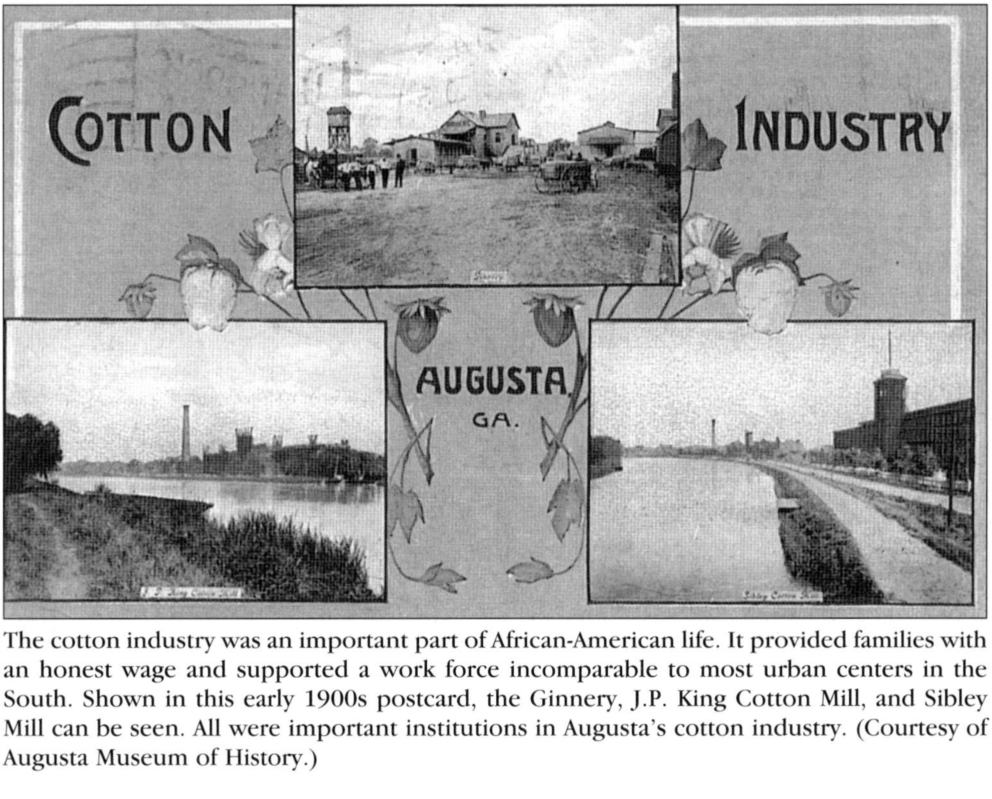

The cotton industry was an important part of African-American life. It provided families with an honest wage and supported a work force incomparable to most urban centers in the South. Shown in this early 1900s postcard, the Ginnery, J.P. King Cotton Mill, and Sibley Mill can be seen. All were important institutions in Augusta's cotton industry. (Courtesy of Augusta Museum of History.)

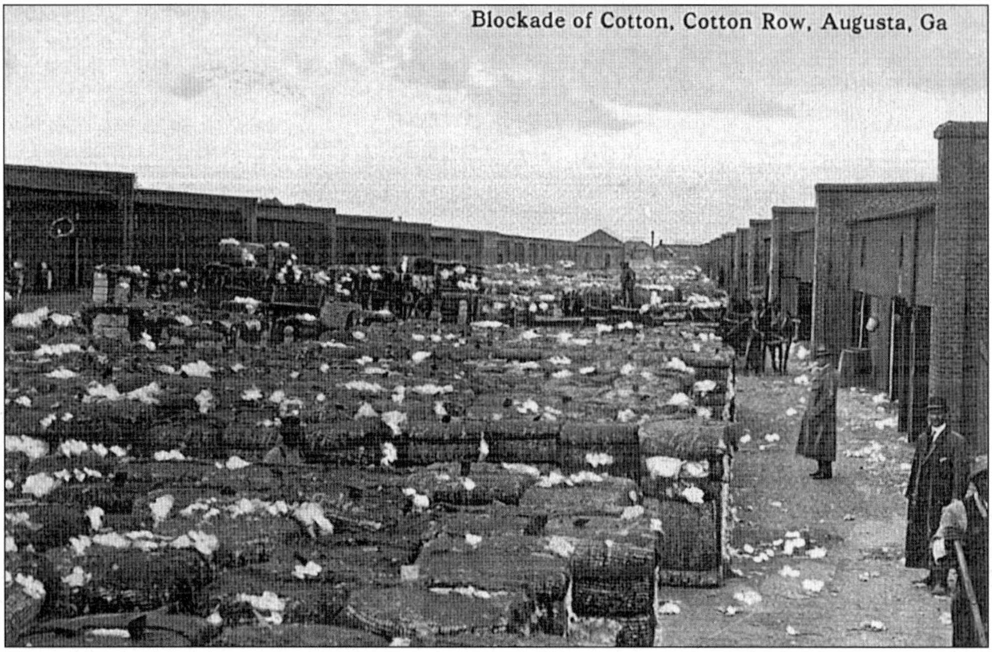

This early 1900s postcard shows a city-block of cotton. Bale after bale can be seen along with African-American men standing near the warehouses. The cotton could span so far that a man could walk across the top of it for a mile. (Courtesy of Milledge G. Murray.)

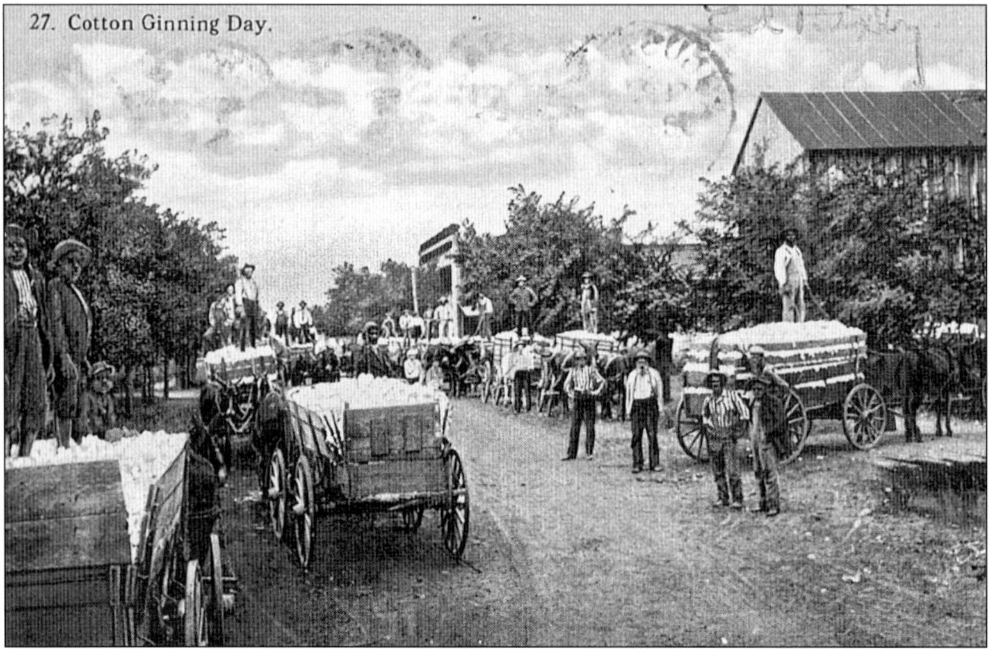

This postcard is titled "Cotton Ginning Day." In the background, African-American men can be seen preparing the wooden wagons for transporting cotton. These men helped make Augusta one of the world's leading cotton industry cities. (Courtesy of Milledge G. Murray.)

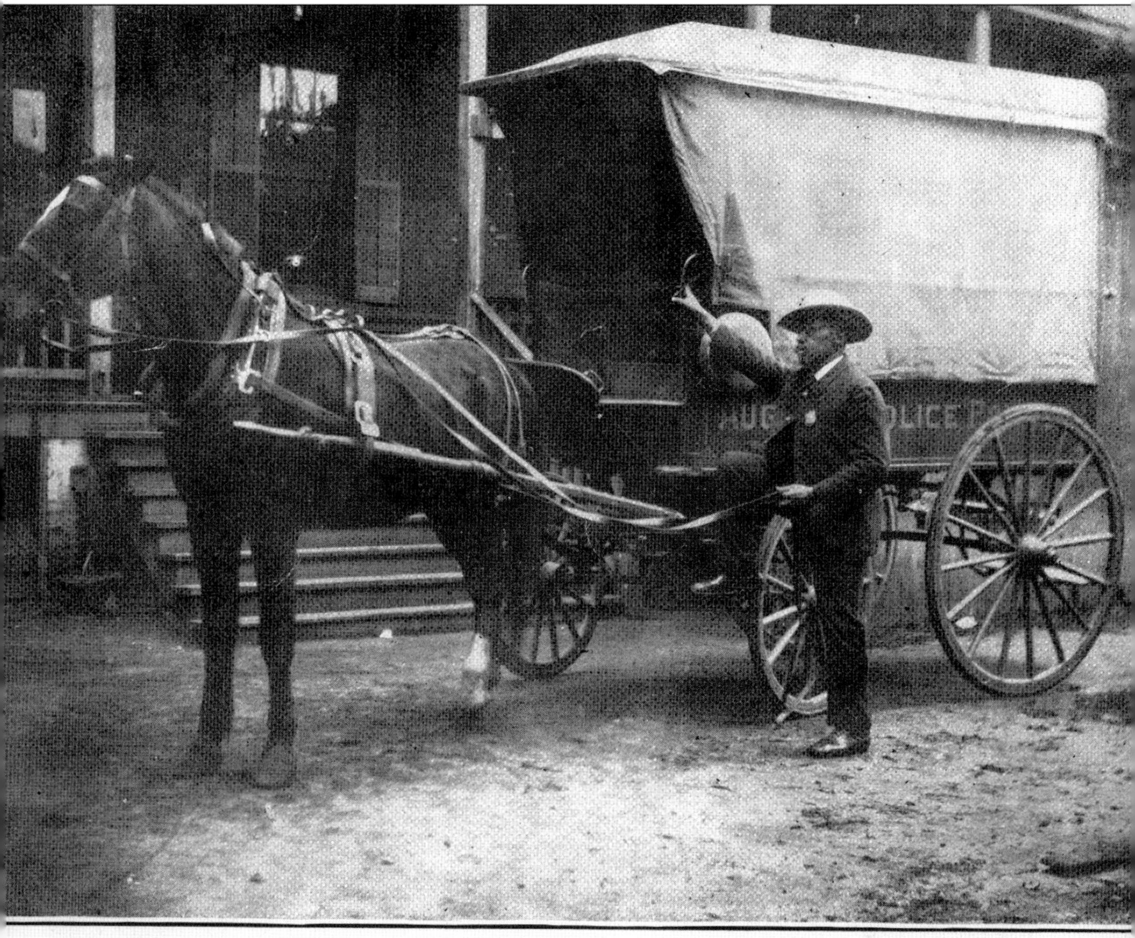

Robert Washington, Janitor and Patrol Driver.

This photograph, dated around 1909, shows an African-American man named Robert Washington, who worked for the Augusta Police Department as a janitor and patrol driver. (Courtesy of Joe Lee, Private Collection.)

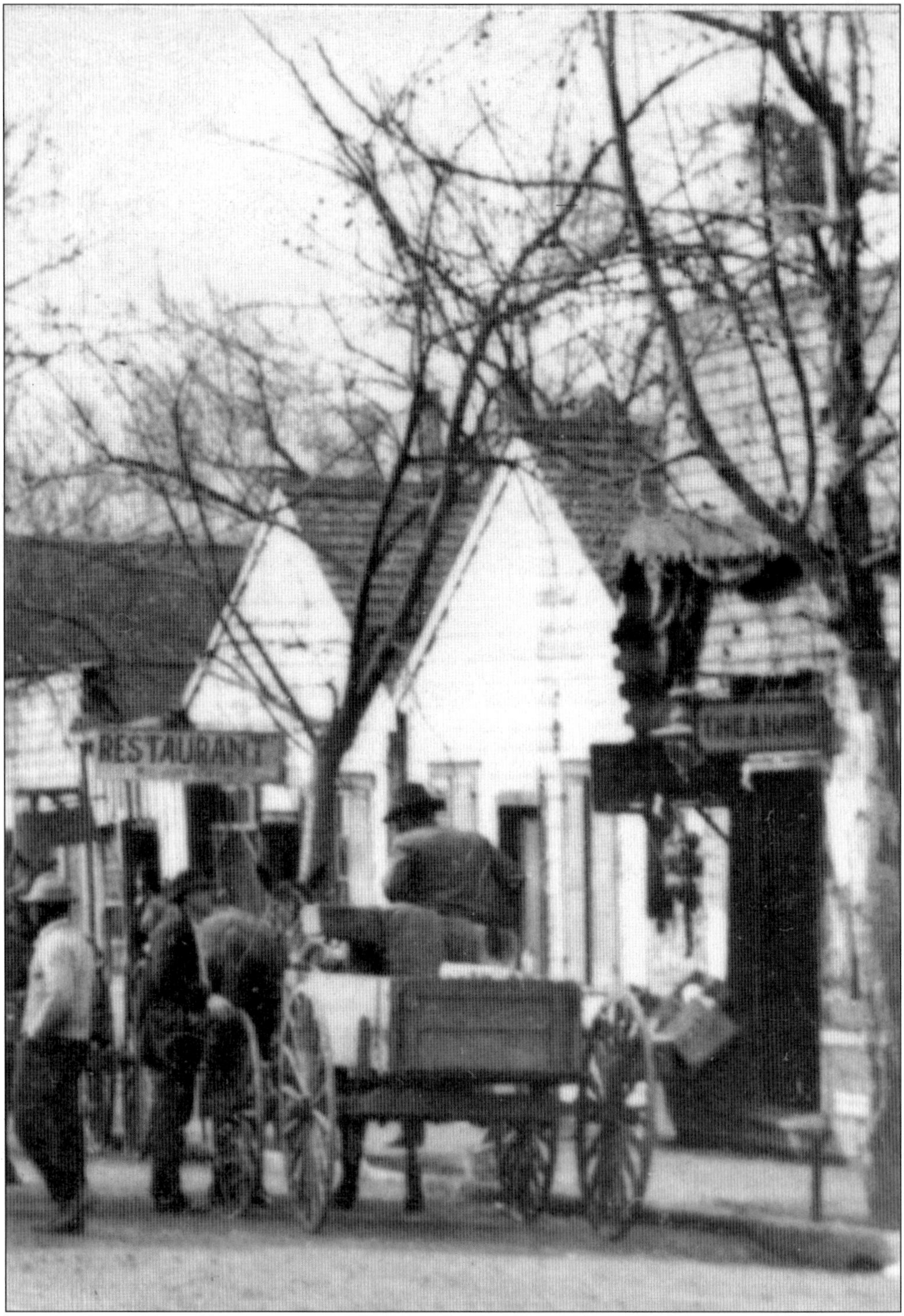

A horse-drawn wagon is driven by an African-American driver at 13th Street, near North Augusta, South Carolina. In the distance, a sign reads "Restaurant" and another one "Theater." (Courtesy of Augusta Museum of History.)

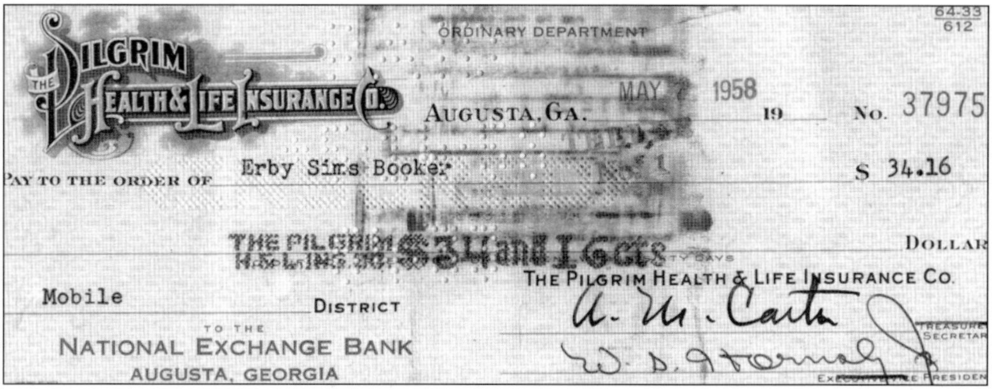

THE PILGRIM HEALTH & LIFE INSURANCE CO.
ORDINARY DEPARTMENT
64-33
612
AUGUSTA, GA. MAY 7 1958 19
No. 37975
PAY TO THE ORDER OF Erby Sims Booker $ 34.16
THE PILGRIM H.&L. INS. CO. $34 and 16 cts
DOLLAR
THE PILGRIM HEALTH & LIFE INSURANCE CO.
Mobile DISTRICT
TO THE
NATIONAL EXCHANGE BANK
AUGUSTA, GEORGIA
TREASURER
SECRETARY
EXECUTIVE VICE PRESIDENT

Pilgrim Health and Life Insurance was located in the middle of the Golden Blocks, now known as Laney Walker Boulevard. A check from the company lists the name of Erby Sims Booker for the amount of $34.16. (Courtesy of Augusta Museum of History.)

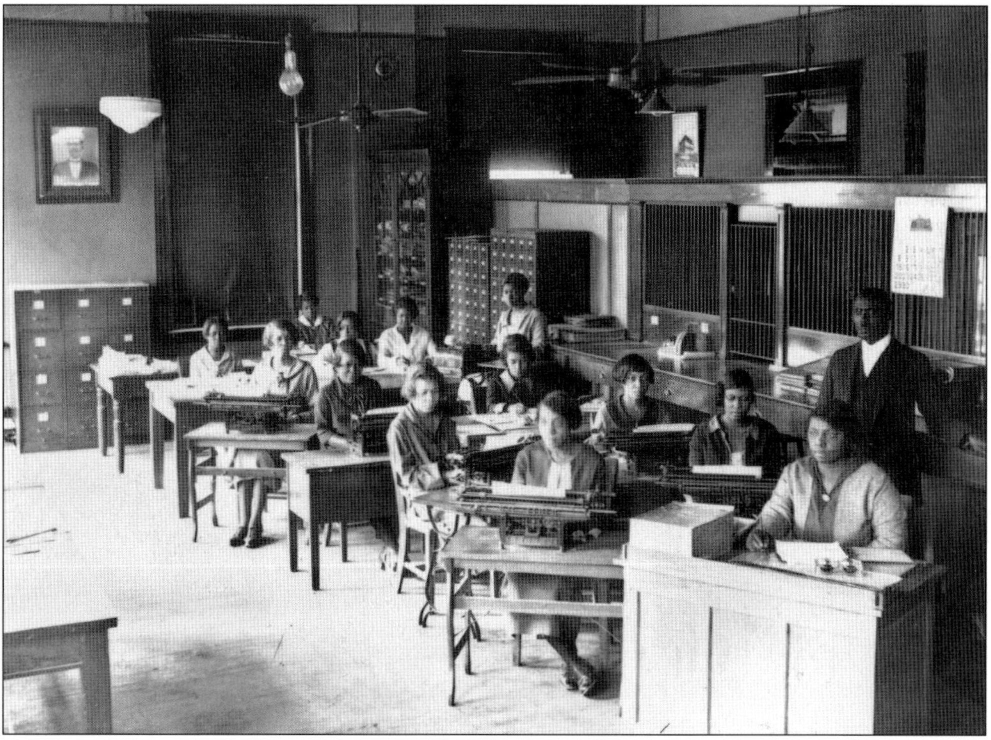

A group of busy employees of the Pilgrim Health and Life Insurance Company stop and pose for a photograph. This photograph shows the interior of the business in the early years of its operation. The company became one of the most influential African-American businesses in the South. (Courtesy of Augusta Museum of History.)

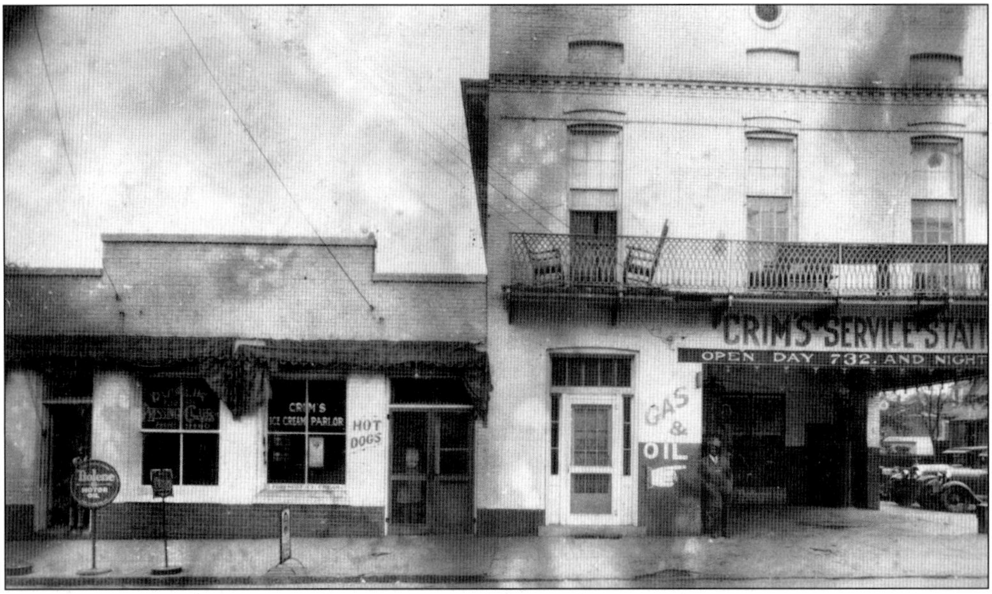

Crims Service Station and Ice Cream Parlor was a popular business in the African-American community. Dublin Pressing Club was next door, with a four-digit phone number of 9460. (Courtesy of Augusta Museum of History.)

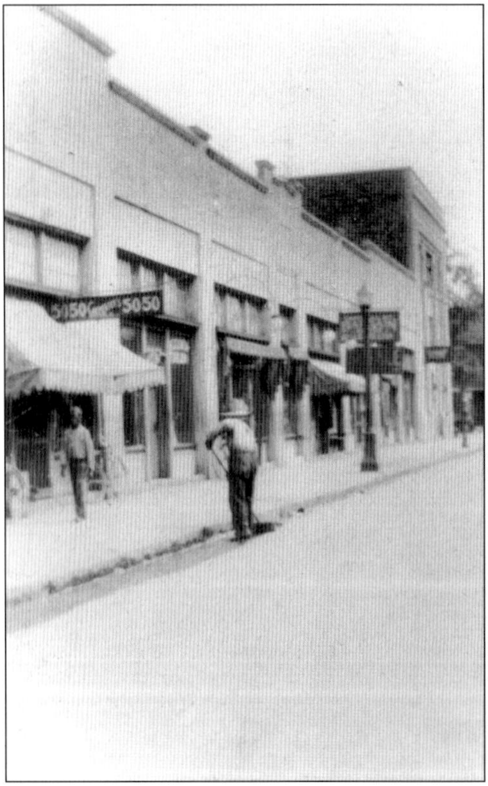

A man sweeps the street in front of several downtown Augusta businesses on Broad Street. A sign in the background advertises The 50/50 store. (Courtesy of Augusta Museum of History.)

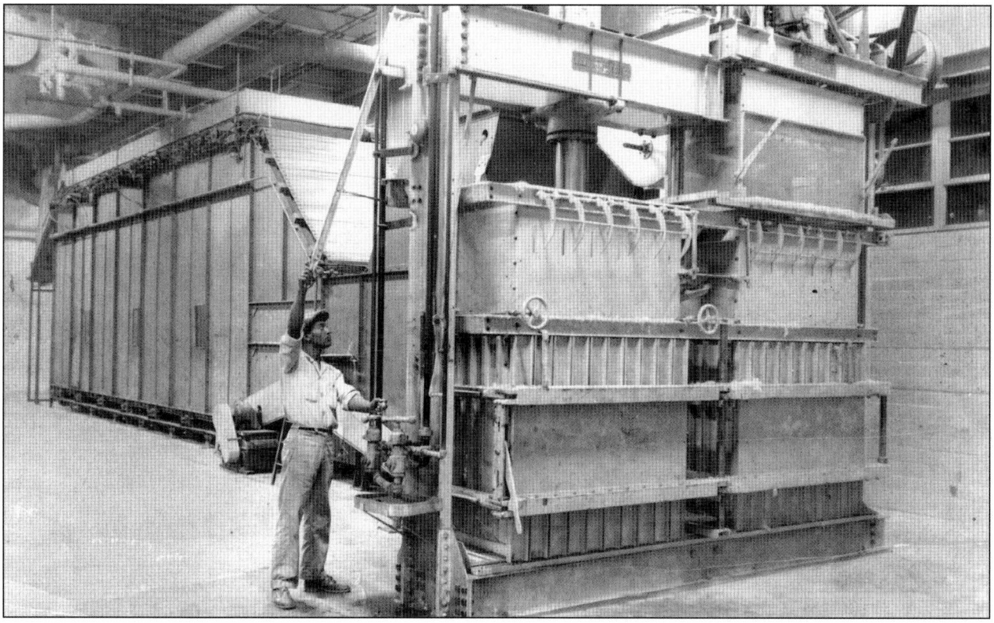

Before the day starts and manufacturing begins, an engineer examines a piece of equipment inside the Riverside Mills. Along with other Augustans, the mill employed many African-American men and was a major contributor to the area's economy. (Courtesy of Augusta Museum of History.)

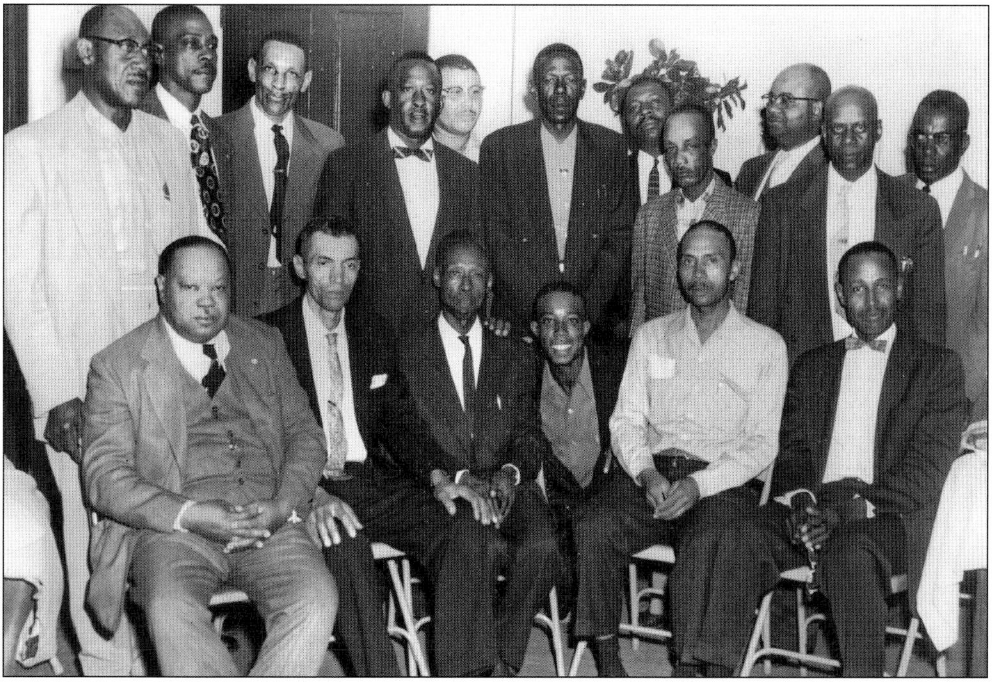

This 1950s photograph shows the Sleeping Car Porters at a professional meeting in Augusta. These men were an important aspect of the railway system. (Courtesy of Augusta Museum of History.)

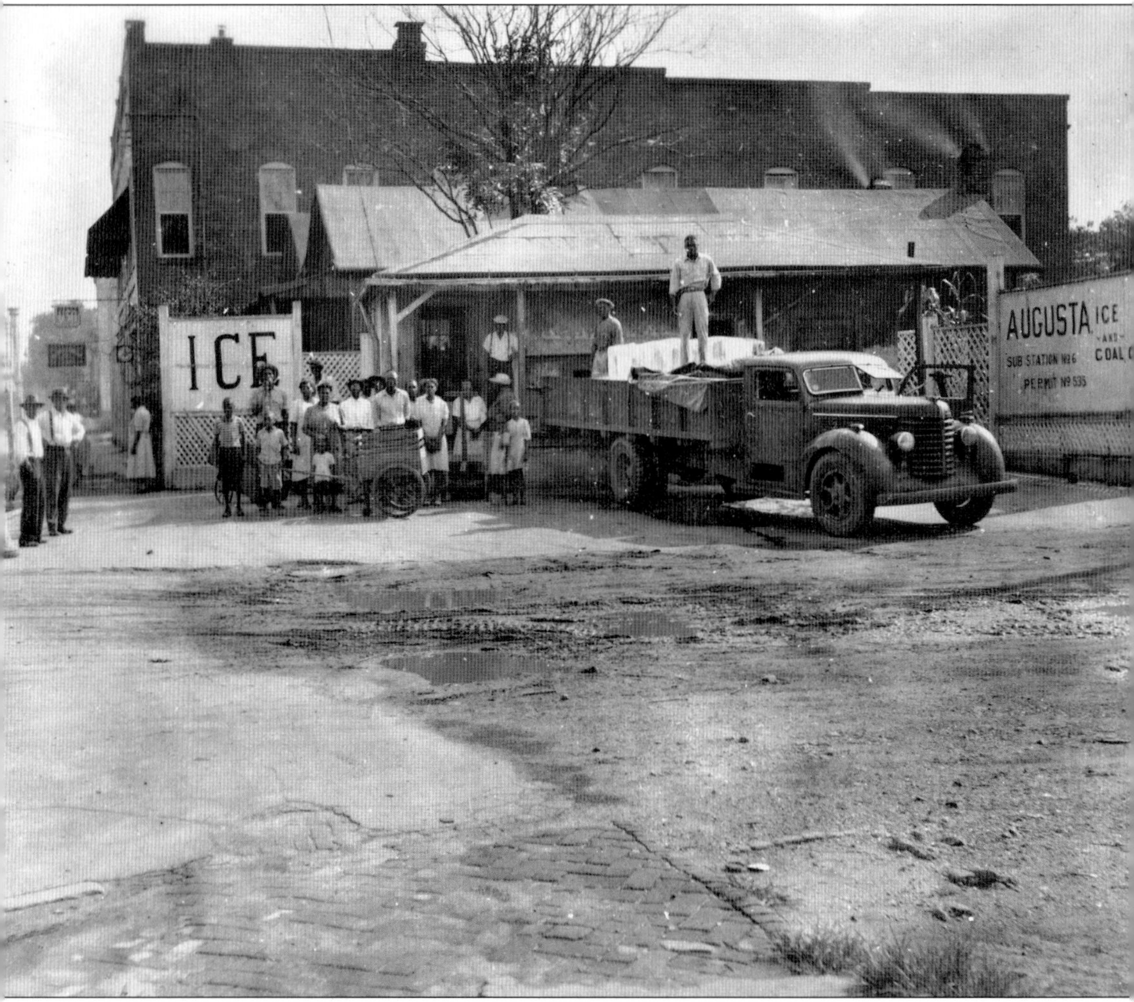

The Augusta Ice and Coal Company was located on 9th Street. It was listed as Sub Station Number 6 and had a permit number of 535. The company was run by African Americans and was located in downtown Augusta. (Courtesy of Augusta Museum of History.)

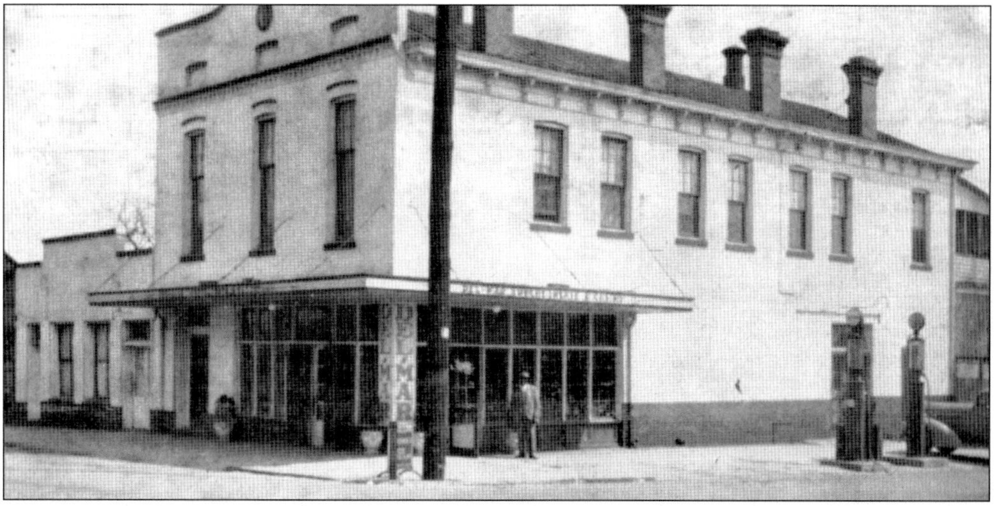

The Del-Mar Casino was called "The Pride of Augusta" and sat in an early African-American business district called the Golden Blocks. All of the businesses in this area were owned and operated by African Americans. Today, the area is known as Laney Walker Boulevard. (Courtesy of Augusta Museum of History.)

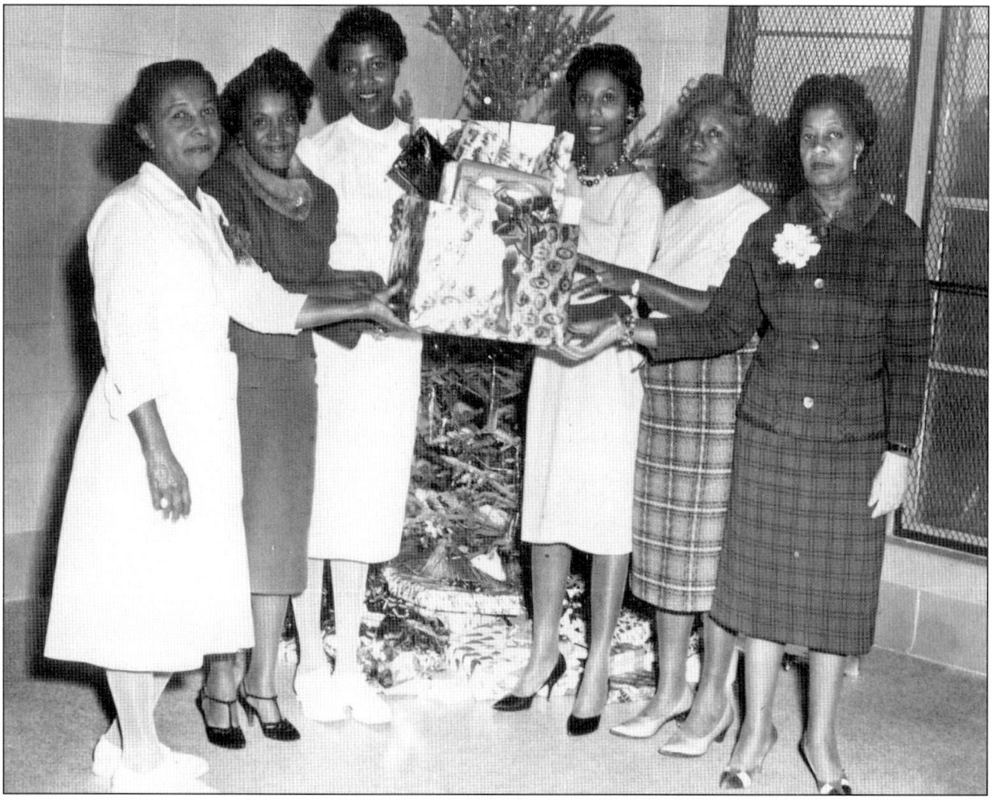

Students from the Registered Nurses School pose in this picture. African-American men and women have contributed to the success of the medical industry in Augusta, which boasts of itself as the largest employer in the county. (Courtesy of Augusta Museum of History.)

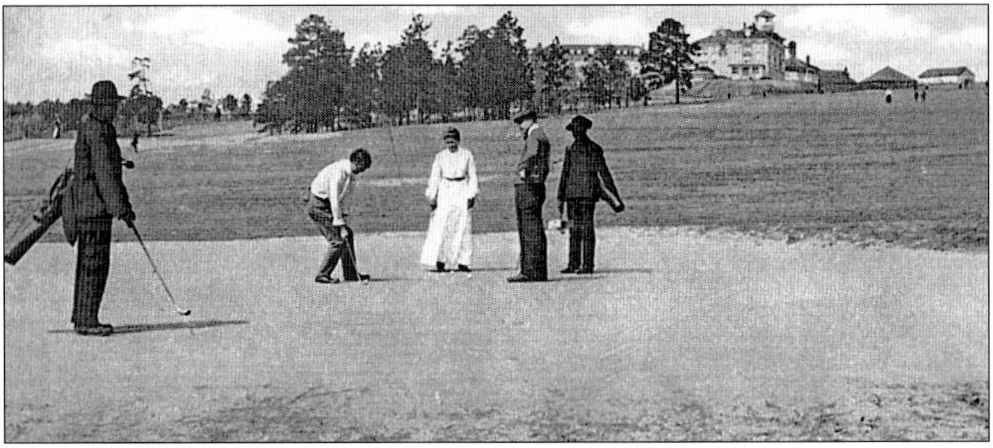

This postcard shows an early glimpse into the world of golf. Near the Hampton Hotel, African-American men working as caddies prepare themselves to hand over a club to a waiting golfer. These men contributed to golf's mounting popularity in Augusta during the turn of the century. (Courtesy of Milledge G. Murray, Private Collection.)

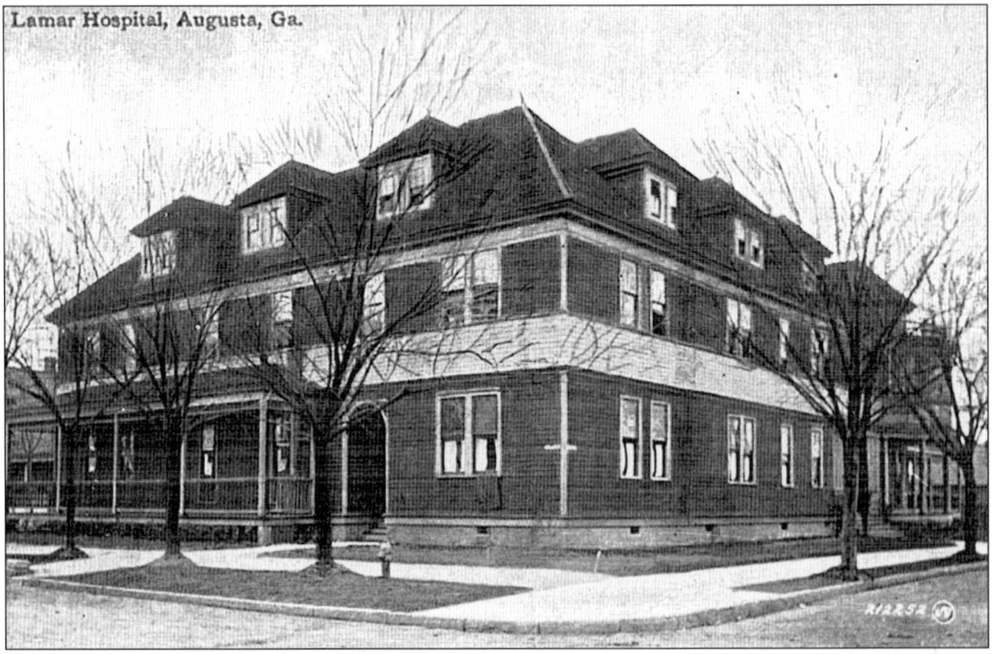

Lamar Hospital was located on Gwinnett Street, at the northwest corner of Harrison Street. Funds for the construction of the hospital were obtained in 1894. The 75-bed building was built for the exclusive care of African Americans and was named after philanthropist Gazeway B. Lamar. In 1911, the hospital caught fire and was destroyed. Tabernacle Baptist church sits on the site today. (Courtesy of Milledge G. Murray.)

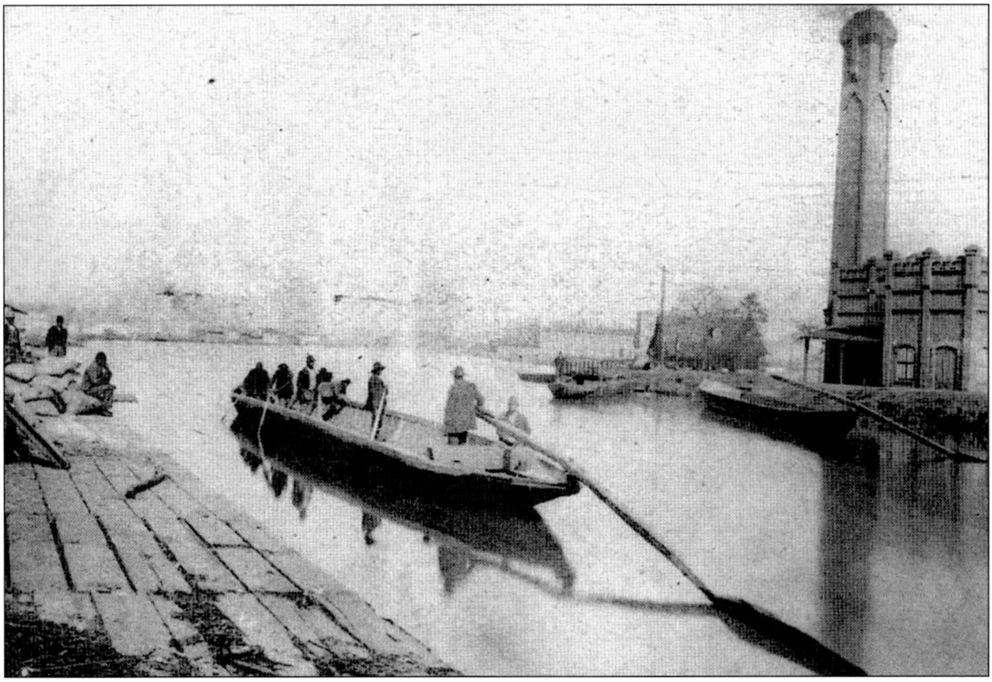

The *Petersburg* boat was used along the Augusta Canal to transport goods. Among the workers that steered the vessels were African Americans. The Augusta Canal Museum memorializes the feats of these men and has replica boats operated by motors for tours of the canal. (Courtesy of Augusta Museum of History.)

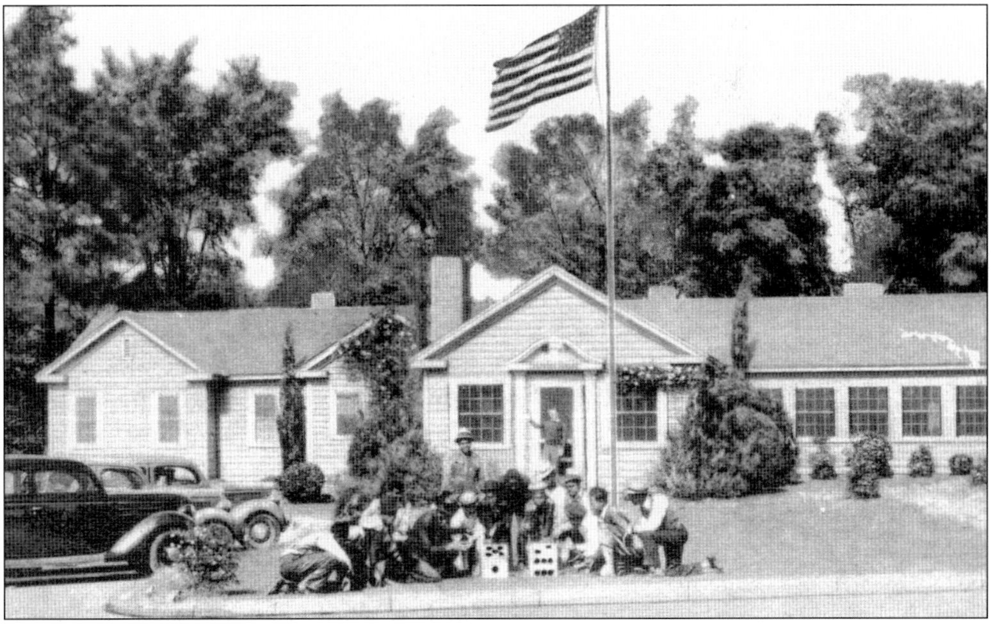

Forest Hills Golf Course was opened in the early 1900s and was a tourist destination for many years. Here, several young men position themselves for a group photograph. These caddies were employed by the golf course. (Courtesy of Augusta Museum of History.)

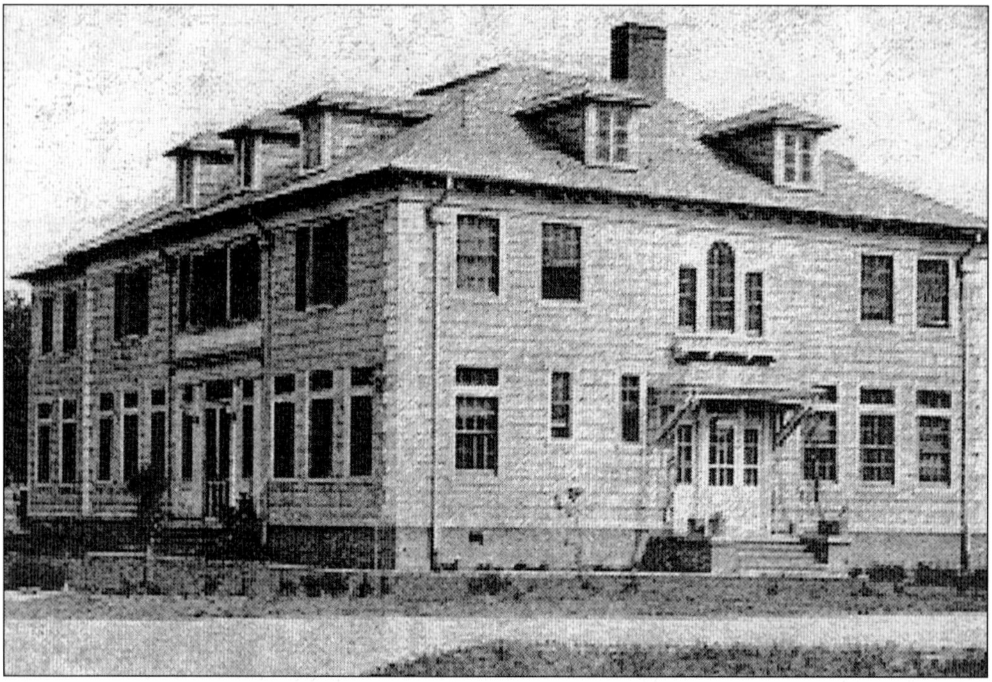

The Bethlehem Community Center's main building is shown in this 1933 photograph. The community center set standards in African-American society as a place that gave back to those in need. (Courtesy of Augusta Museum of History.)

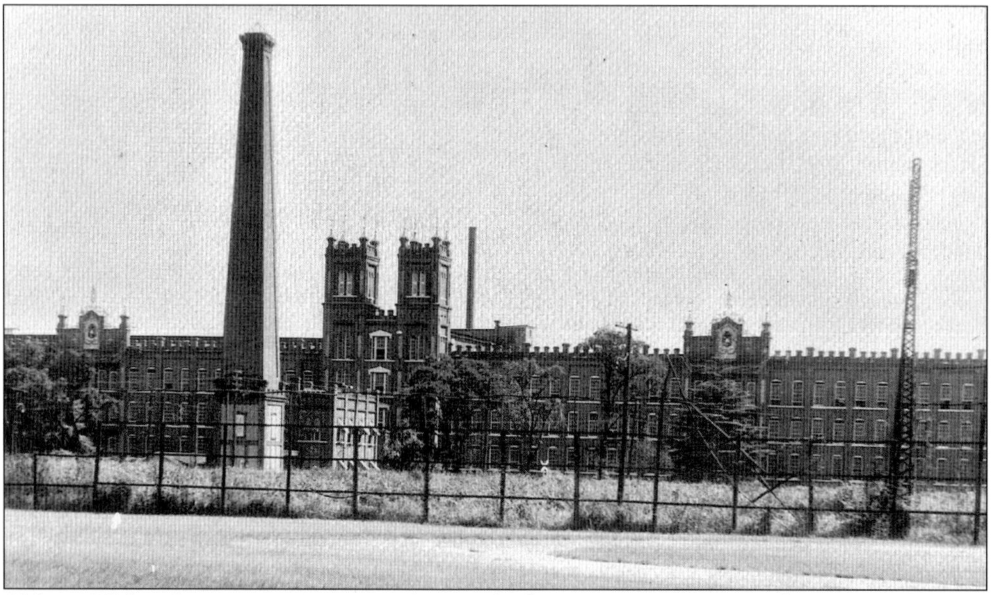

Sibley Mill has been a constant employer of African Americans over the years. This was especially true during the earlier part of the 20th century. The history of the site is impressive and it is the former site of the Confederate Powderworks. The lone standing chimney column is the last remnant of the works that supplied gunpowder to the Confederacy. (Courtesy Sean Joiner, Private Collection.)

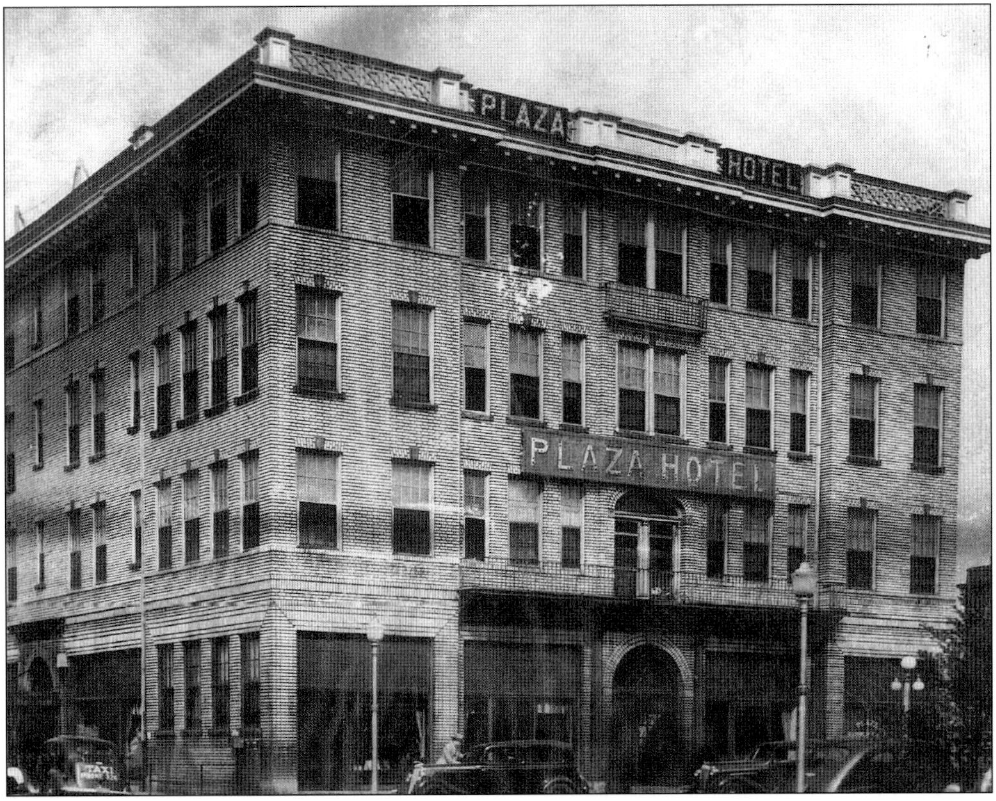

The Plaza Hotel in downtown Augusta was a ritzy place for vacationers and businessmen visiting the area. The hotel was an important employer of African Americans during the early 1900s, especially during the Great Depression, when employment was hard to find. (Courtesy Sean Joiner, Private Collection.)

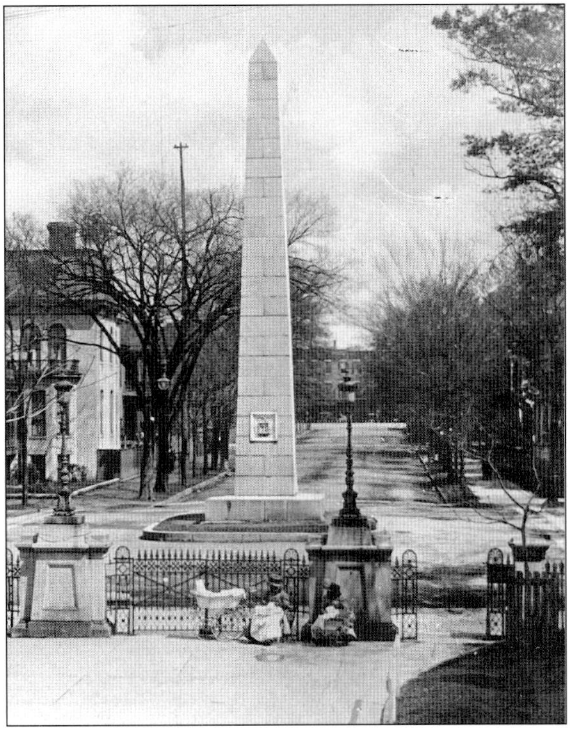

Seated outside the Founder's Monument, African-American nannies tend to the needs of their small charges. This scene is in front of the old courthouse, facing north. (Courtesy of Sean Joiner, Private Collection.)

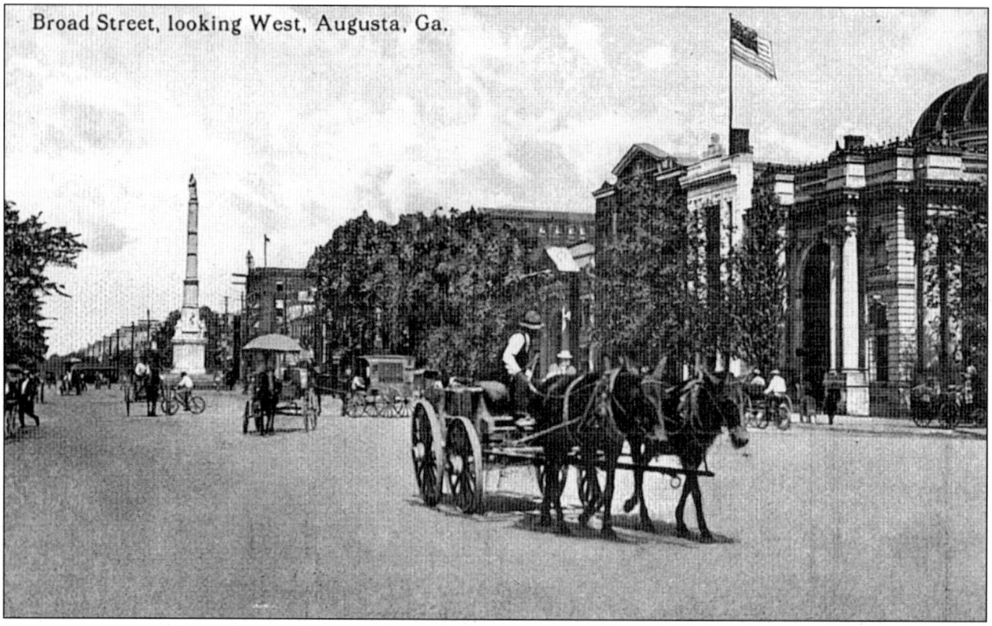

Driving a wagon pulled by mules, this African-American man looks back west on Broad Street at the traffic and buildings behind him. This scene is dated from the early 1900s. (Courtesy of Milledge G. Murray, Private Collection.)

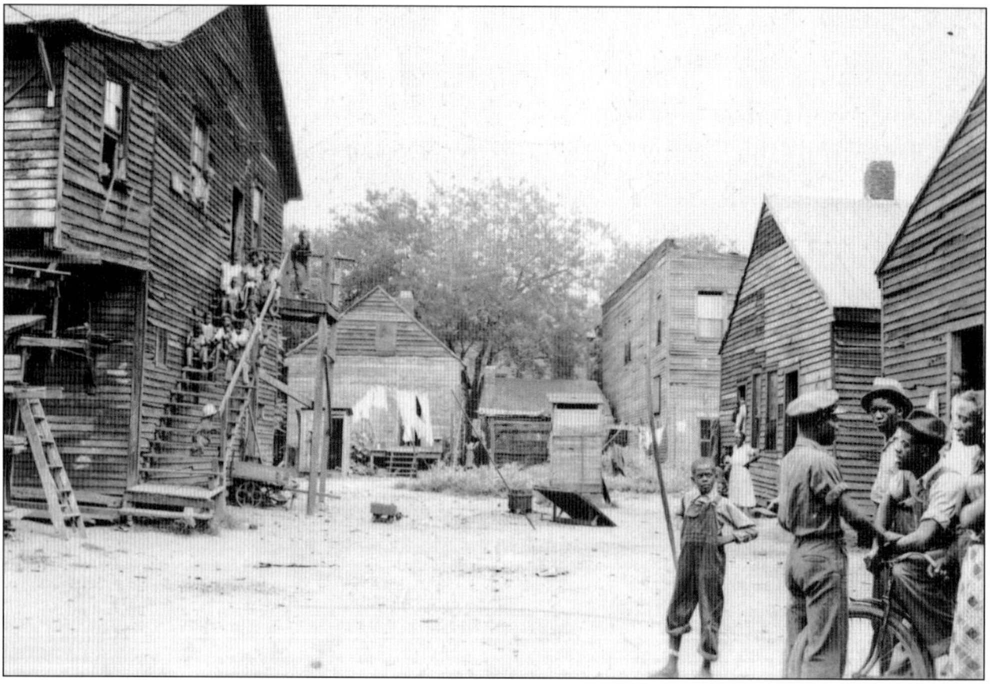

Behind the houses on Telfair Street, children talk on the steps while another group talks to an African-American man sitting on a bicycle. (Courtesy of Augusta Museum of History.)

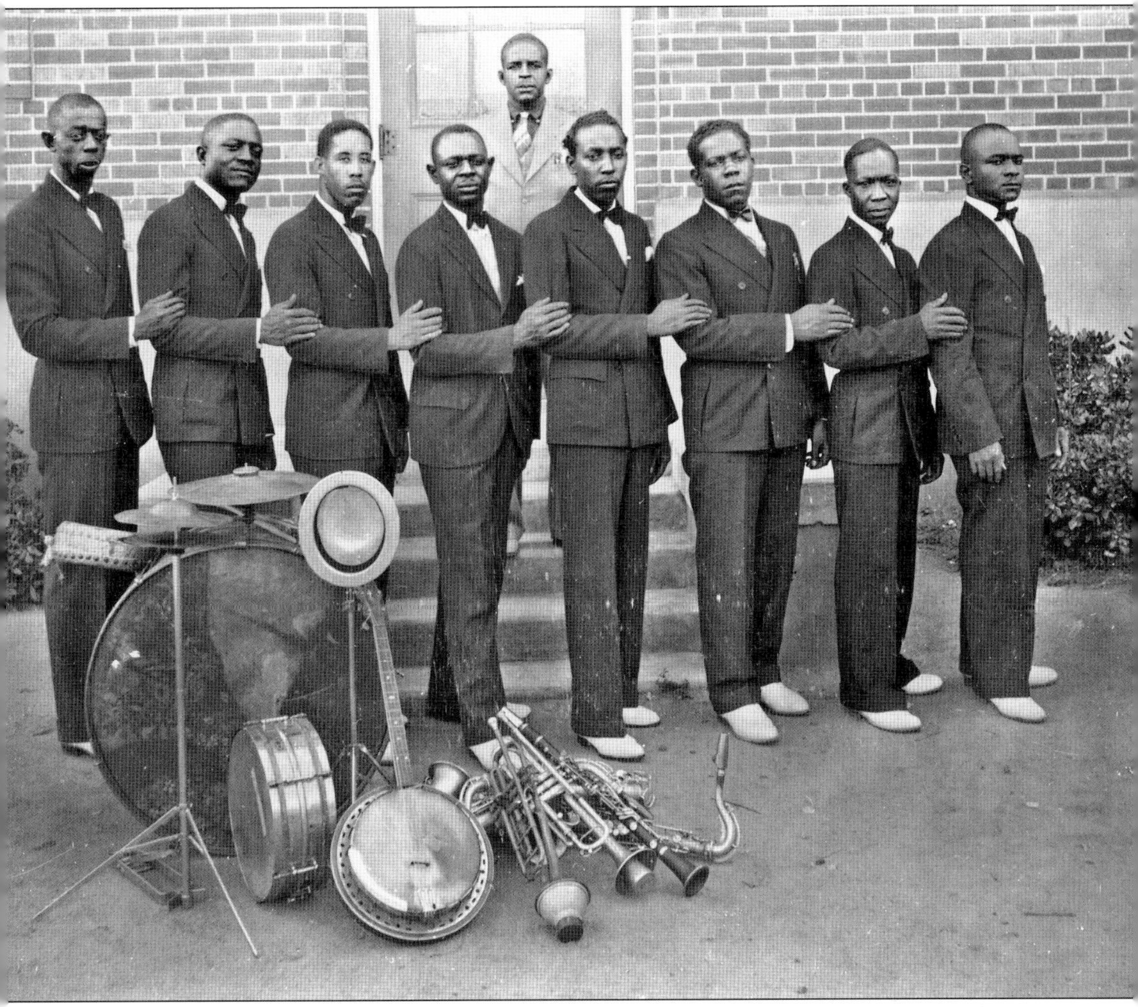

A group of musicians pose for a photograph. These men were part of a swing and jazz group from Augusta. (Courtesy of Augusta History Museum.)

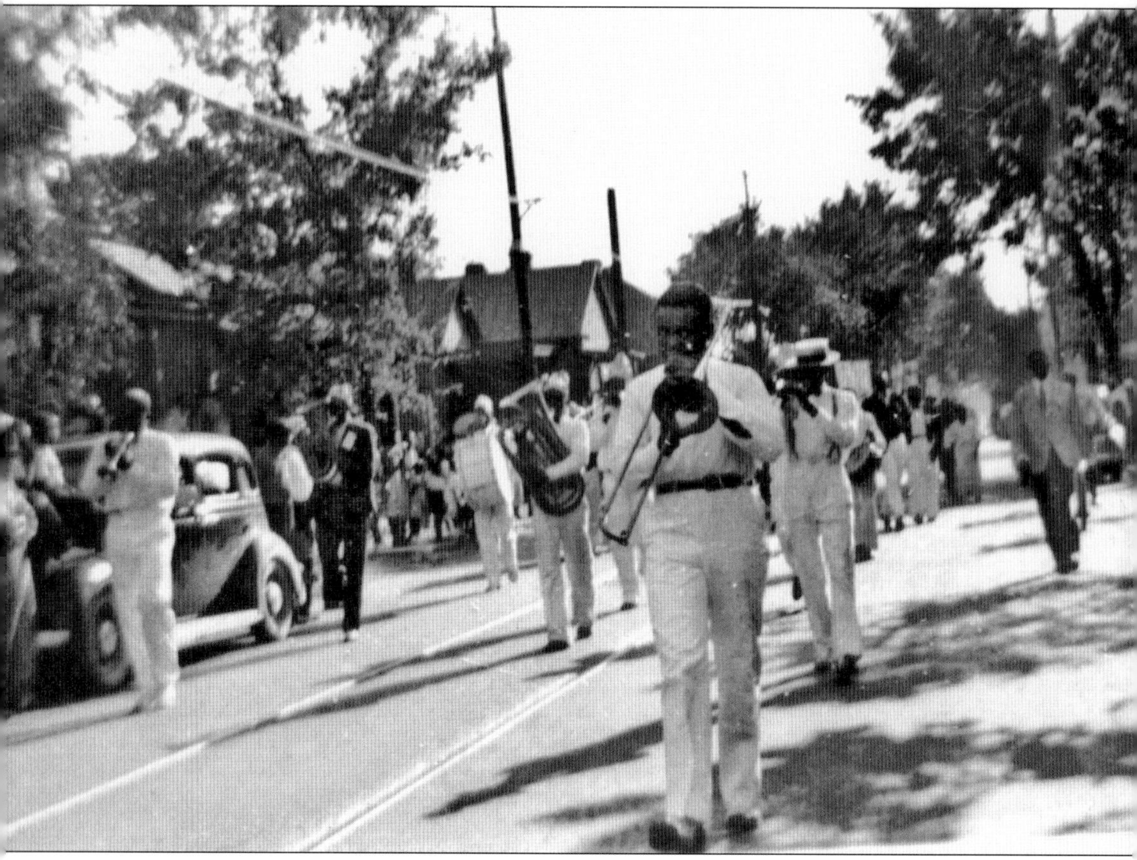

The Daddy Grace parade is led down Laney Walker Boulevard by a group of musicians. This was an important day of celebration for the African-American community, in honor of Daddy Grace, a noted charismatic African-American minister. (Courtesy of Milledge Murray, Private Collection.)

Six
RURAL LIFE

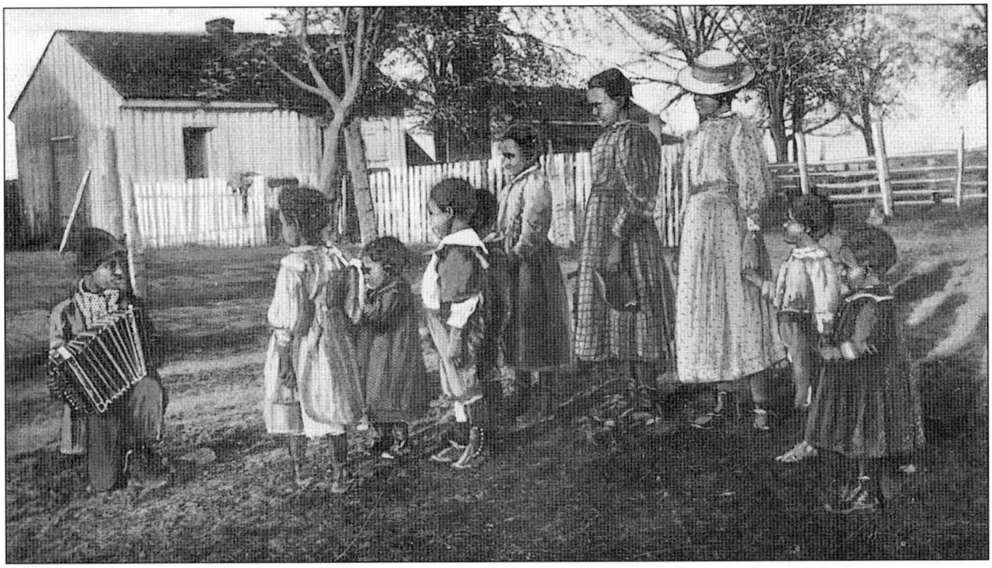

In the rural countryside, a group of children stand by and watch as another plays an accordion. They are in their Sunday best and are waiting to attend services with their parents. (Courtesy of Sean Joiner, Private Collection.)

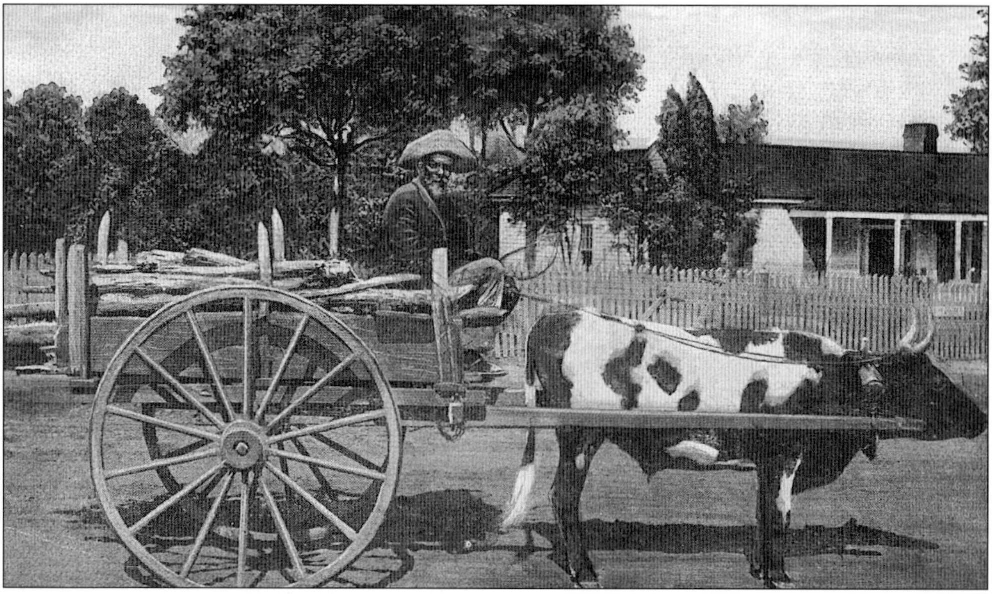

A beast of burden pulls a wagon driven by an elderly man in the countryside outside Augusta. The cart is carrying a load of wood. (Courtesy of Sean Joiner, Private Collection.)

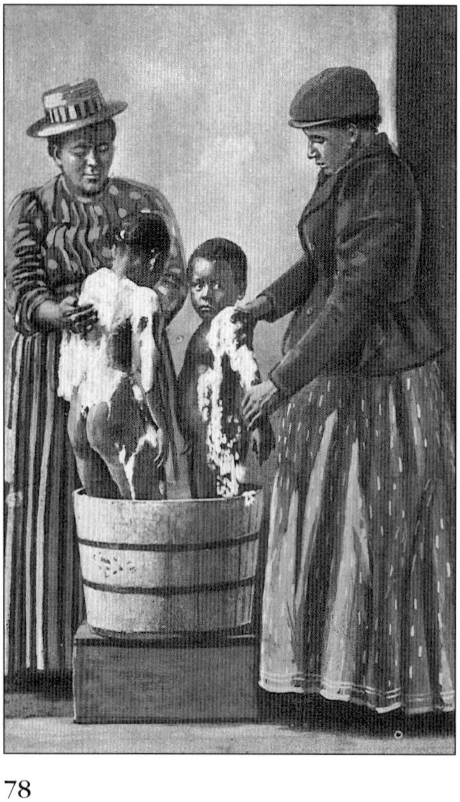

In this photograph, two women wash their children in a tub. Daily life in the late 1800s was laborious, especially considering water had to be carried back and forth for washing. Handmade lye soap was often used during this period. (Courtesy of Sean Joiner, Private Collection.)

This photograph was taken in the early part of the 20th century. Having the time to learn to play such an instrument as the fiddle was a luxury. (Courtesy of Sean Joiner, Private Collection.)

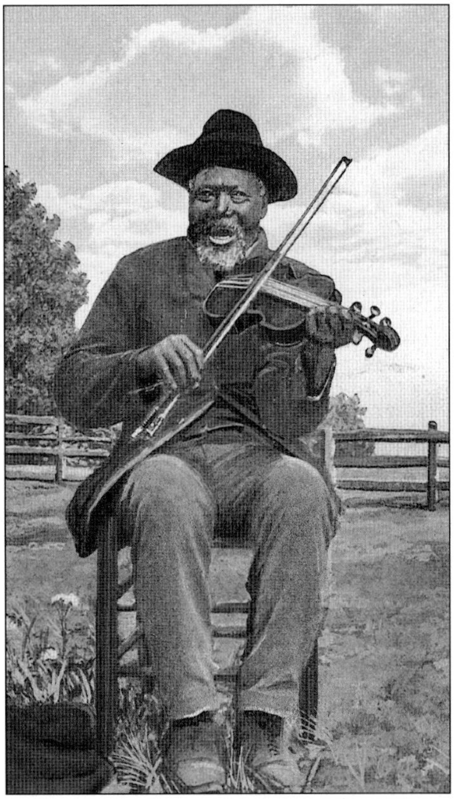

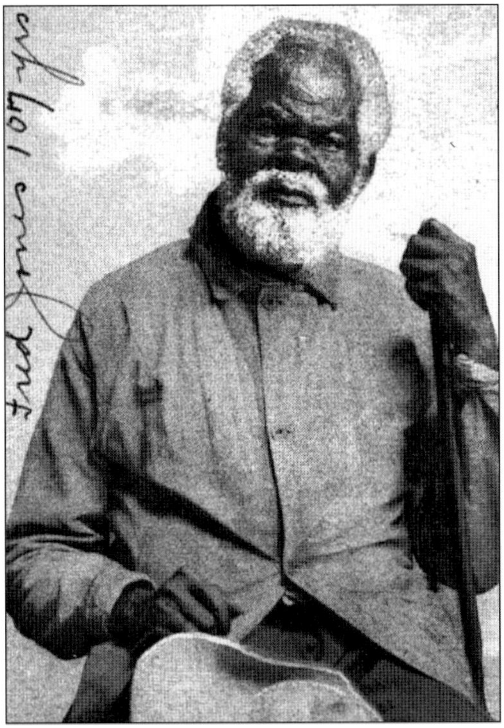

The man in this photograph is identified as Fred Jones and is listed as being 107 years old. He resided on the opposite side of the Savannah River, in Aiken County, South Carolina. (Courtesy of Sean Joiner, Private Collection).

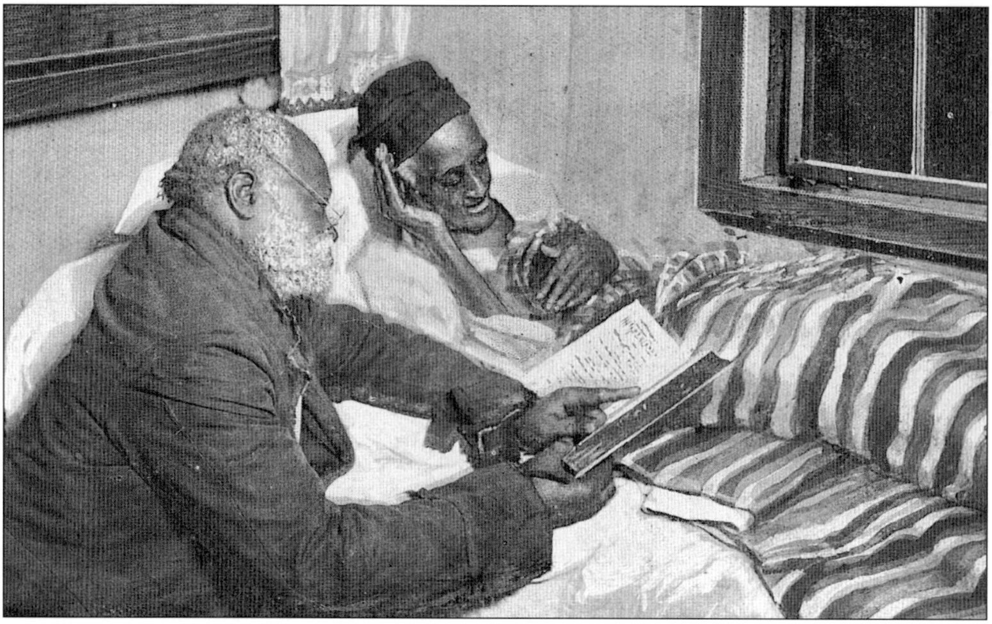

Mr. Jones reads from the Bible to his beloved wife. Her age and name at the time of the photograph is unknown. (Courtesy of Sean Joiner, Private Collection).

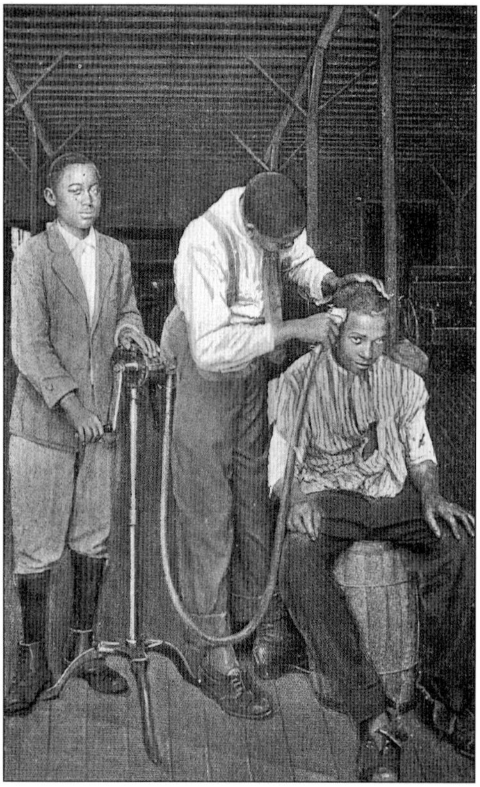

Every couple of weeks, these young men would have their hair cut. It was not uncommon for several people to buy a set of clippers to save money. (Courtesy of Sean Joiner, Private Collection.)

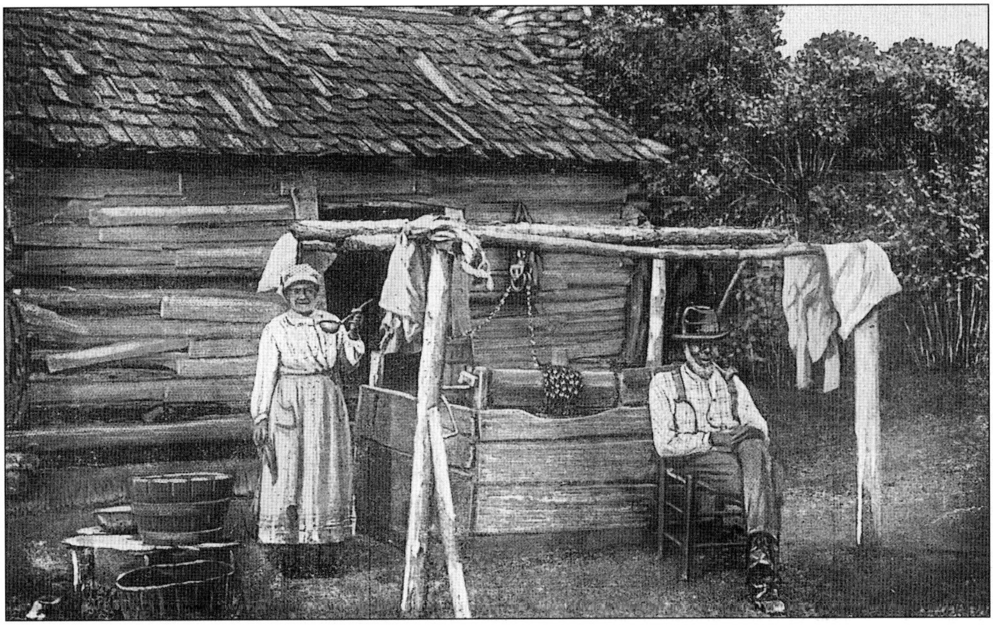

An elderly man sits outside his home in the rural Augusta countryside while his wife hangs laundry. (Courtesy of Sean Joiner, Private Collection.)

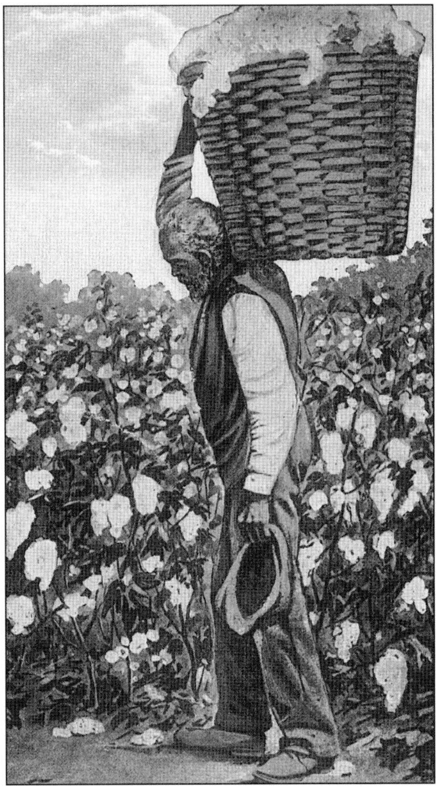

An unknown African-American man carries a basket of cotton on his shoulders. Even after the Civil War, cotton was picked by hand. Former slaves worked alongside tenant farmers to make a living. The average load hauled per day was about 300 pounds. (Courtesy of Sean Joiner, Private Collection.)

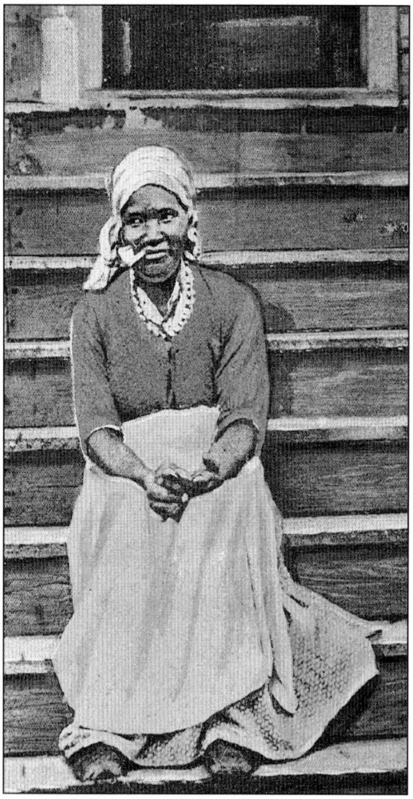

An elderly woman sits on the steps of her rural house, somewhere in south Augusta during the early 1900s. Notice she is smoking a pipe. This practice, along with using snuff, was not unusual among country folk. (Courtesy of Sean Joiner, Private Collection.)

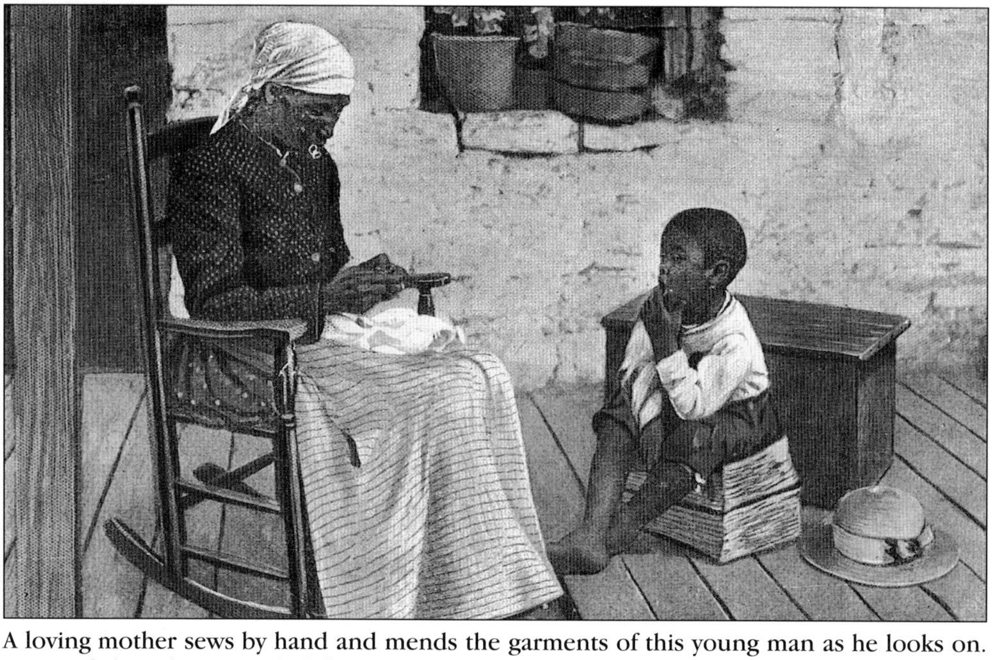

A loving mother sews by hand and mends the garments of this young man as he looks on. Many of the talents needed for the common good of the family were transferred from generation to generation. (Courtesy of Sean Joiner, Private Collection.)

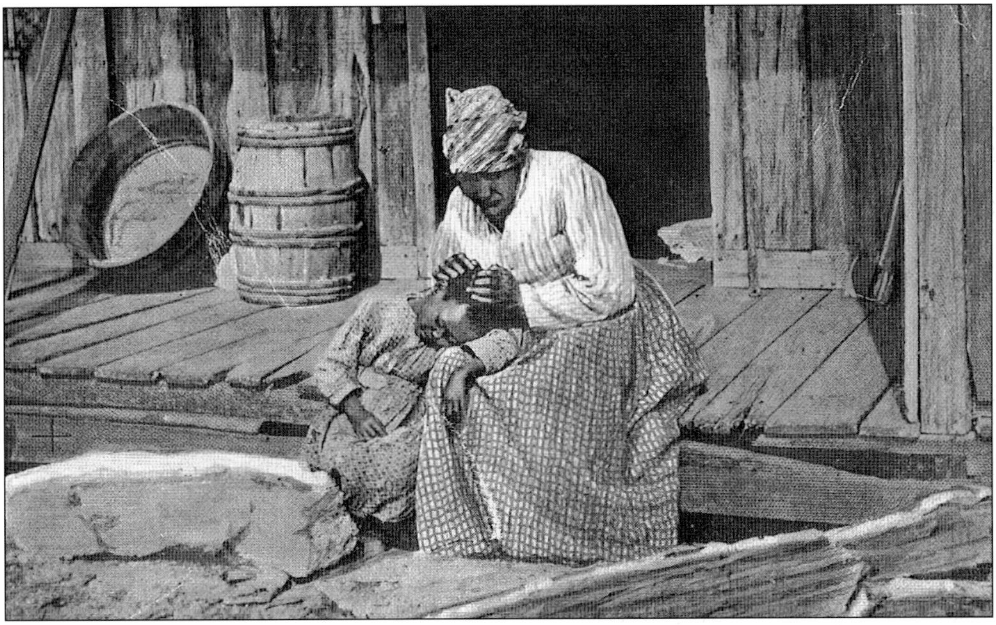

This woman cradles the head of a child as she looks for parasites in her hair. This was an unpleasant—but necessary—task in everyday rural life during the early 20th century. (Courtesy of Sean Joiner, Private Collection.)

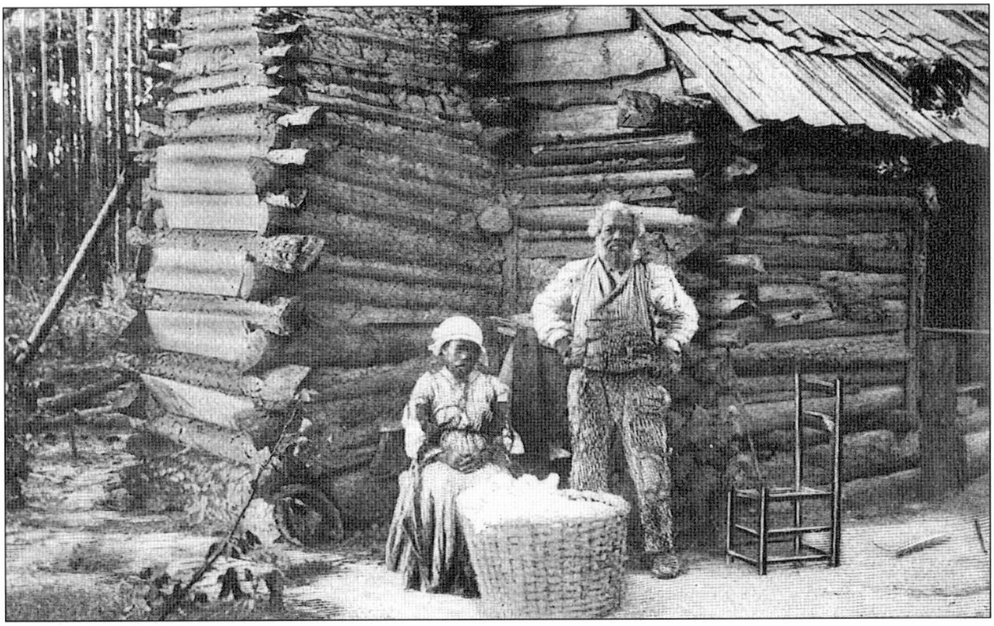

An elderly man stands while his wife sits outside their log cabin home in the countryside of Augusta. Most homes were constructed of hand hewn logs. (Courtesy of Sean Joiner, Private Collection.)

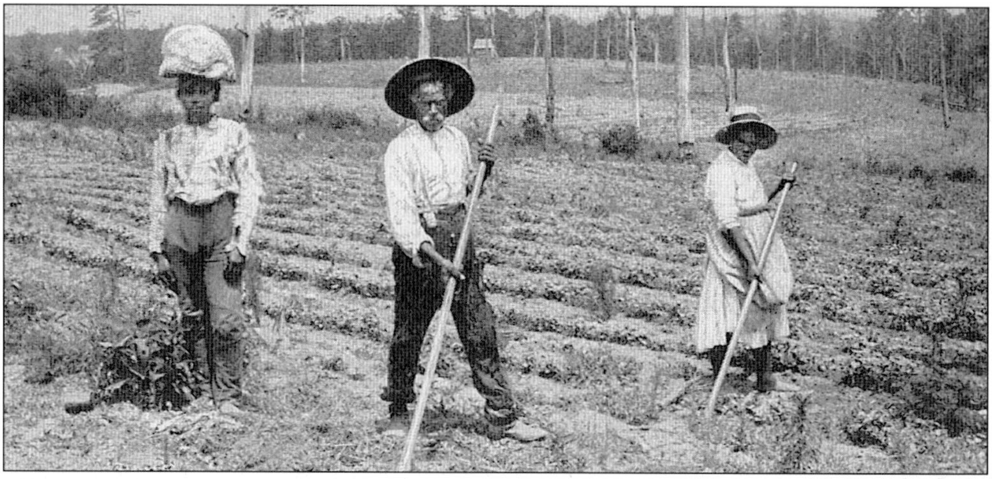

This tenant farmer and his family work the ground to keep their crops in pristine condition. This was not an easy task. Most of the time, the whole family contributed to this process. (Courtesy of Sean Joiner, Private Collection.)

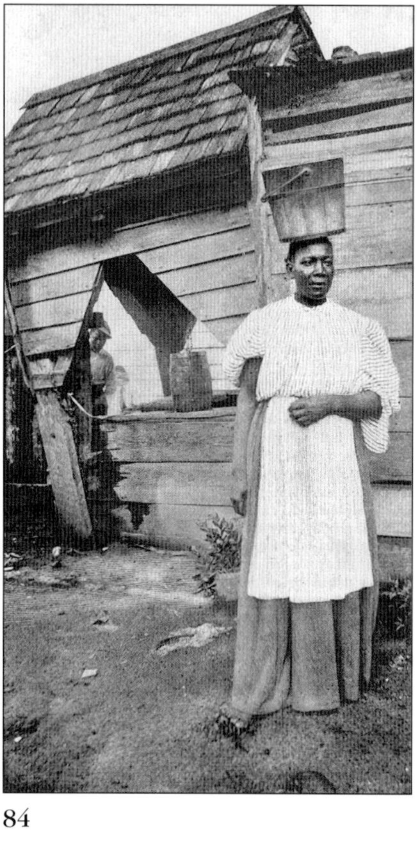

Gathering water from the well was a daily chore taken care of by the women and children. This task could become very tiring, but with no running water it was unavoidable. (Courtesy of Sean Joiner, Private Collection.)

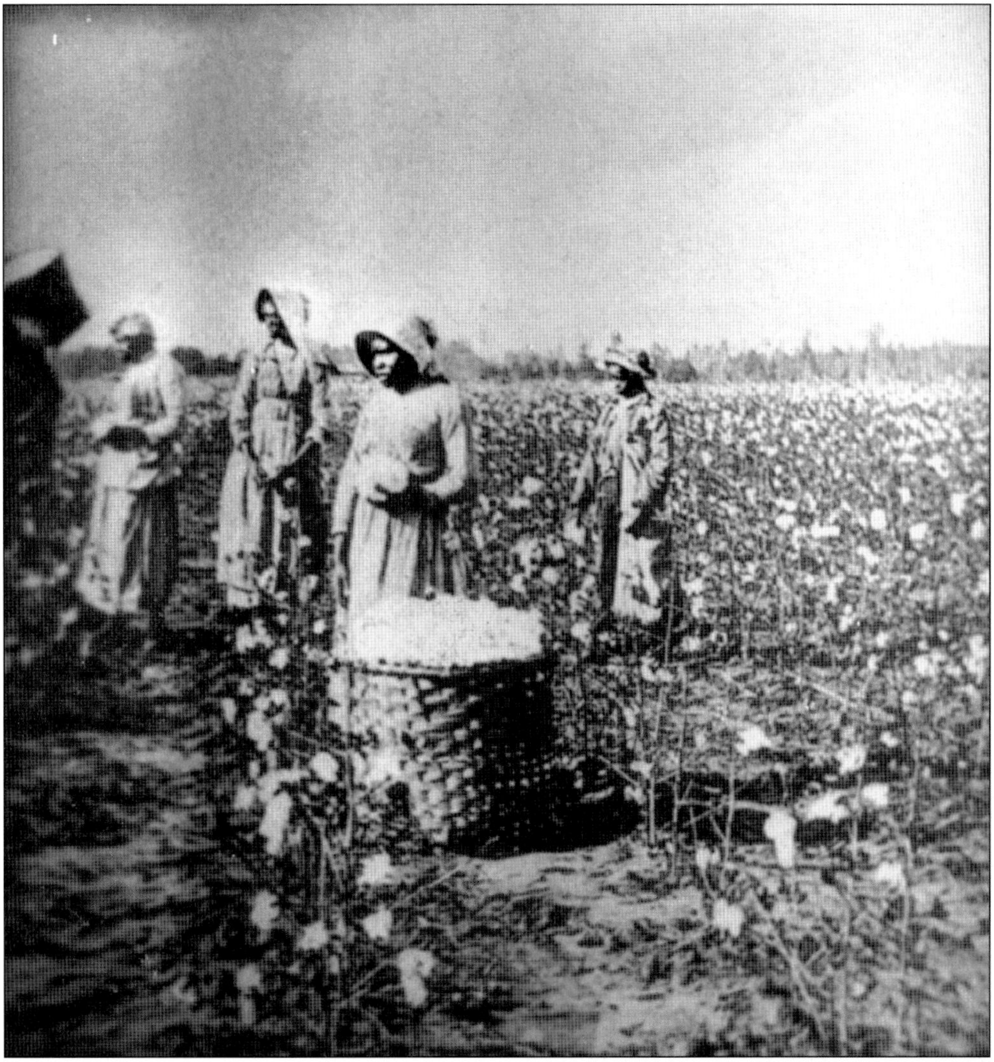

This photograph shows four African-American women cultivating cotton by hand. This was a laborious task, but was necessary at the turn of the century, especially for the black population that depended on the cotton season to sustain their families. (Courtesy of Special Collections, Reese Library, Augusta State University.)

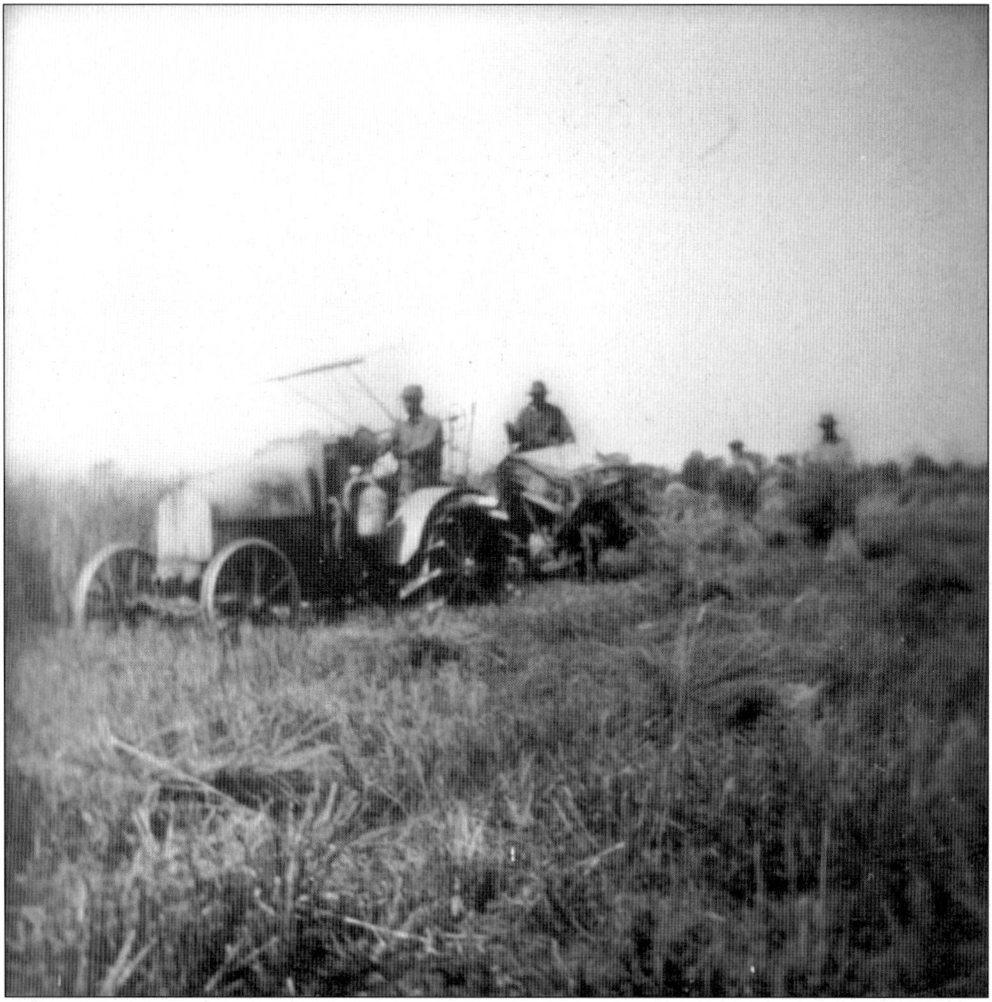

Riding a tractor, this African-American harvests a field of wheat. In the background can be seen several more people working diligently. (Courtesy of Special Collections, Reese Library, Augusta State University.)

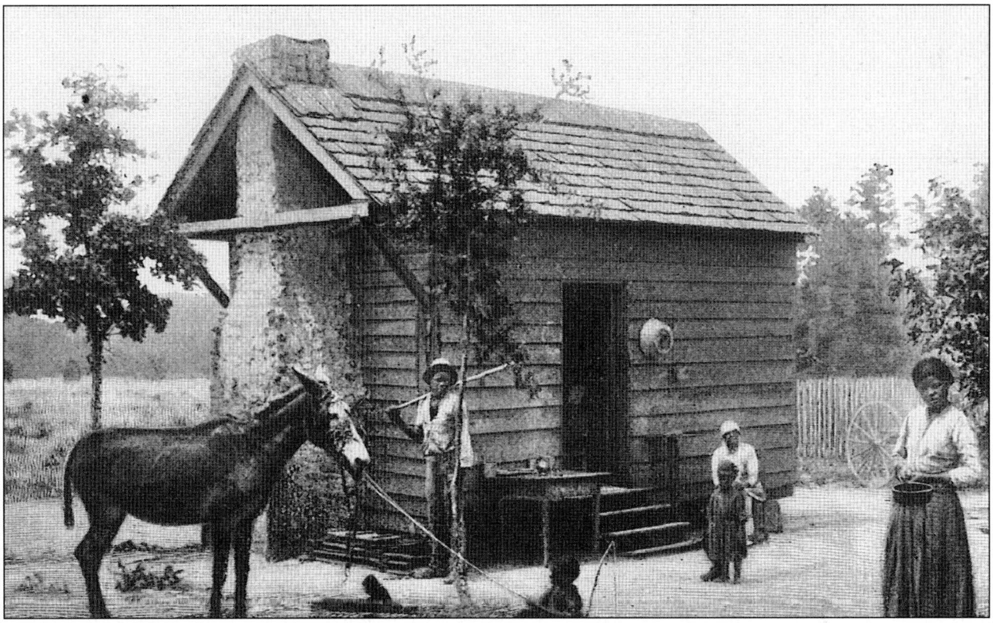

This 1898 photograph shows the hard rural life outside of the city that many endured. This is a simple, single-story building with only one room. In the background, a mother tends to her child while another plays with a mule. (Courtesy of Sean Joiner, Private Collection.)

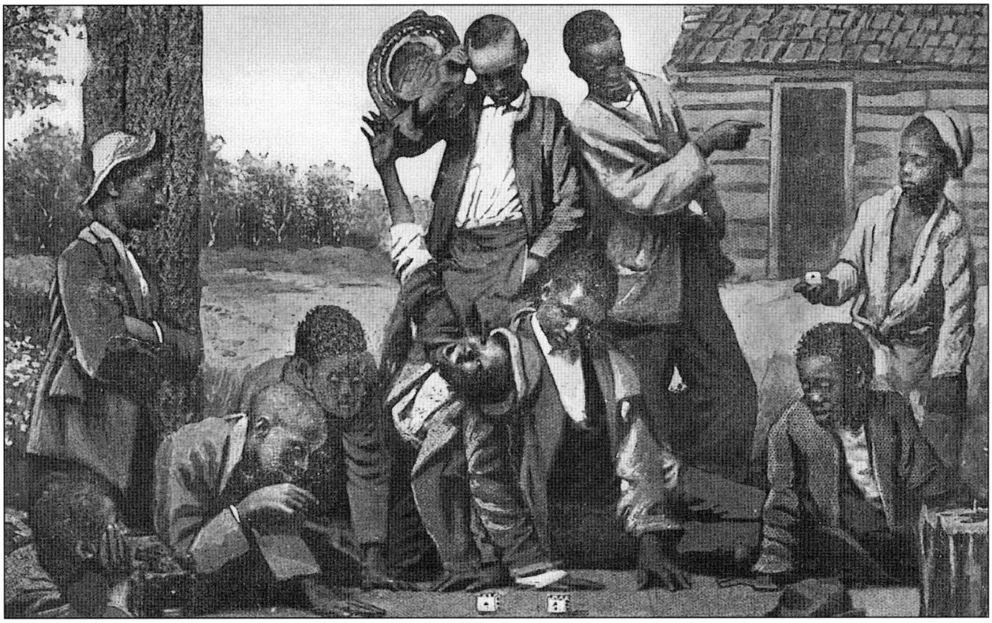

A group of children play a game of dice. After the chores were done, this type of activity was a favorite for many rural people. Marbles and hopscotch were also played to pass the time. (Courtesy of Sean Joiner, Private Collection.)

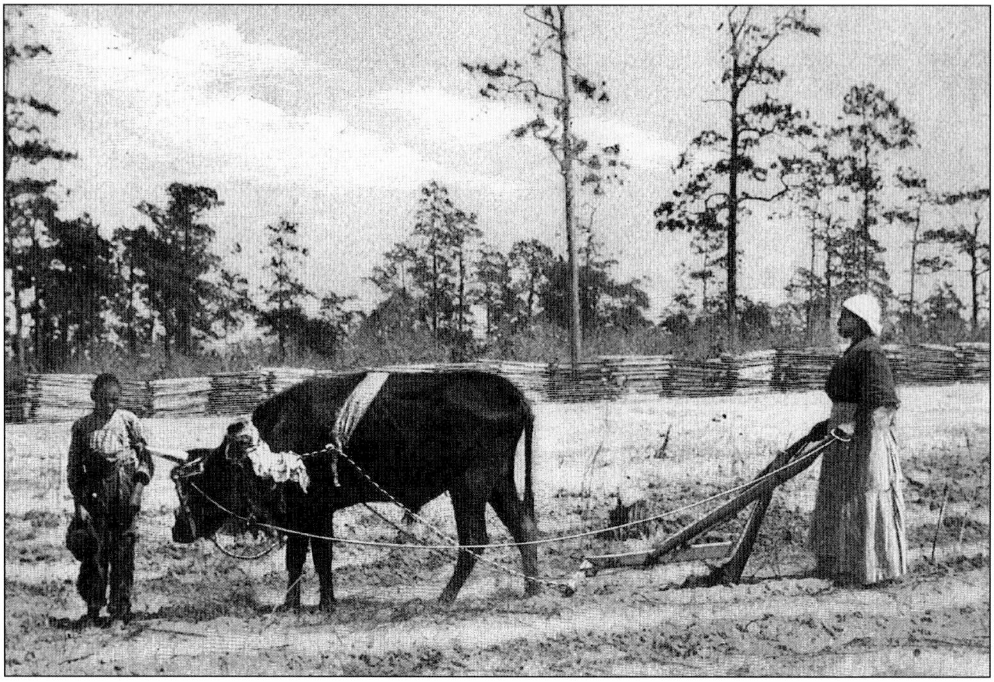

A woman tends to her fields and crops with this ox that is tied to a cultivator. Standing on the opposite side is a small boy waiting to help her if needed. (Courtesy of Sean Joiner, Private Collection.)

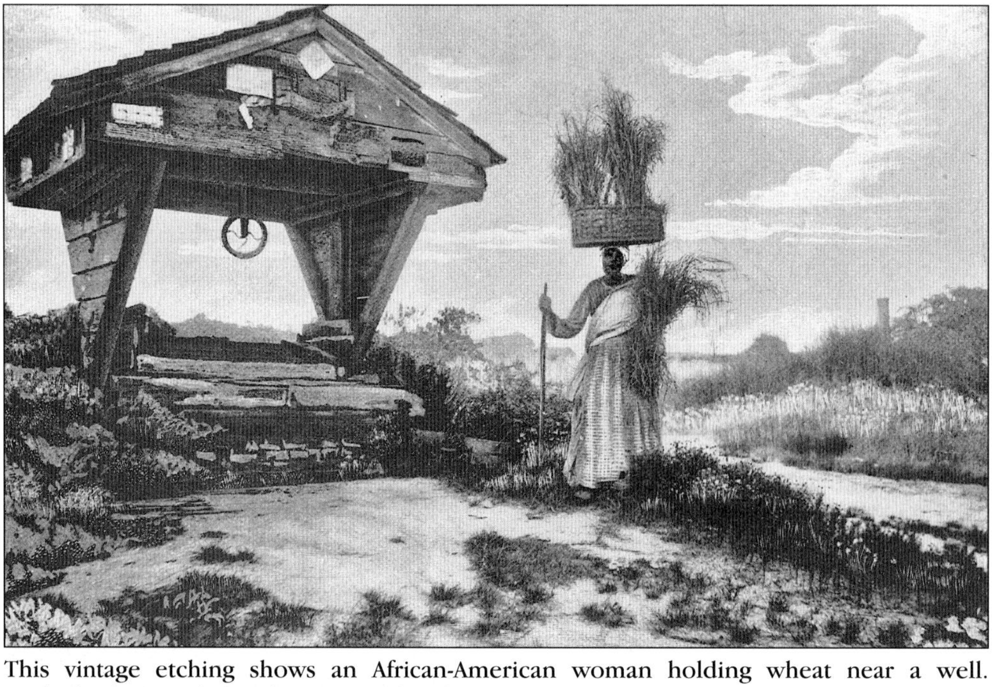

This vintage etching shows an African-American woman holding wheat near a well. In the background, the chimney stacks of a mill can be seen. (Courtesy of Augusta Museum of History.)

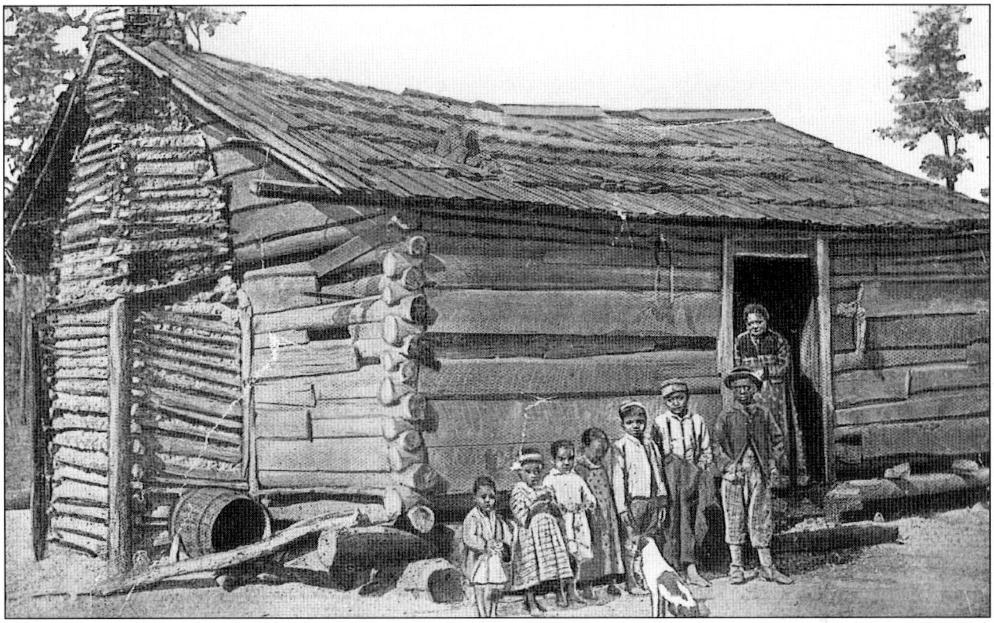

A group of seven children, their mother, and a dog pose next to their house at an unidentified location in rural Richmond County. (Courtesy of Sean Joiner, Private Collection.)

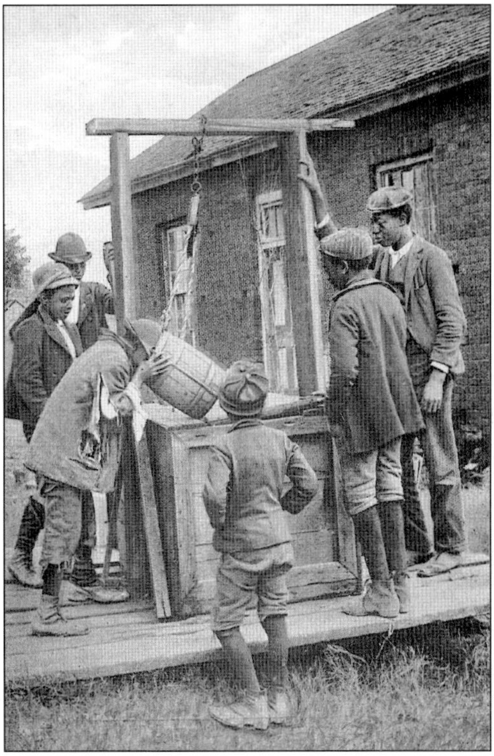

A group of young men and boys take a drink from a well during a hot spring day. Lunchtime is almost over. One more quick game can be finished off before the bell rings. (Courtesy of Sean Joiner, Private Collection.)

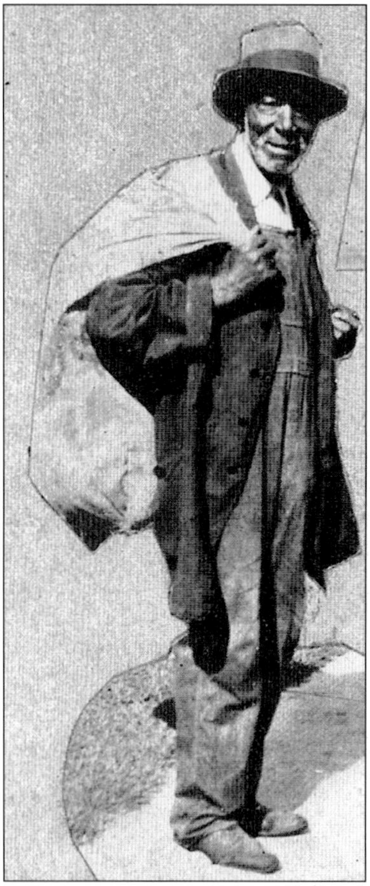

This is an unidentified African-American man in Augusta. (Courtesy of Gerald Smith Ph.D., Private Collection.)

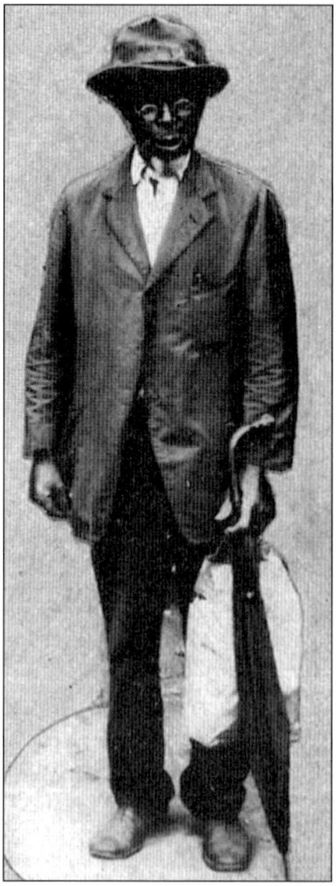

Here is another unidentified African-American man in Augusta. His attire, umbrella, and bag suggest a visit to town. (Courtesy of Gerald Smith Ph.D., Private Collection.)

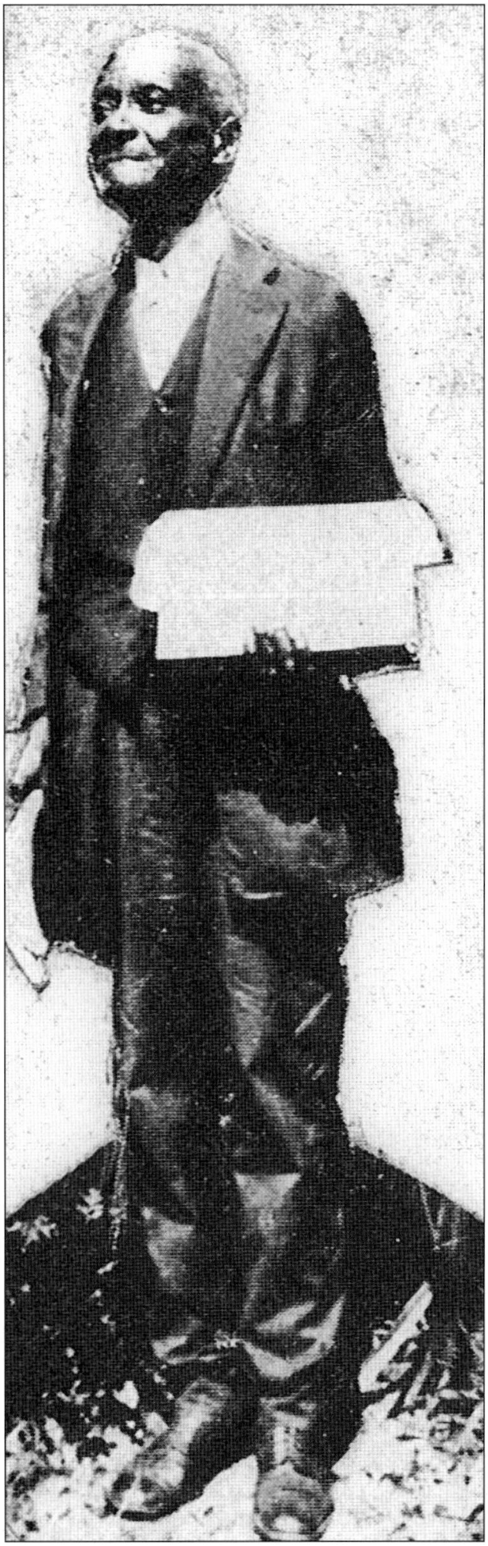

Pictured here is an unidentified African-American man in Augusta. His bearing and bible suggest that perhaps he serves as a minister. (Courtesy of Gerald Smith Ph.D., Private Collection.)

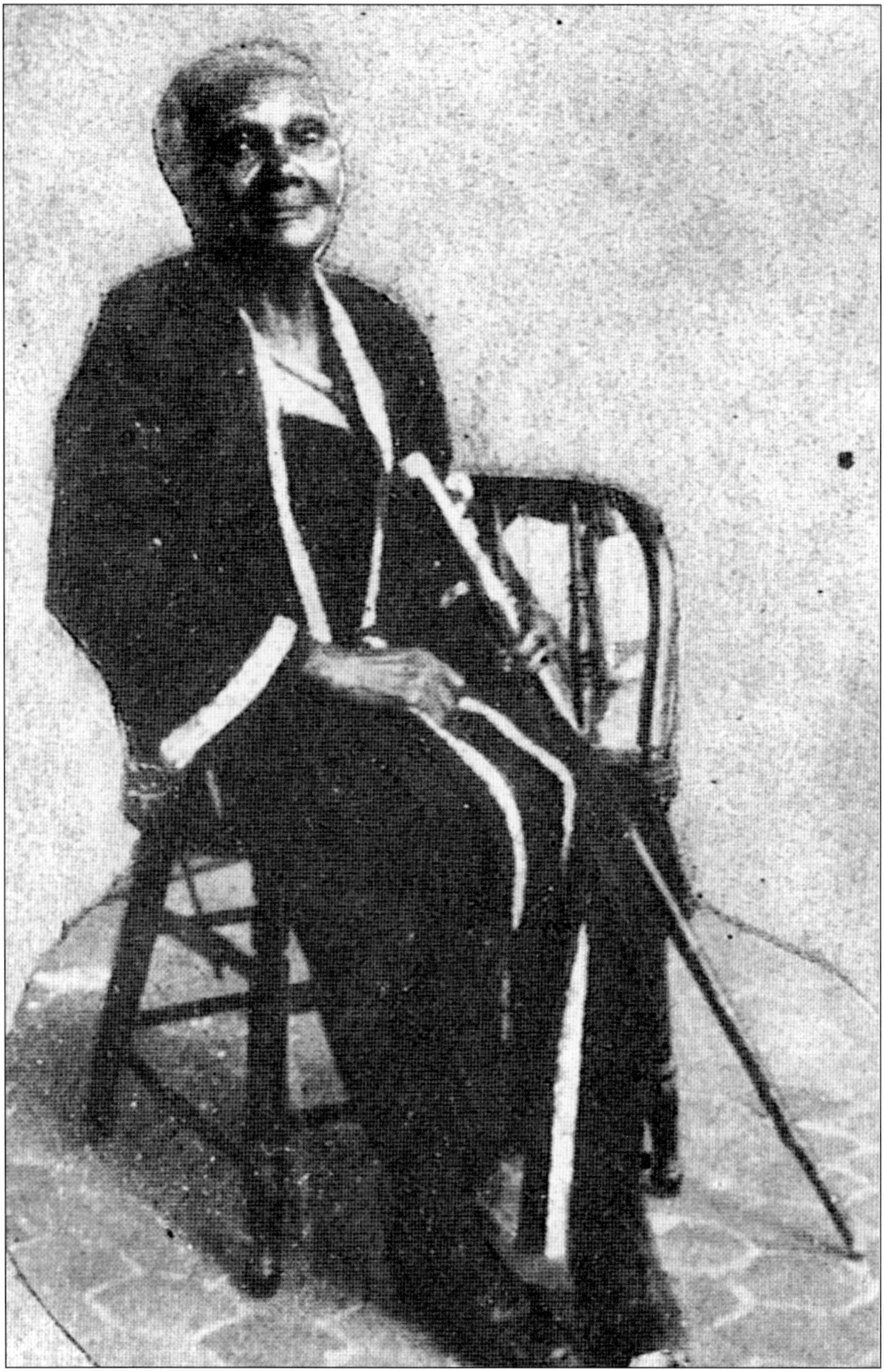

This is an unidentified African-American woman in Augusta. (Courtesy of Gerald Smith Ph. D., Private Collection.)

Seven
Schools of the Environs

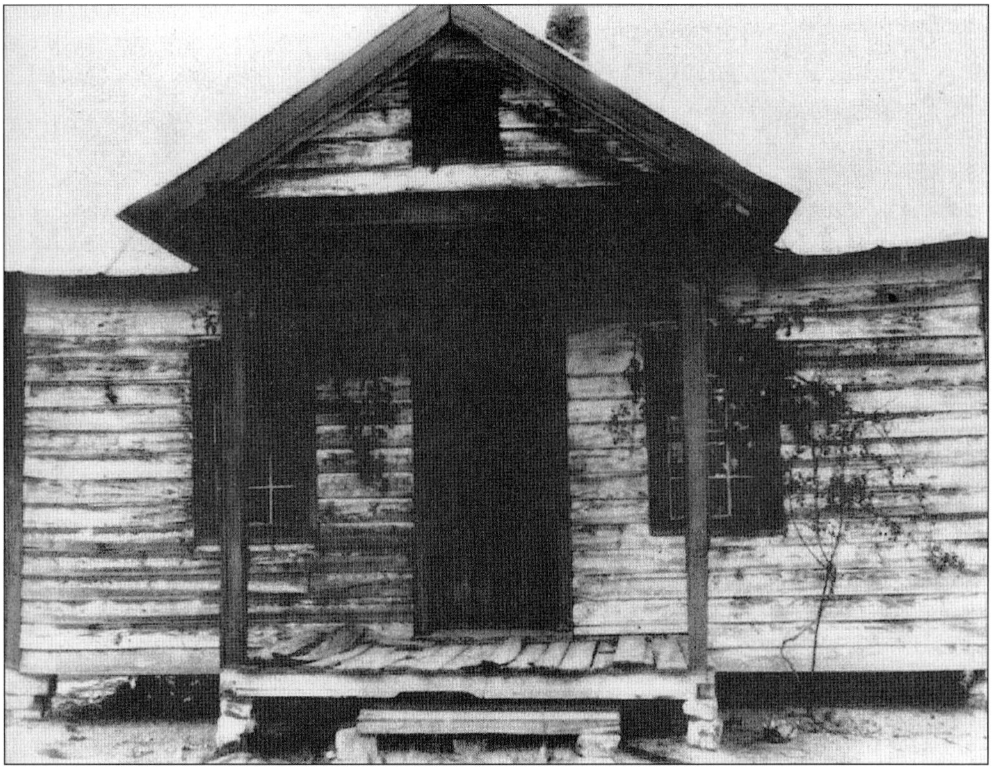

Around 1930, the Steiner School for Negroes was a small, one-room school house in Columbia County. (Courtesy of Gerald Smith Ph.D., Private Collection.)

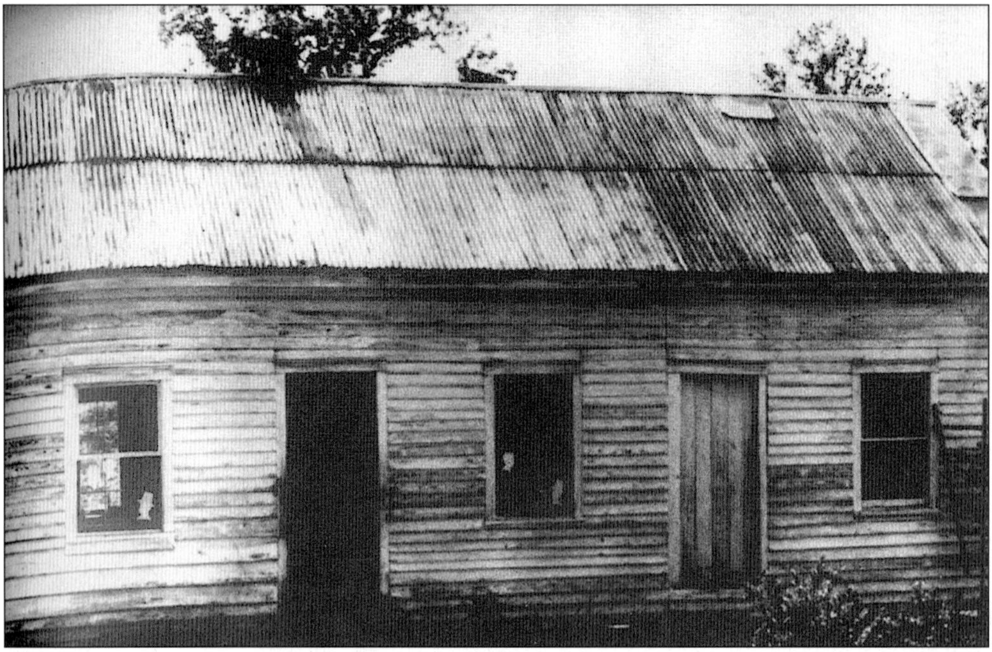

Mount Moriah School for Negroes was located in Columbia County around 1930. (Courtesy of Gerald Smith Ph.D., Private Collection.)

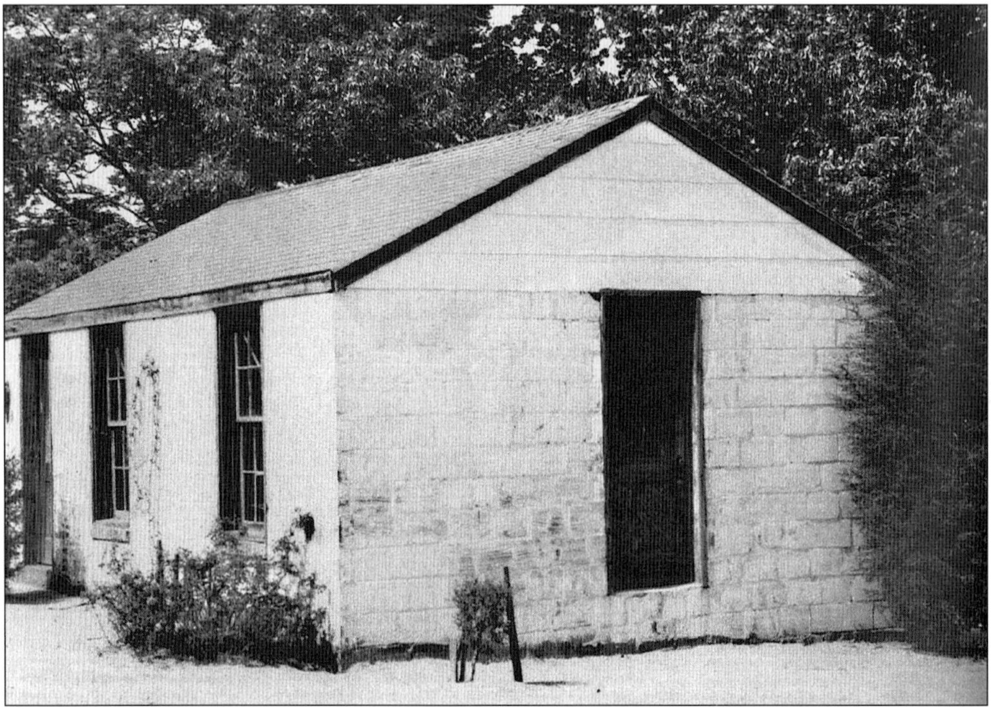

The Steiner School for Negroes was a small school. Here, it is shown after its restoration in the 1950s. (Courtesy of Gerald Smith Ph.D., Private Collection.)

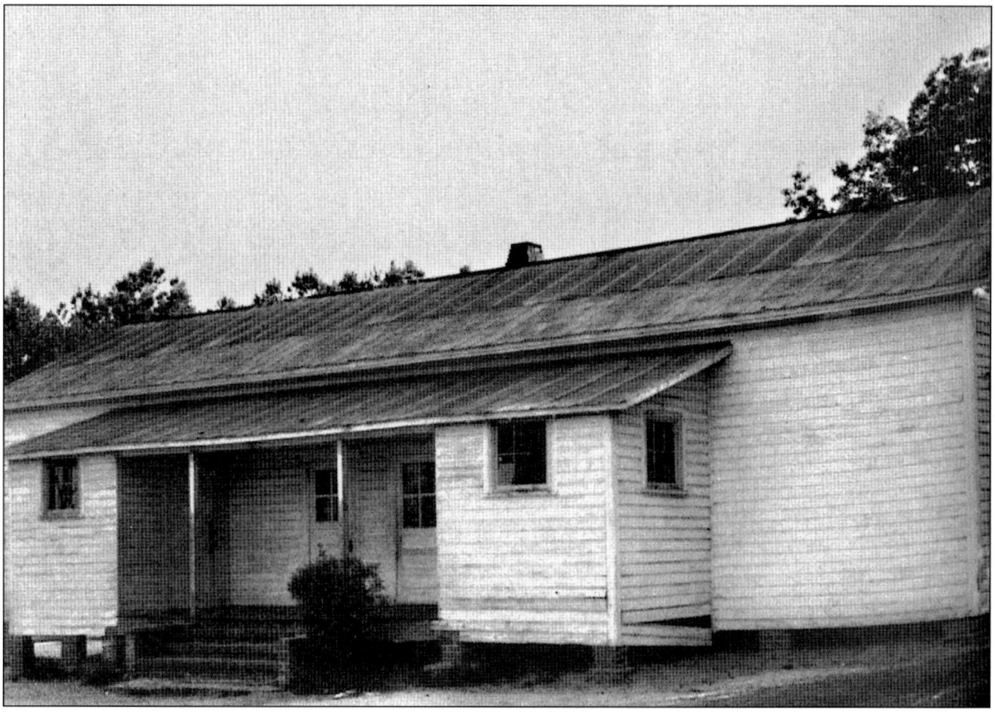

This photograph of the Oakey Grove School is from the 1950s. (Courtesy of Gerald Smith Ph.D., Private Collection.)

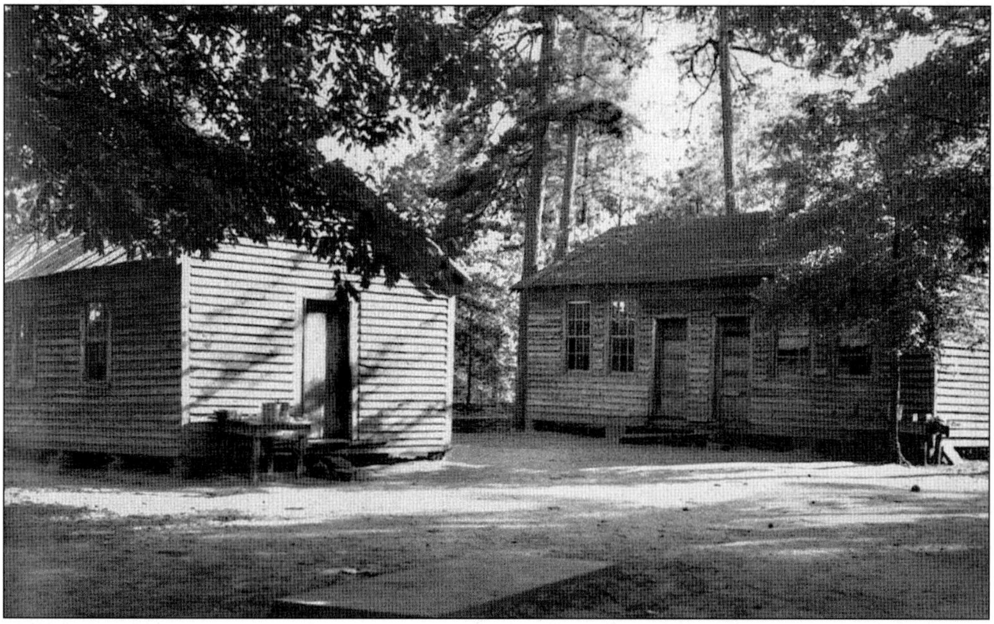

These two buildings were used to house African-American children from first through twelfth grade. This photograph dates to the 1950s. (Courtesy of Gerald Smith Ph.D., Private Collection.)

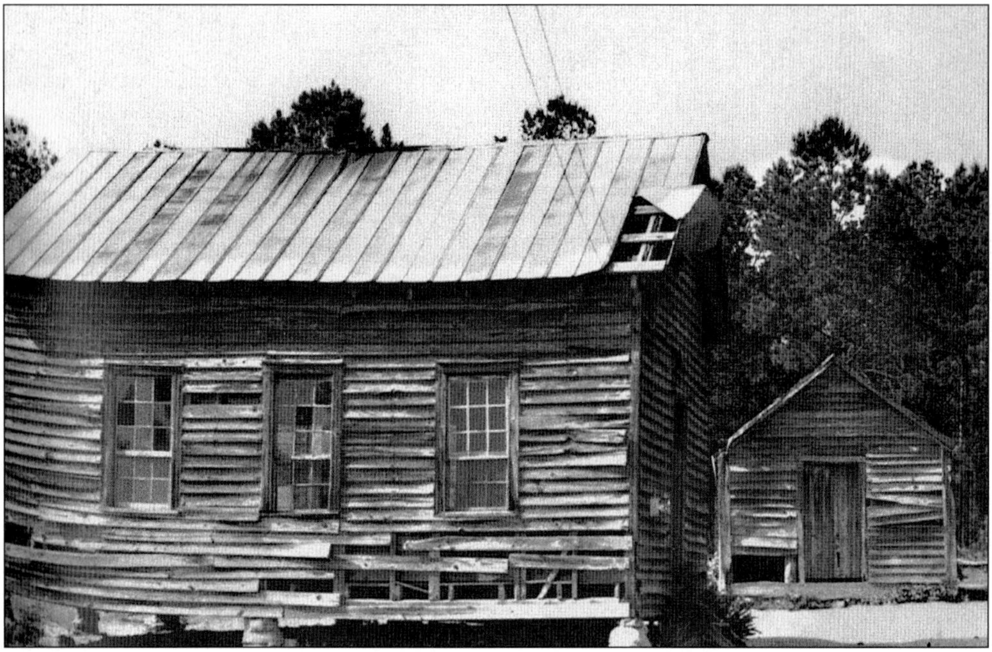

Although these two wooden buildings are dilapidated, they were some of the only structures used for African-American schoolhouses. This is the Popular Springs School, dating around 1940. (Courtesy of Gerald Smith Ph.D., Private Collection.)

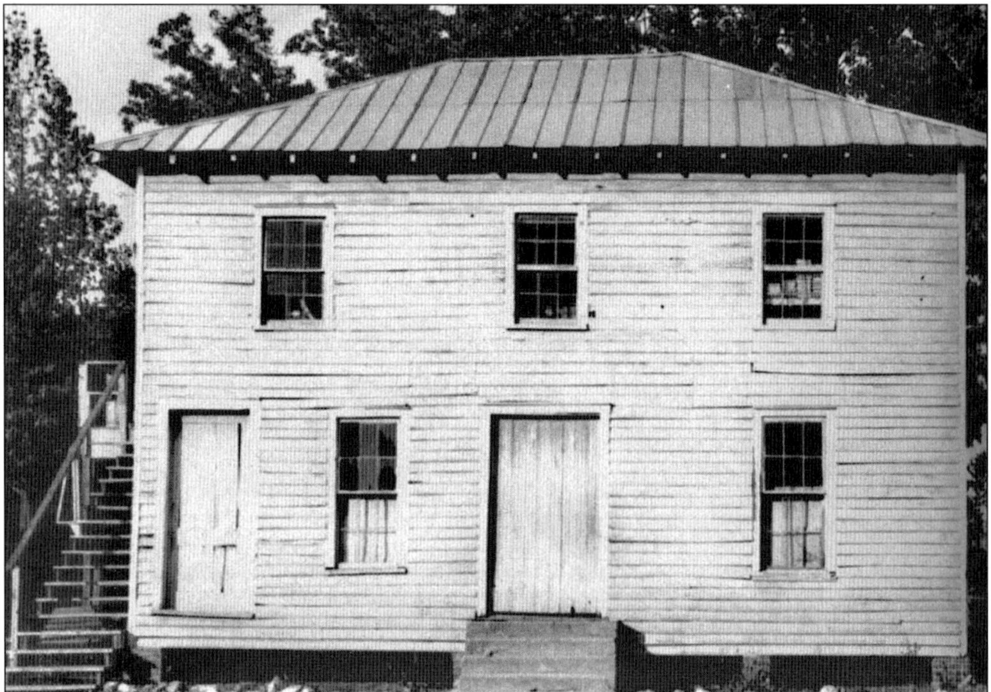

This is the Gospel Water Branch School, an African-American school dating to the 1950s. (Courtesy of Gerald Smith Ph.D., Private Collection.)

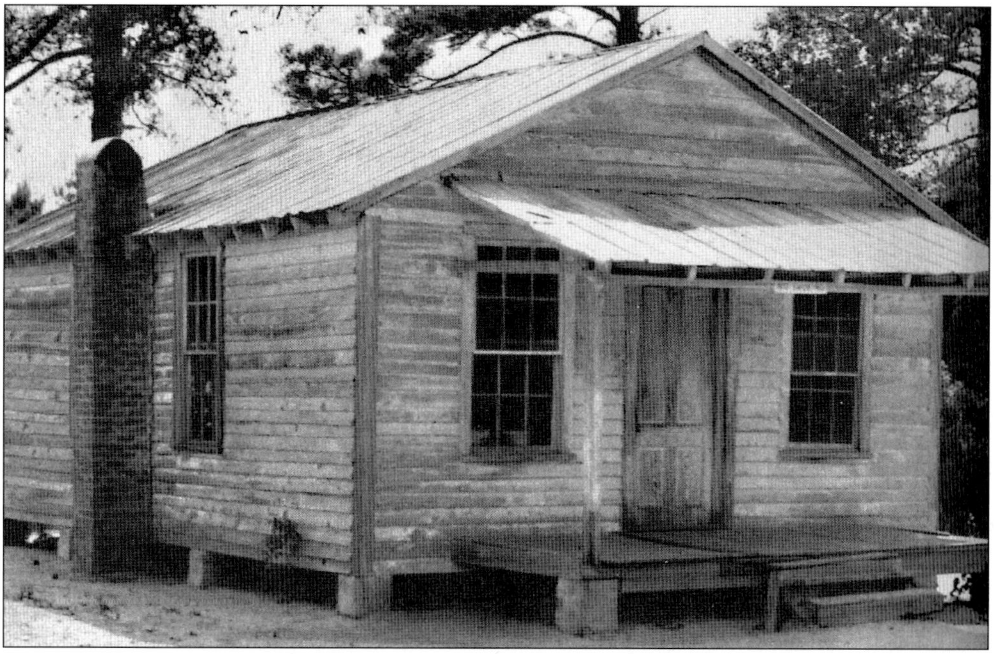

The Jerusalem School shown here dates to around 1950. Many African-American schools were sponsored by local African-American churches. (Courtesy of Gerald Smith Ph.D., Private Collection.)

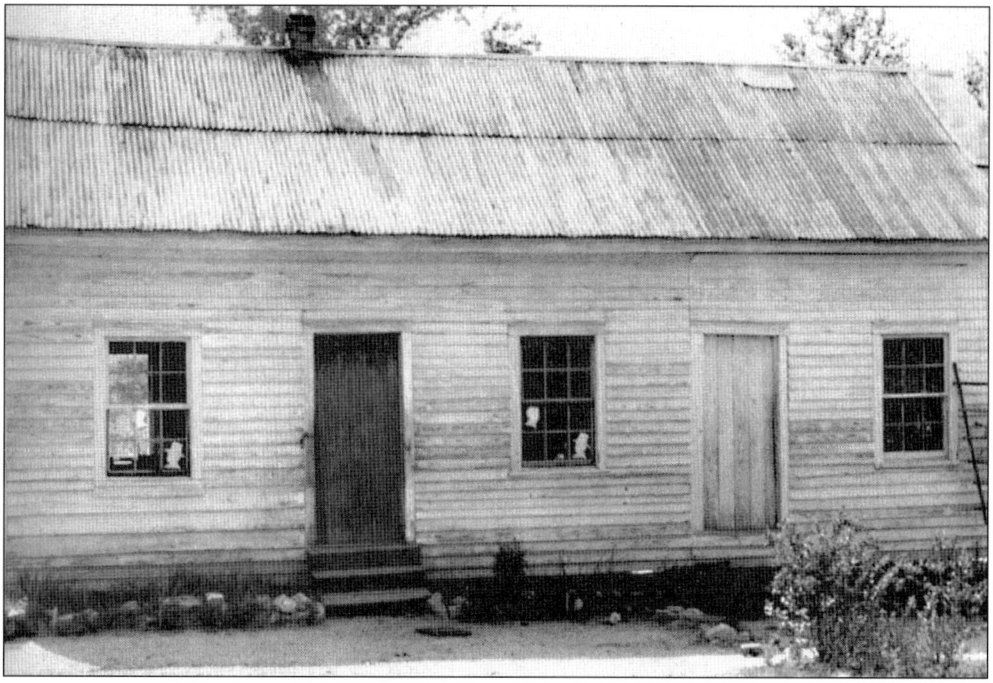

The Lamkin Grove School is an African-American school dating to 1950. (Courtesy of Gerald Smith Ph.D., Private Collection.)

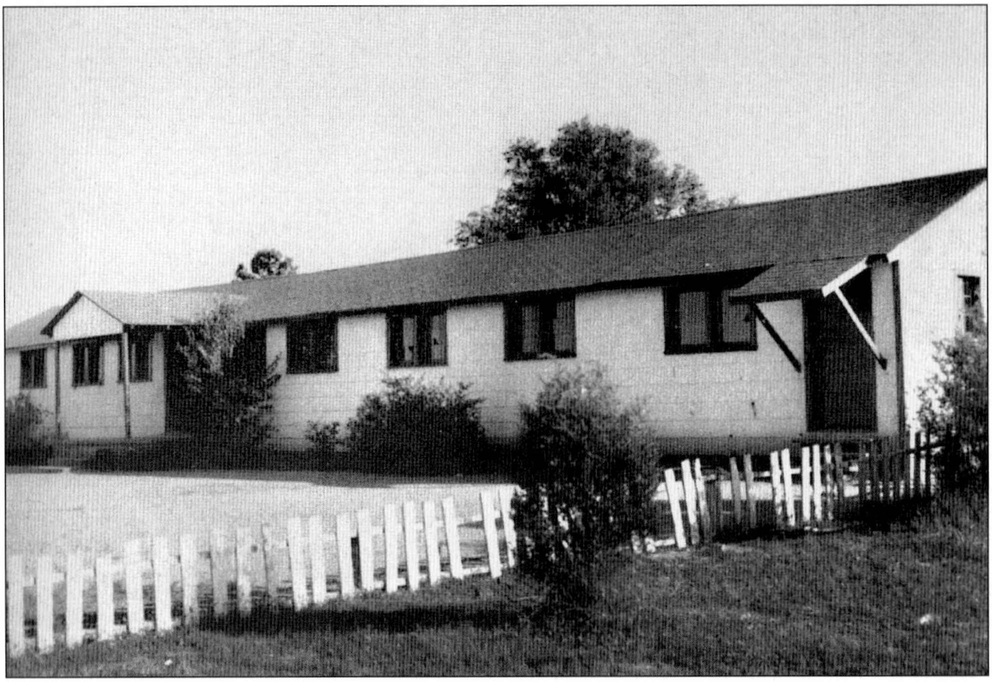

The Gibbs School dates to the 1950s and served the African-American community in Columbia County for many years. (Courtesy of Gerald Smith Ph.D., Private Collection.)

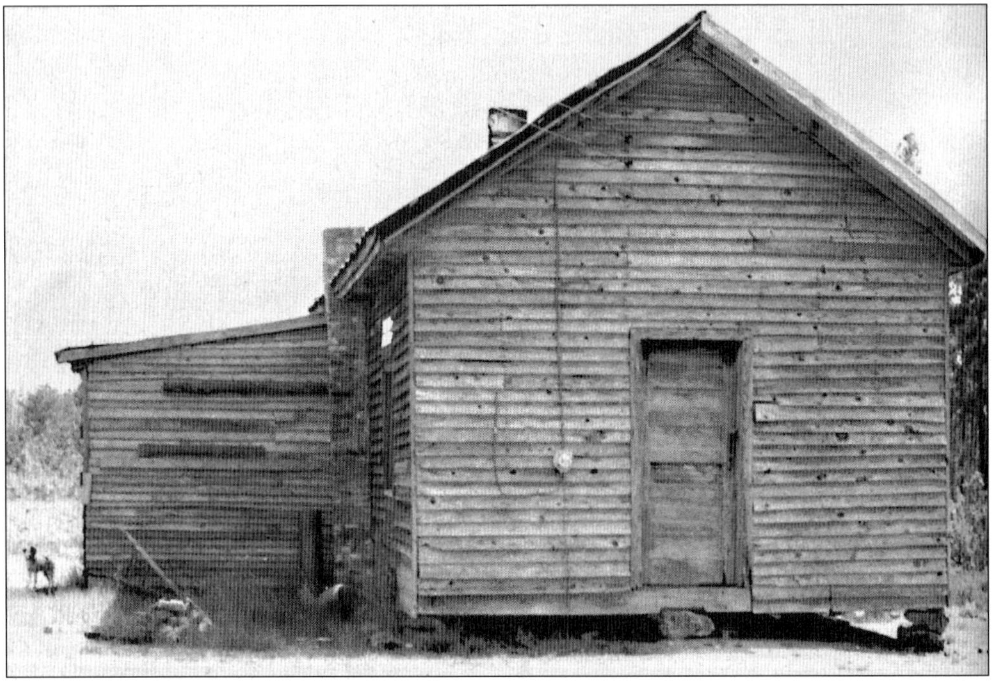

Clary Grove School was a small, humble wooden building in desperate need of repair. (Courtesy of Gerald Smith Ph.D., Private Collection.)

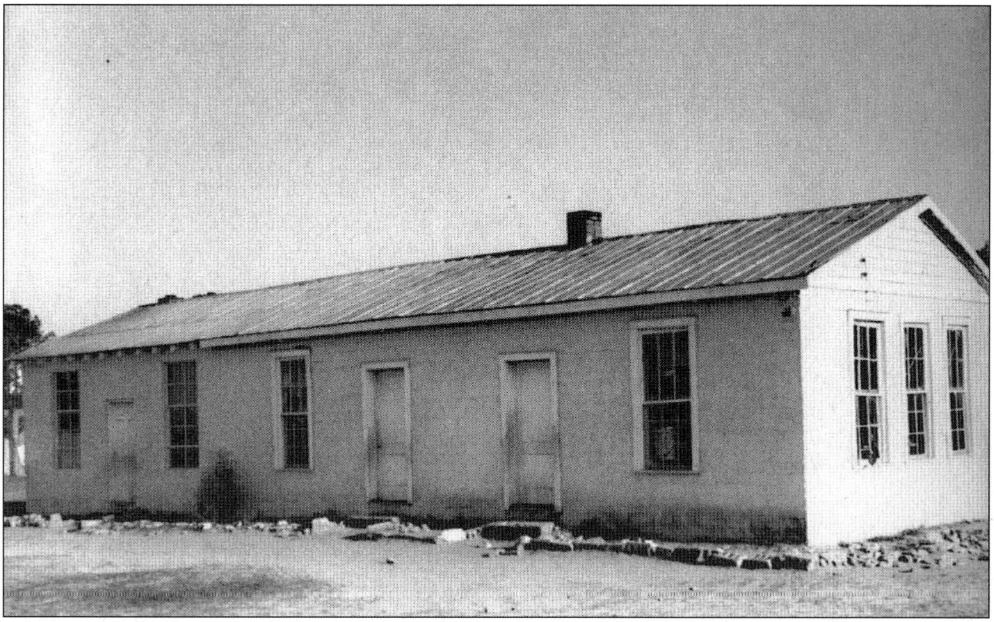

Dating to before the 1950s, the Macedonia School for African-Americans was situated in the rural District Of Columbia County. (Courtesy of Gerald Smith Ph.D., Private Collection.)

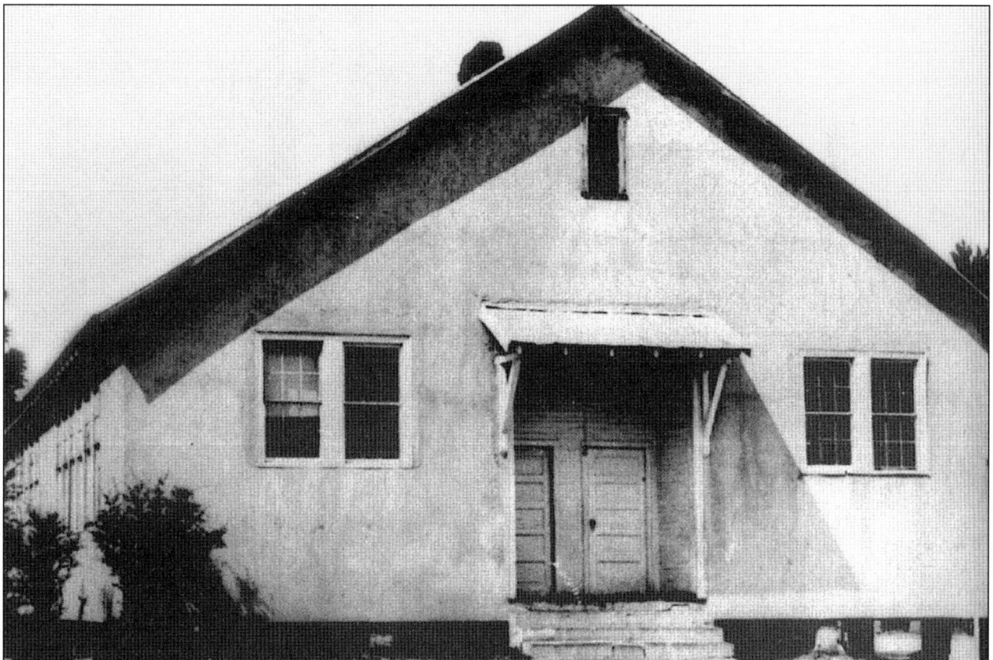

In the 1940s, Pollard's Academy for African Americans was located in Harlem. (Courtesy of Gerald Smith Ph.D., Private Collection.)

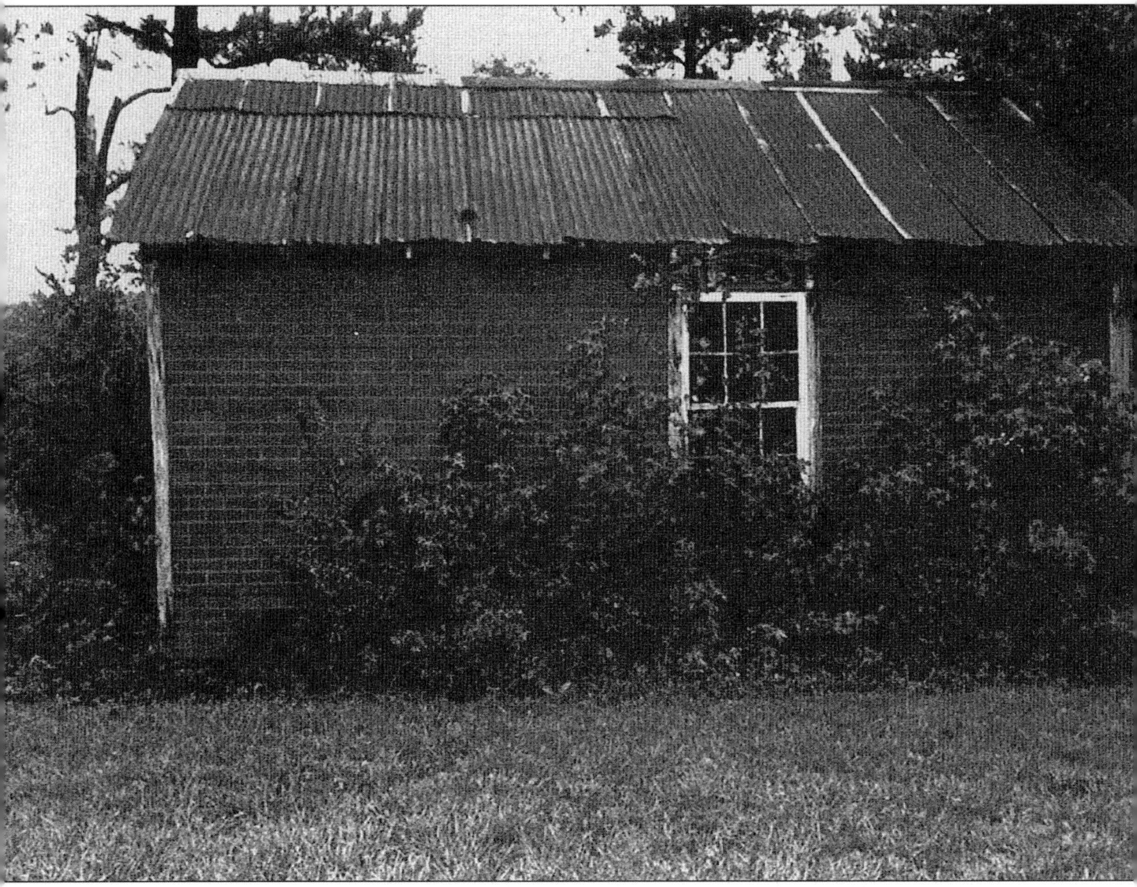

Mount Enon School for African Americans was located in Evans and was a small, one-room schoolhouse. (Courtesy of Gerald Smith, Ph.D., Private Collection.)

Eight
Coming Together

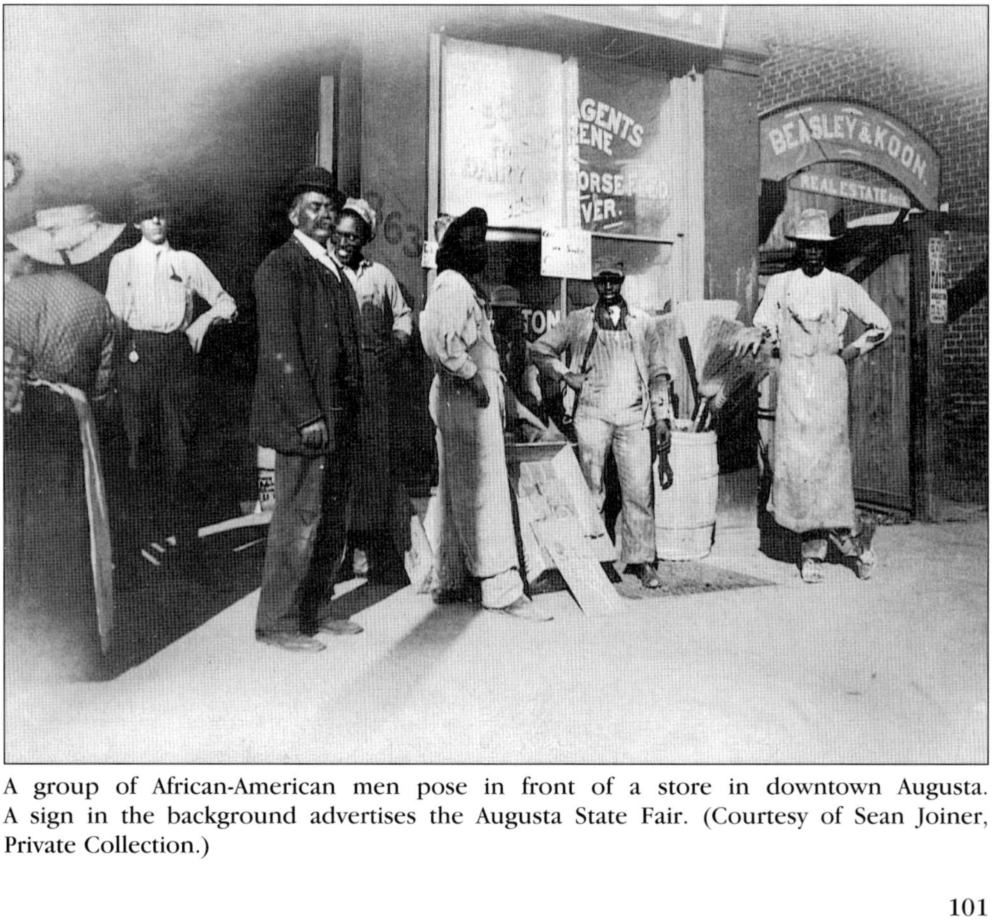

A group of African-American men pose in front of a store in downtown Augusta. A sign in the background advertises the Augusta State Fair. (Courtesy of Sean Joiner, Private Collection.)

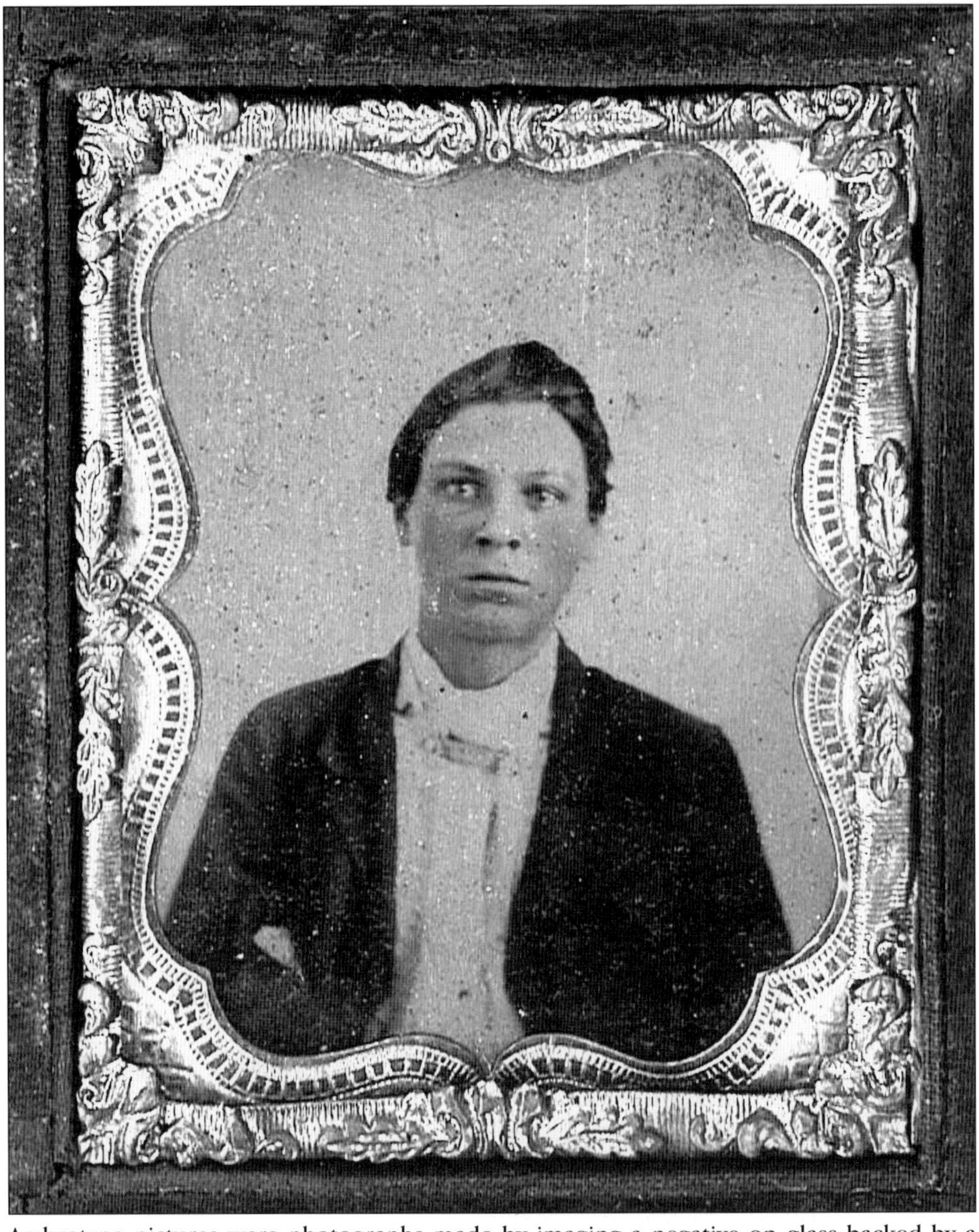

Ambrotype pictures were photographs made by imaging a negative on glass backed by a dark surface. Shown here is an ambrotype taken in Augusta of an unknown African-American woman. This is a rarity from the middle 19th century. (Courtesy of Gerald Smith Ph.D., Private Collection.)

There are hundreds of people attending this baptism. The photograph was taken sometime in the 1940s. (Courtesy of Milledge G. Murray, Private Collection.)

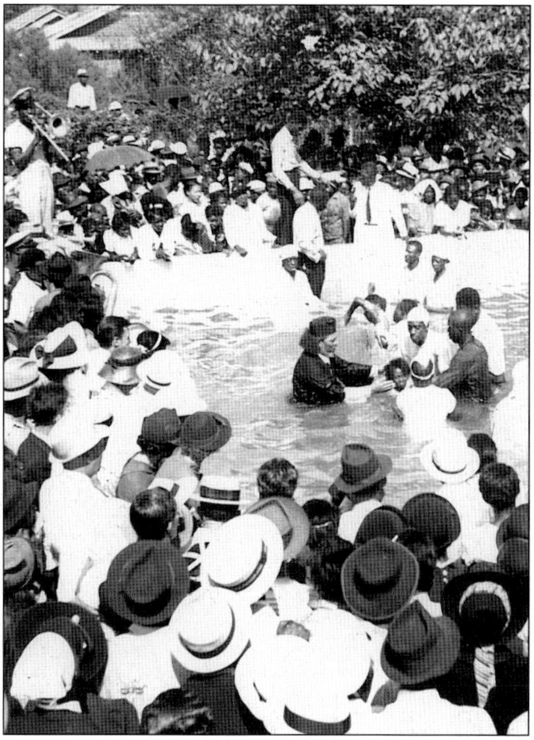

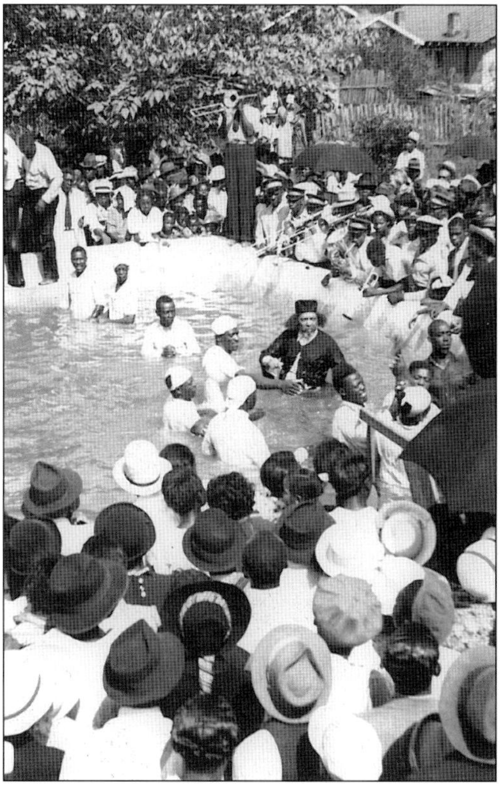

This is a baptism with celebrations in the background. A band plays religious tunes as musicians watch from a distance. (Courtesy of Milledge Murray, Private Collection.)

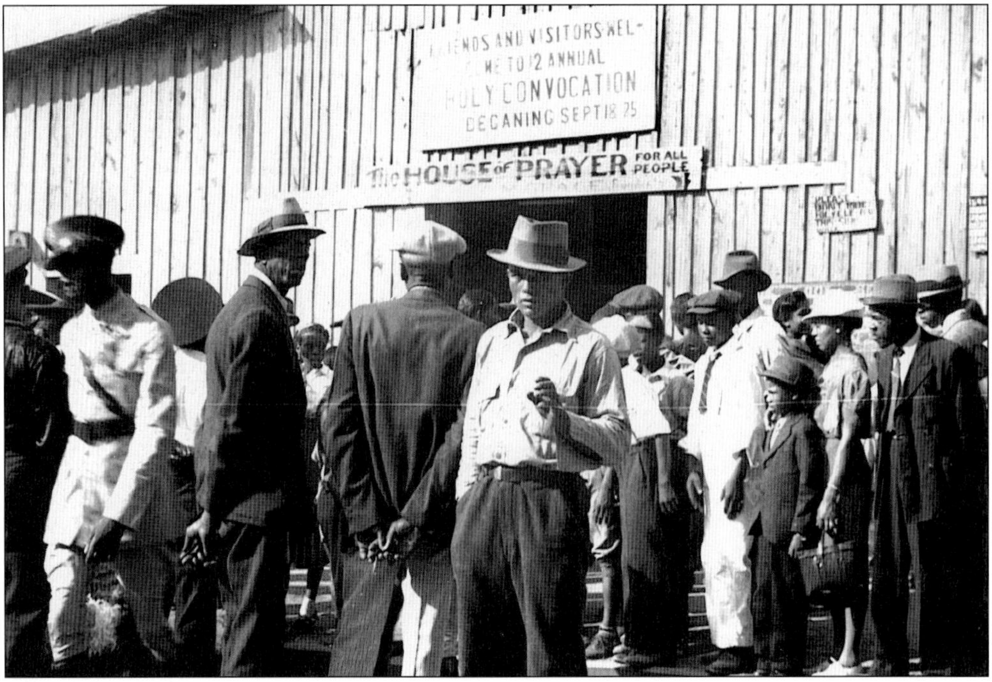

This handsome African-American man stands in front of the House of Prayer for All People. The sign above his head reads "Friends and visitors welcome to the 2nd annual Holy Convocation beginning September 25th." Another sign reads "Don't leave bicycles on this side." (Courtesy of Sean Joiner, Private Collection.)

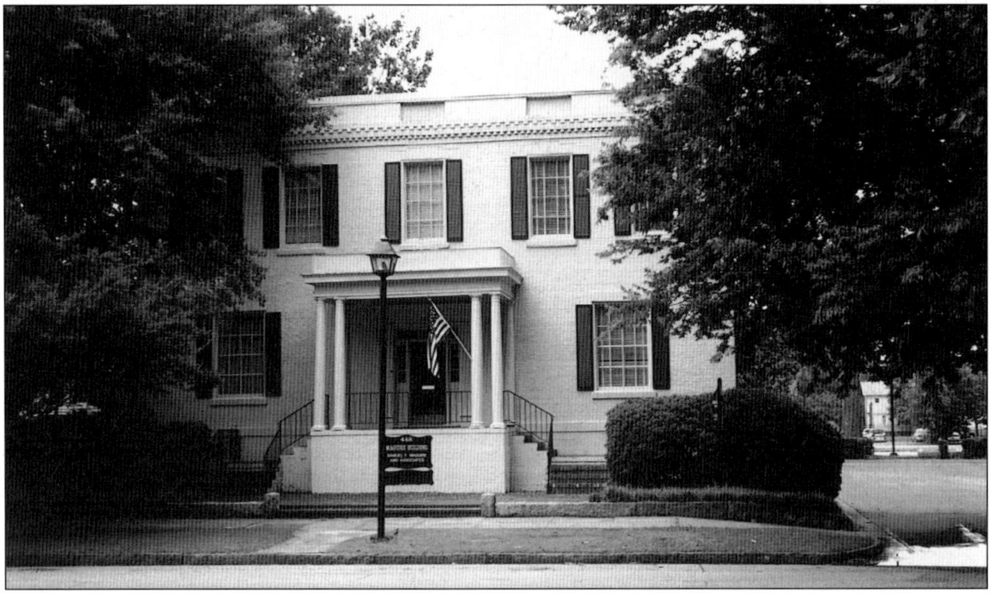

Born during the antebellum era, Amanda America Dickson was the daughter of a white planter. After her father died, she inherited his estate and moved to Augusta, where she lived in the house shown here. She became one of the wealthiest black women in the country. (Courtesy of Sean Joiner, Private Collection.)

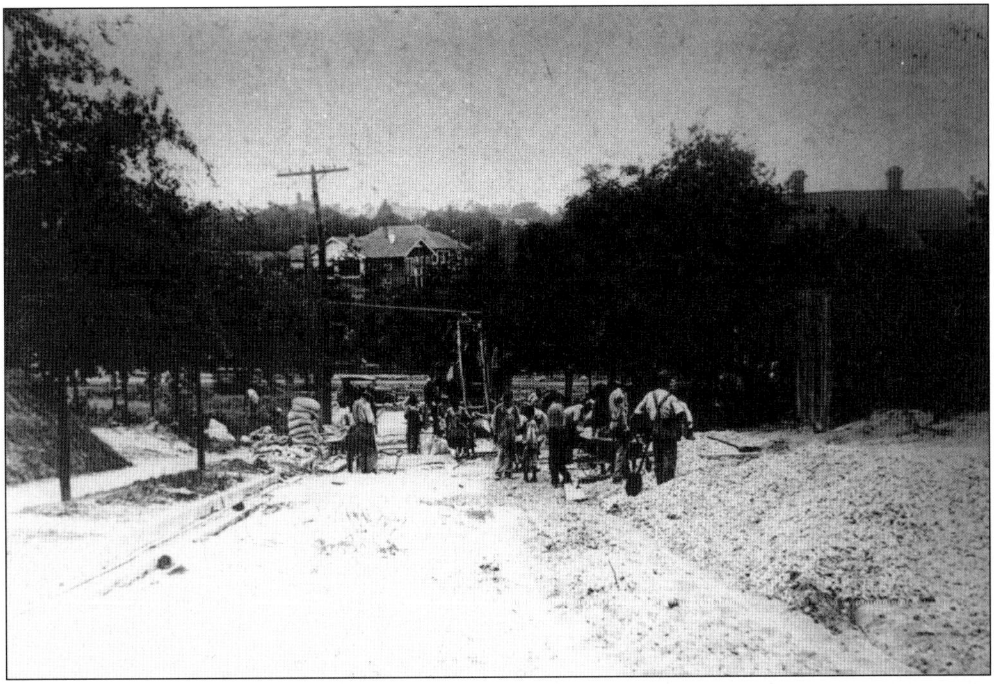

This is a vintage image of several African-American men paving a section of Walton Way in the Hill area of Augusta. (Courtesy of Special Collections, Reese Library, Augusta State University.)

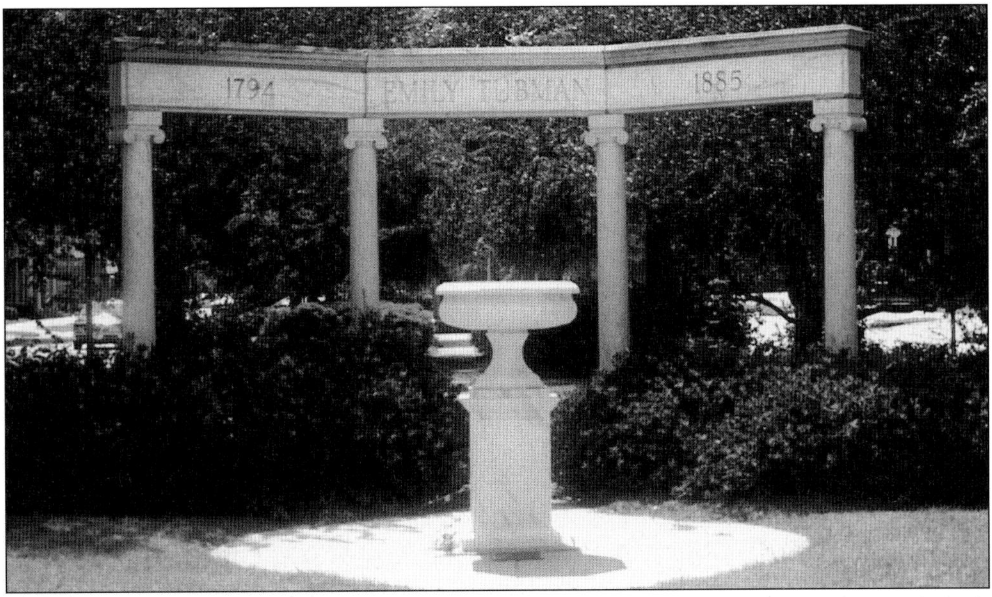

Augusta and the African-American community greatly benefited from the efforts of Emily Tubman. A monument was erected in her honor and is the only one in Augusta dedicated to a female. After her husband's death, she freed the slaves they owned and paid passage for them back to Africa. (Courtesy of Sean Joiner, Private Collection.)

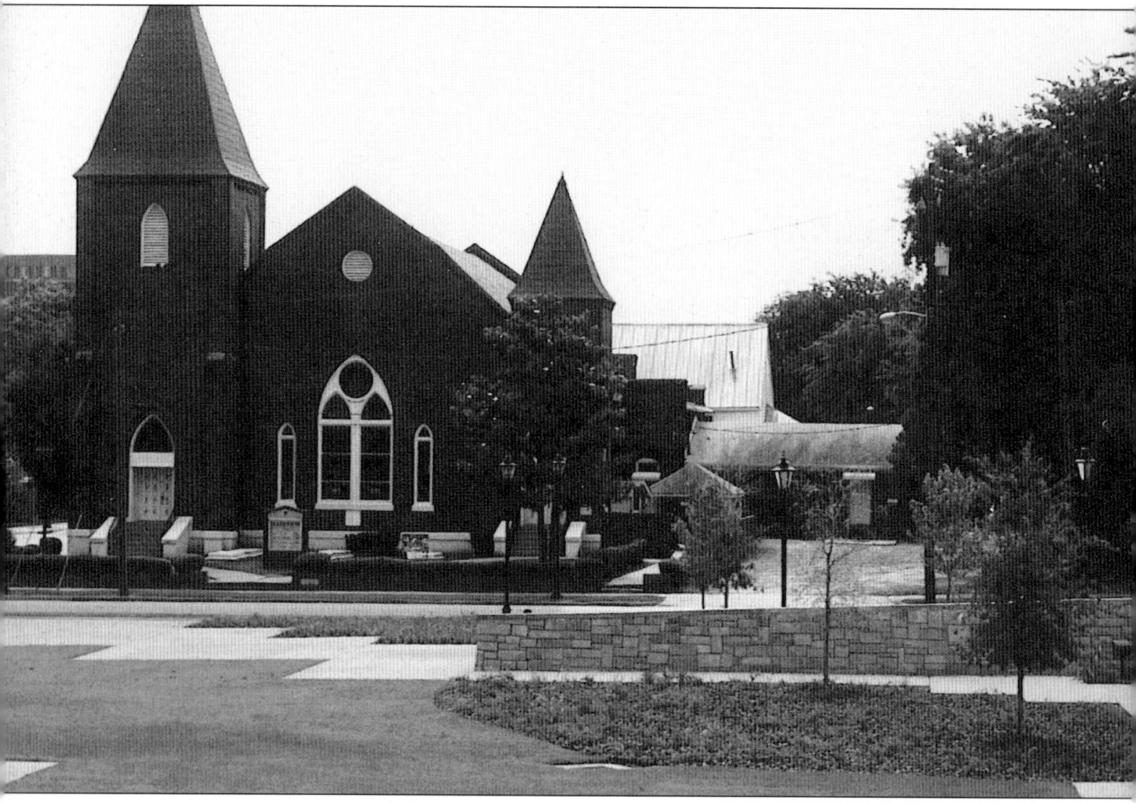

Shown here is the Springfield Baptist Church as it looks today. (Courtesy of Sean Joiner, Private Collection.)

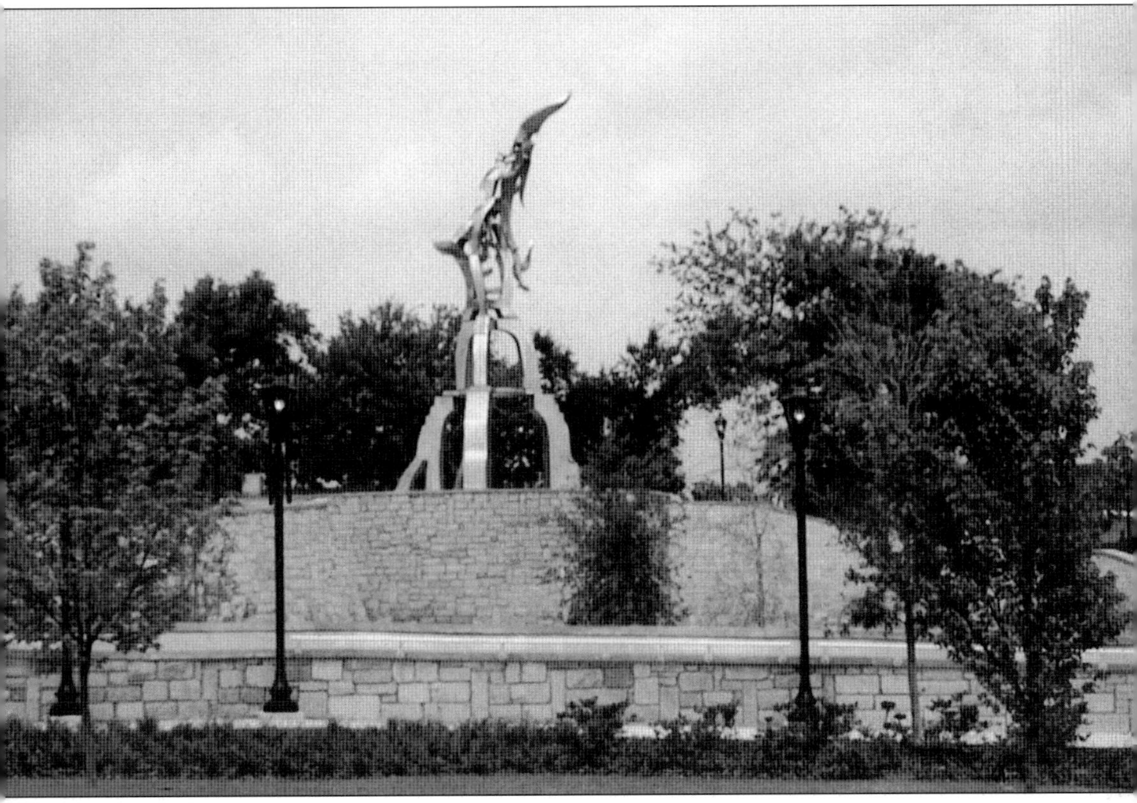

The Springfield Baptist Church Park sits across the street from the church. The large piece of artwork that towers above the landscape is the focus point of the site. (Courtesy of Sean Joiner, Private Collection.)

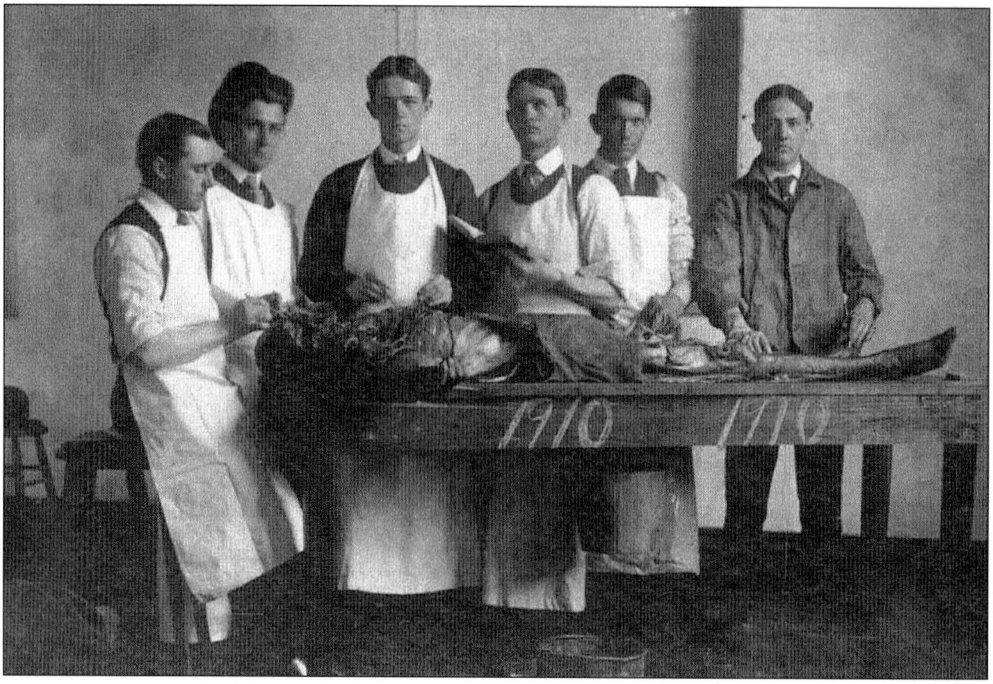

This vintage photograph shows Medical College of Georgia doctors performing an autopsy on an African-American man. This was not an uncommon practice during the early 20th century. The corpses were used for medical research and educational purposes. (Courtesy of Gerald Smith Ph.D.)

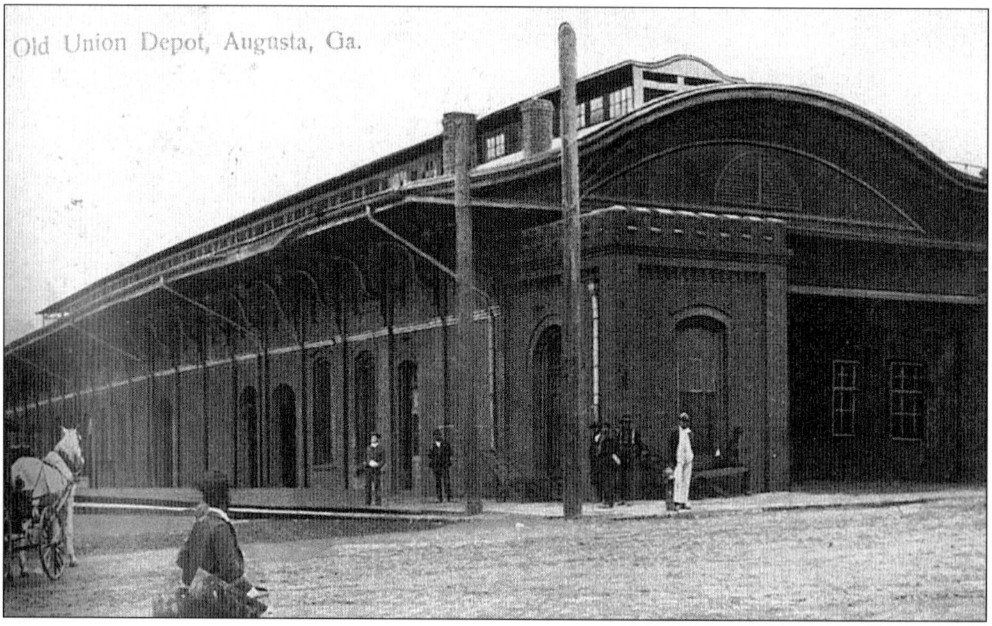

This early postcard of the Old Union Depot in Augusta shows a small African-American child looking at the entrances to the station. Standing next to the entrances are several African-American men. (Courtesy of Augusta Museum of History.)

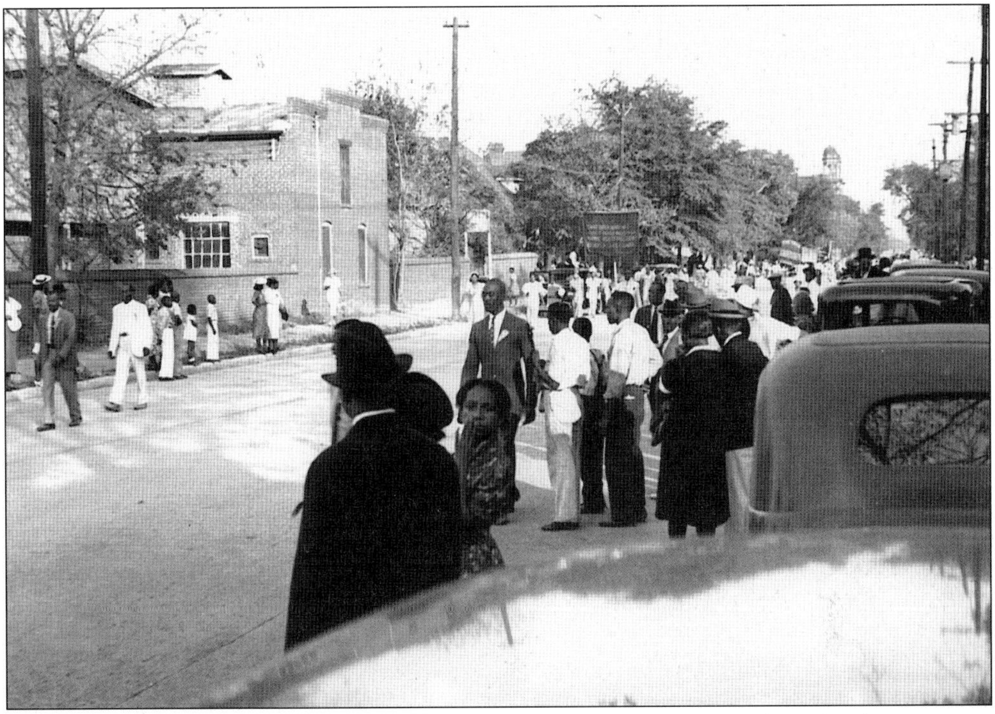

Several people watch as a parade passes by on Laney Walker Boulevard. The men are dressed in sharp suits and the children are in their Sunday best. (Courtesy of Milledge Murray, Private Collection.)

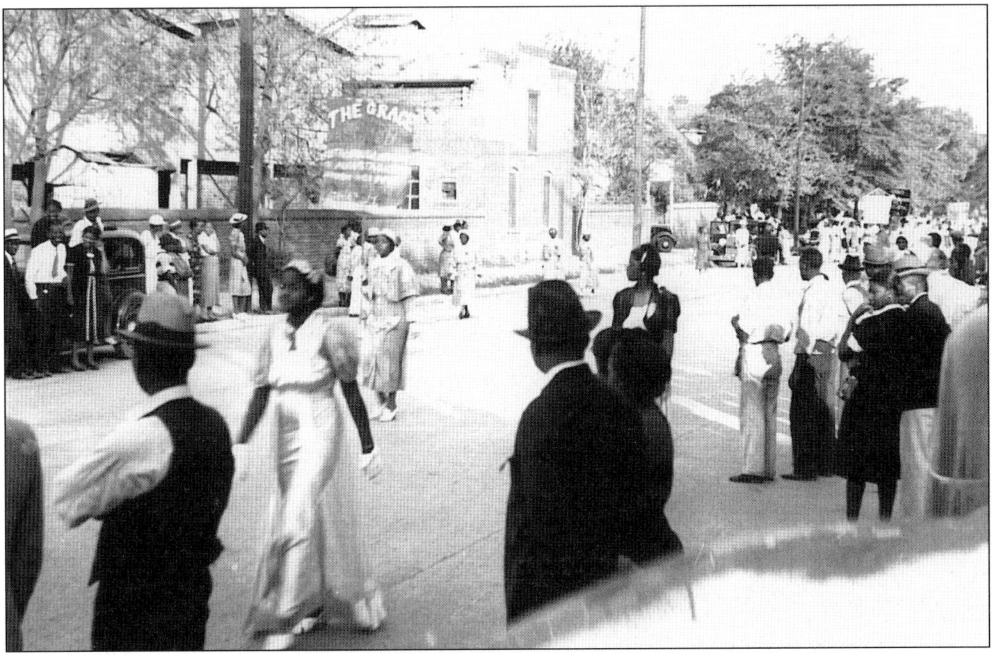

The women marching in this parade on Laney Walker Boulevard are wearing their smartest dresses for the occasion. (Courtesy of Milledge G. Murray, Private Collection.)

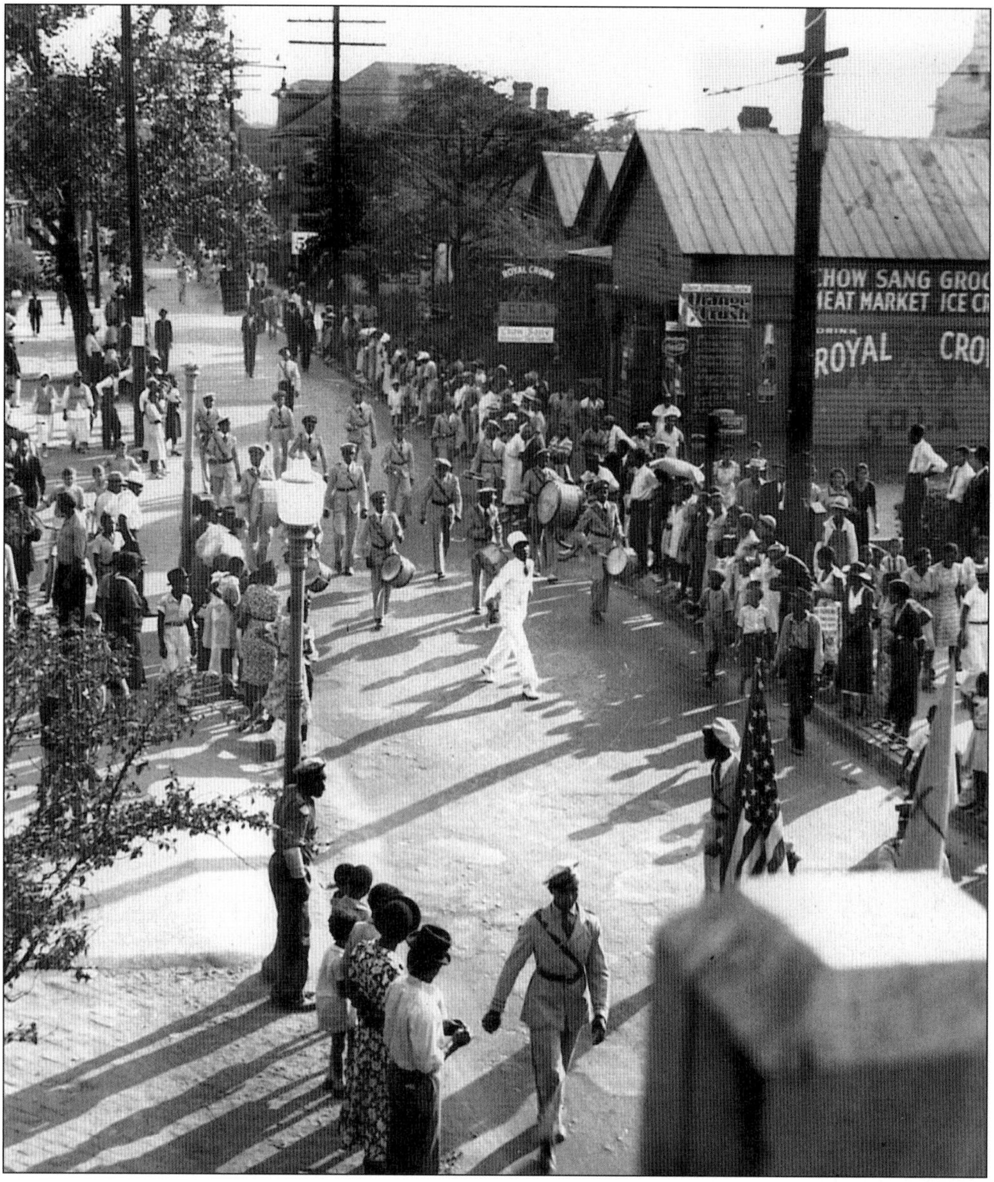

The Daddy Grace Parade was a joyful event; here, a band marches through the streets in celebration. (Courtesy of Milledge G. Murray, Private Collection.)

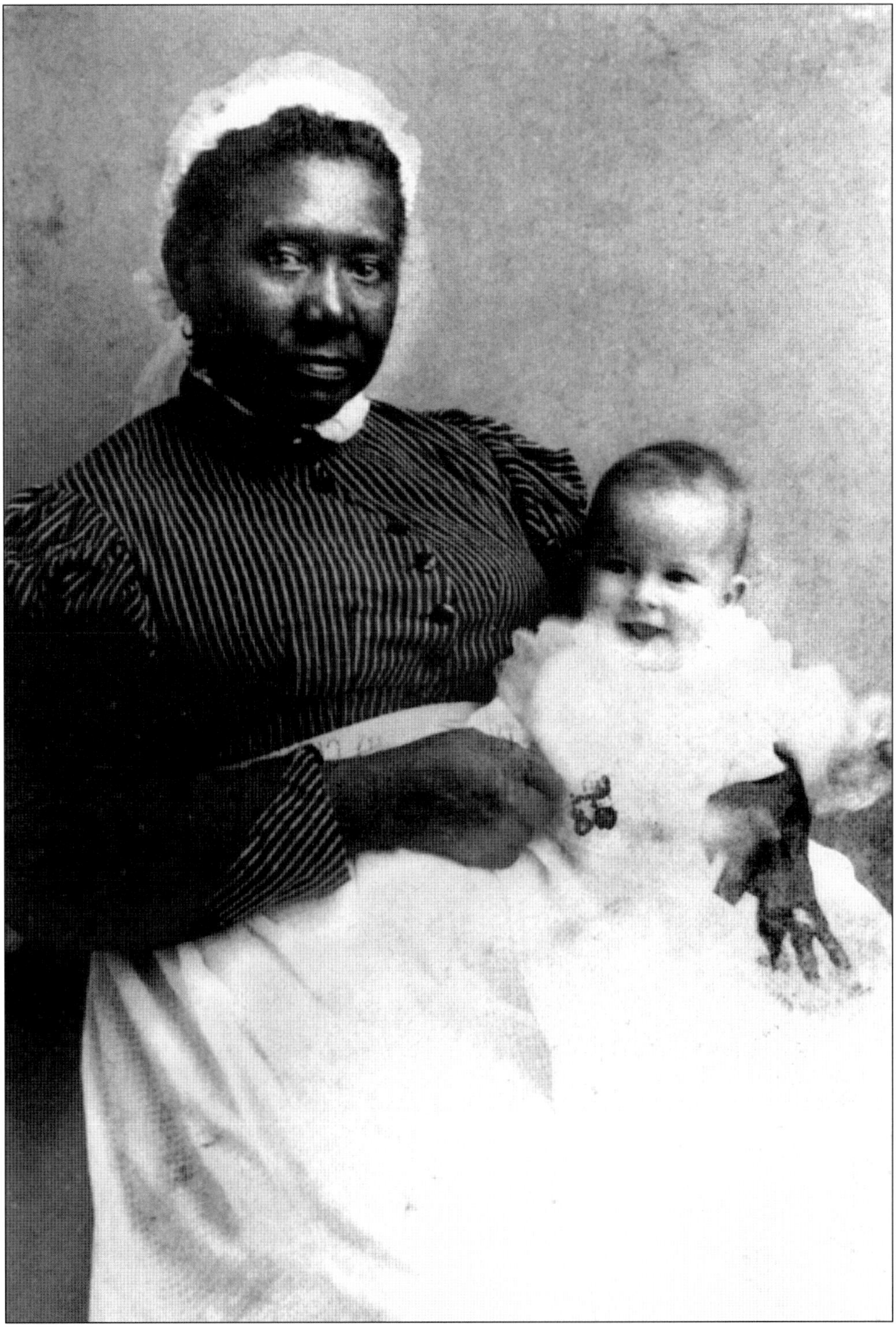

This photograph shows an unidentified Augusta nanny holding a small child. (Courtesy of Special Collection, Reese Library, Augusta State University.)

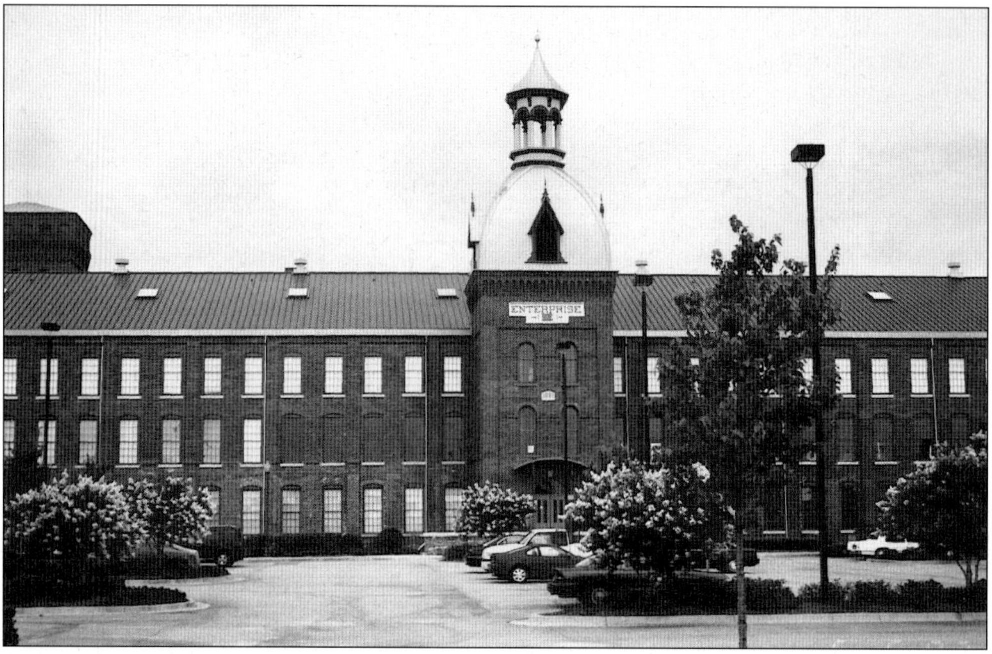

The Enterprise Mill employed hundreds of people in Augusta during its time as a textile mill. (Courtesy of Sean Joiner, Private Collection.)

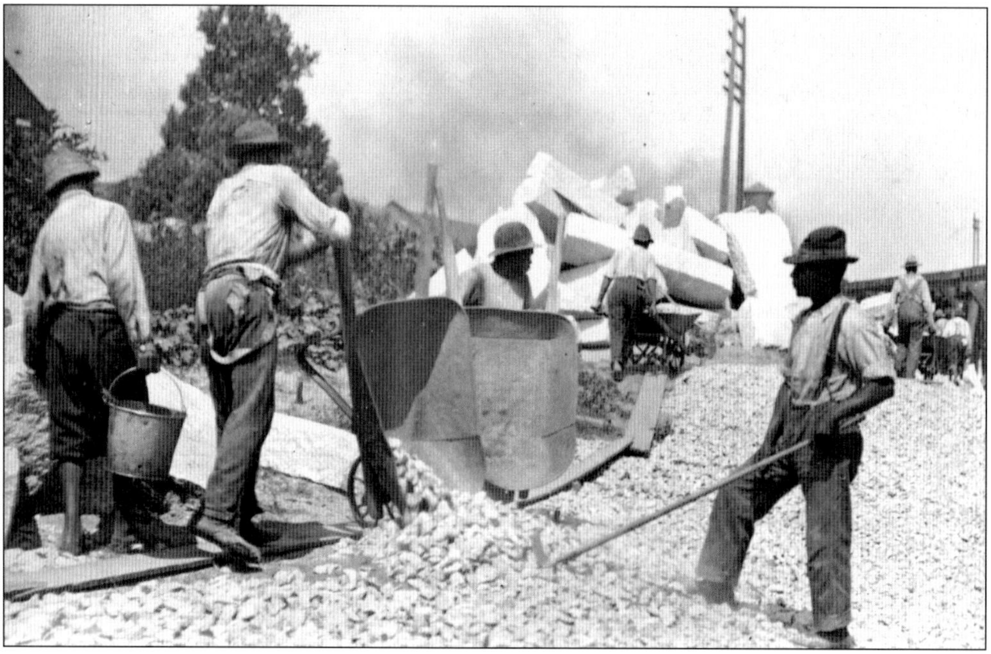

These men are working hard to build the levee in downtown Augusta near the Savannah River. (Courtesy of Augusta Museum of History.)

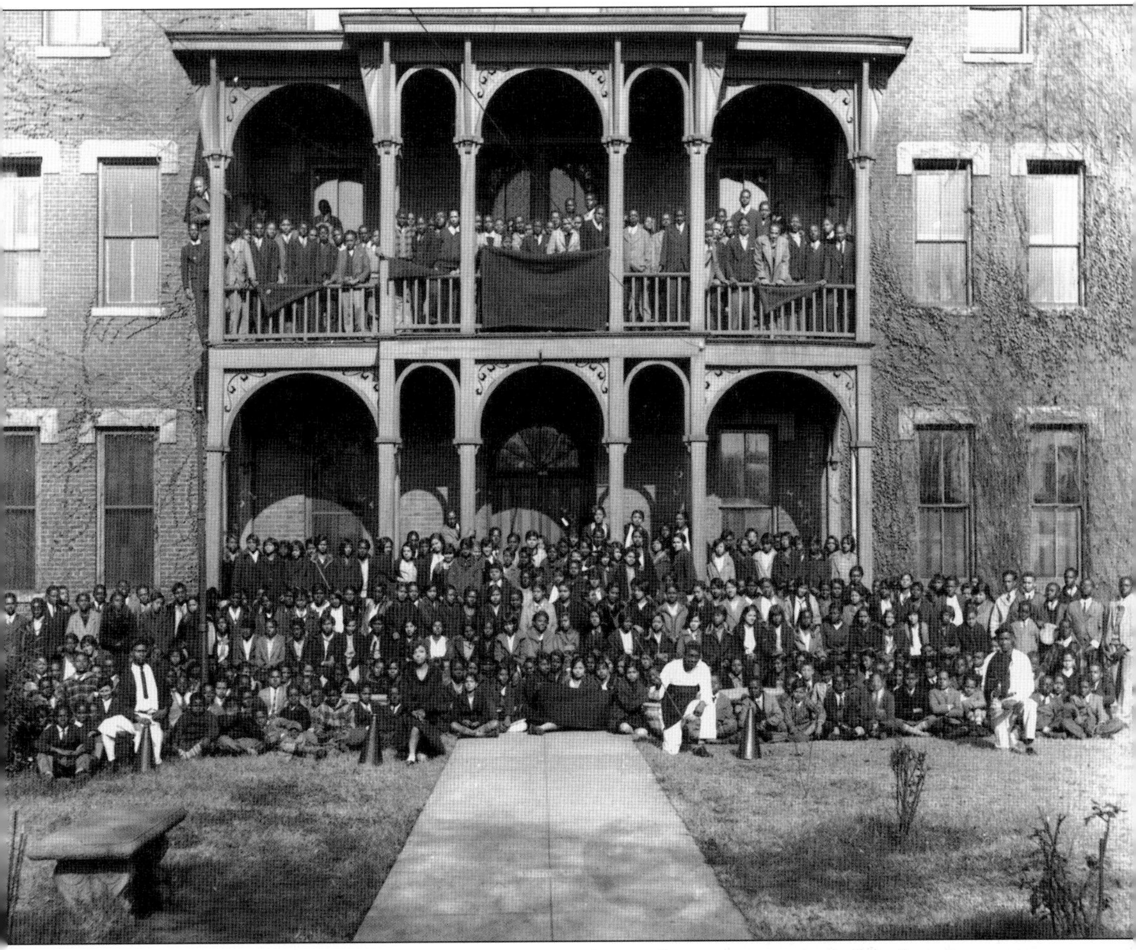

This large group photograph shows a number of students and faculty from an unidentified school in Augusta posing in front of a school building. (Courtesy of Augusta Museum of History.)

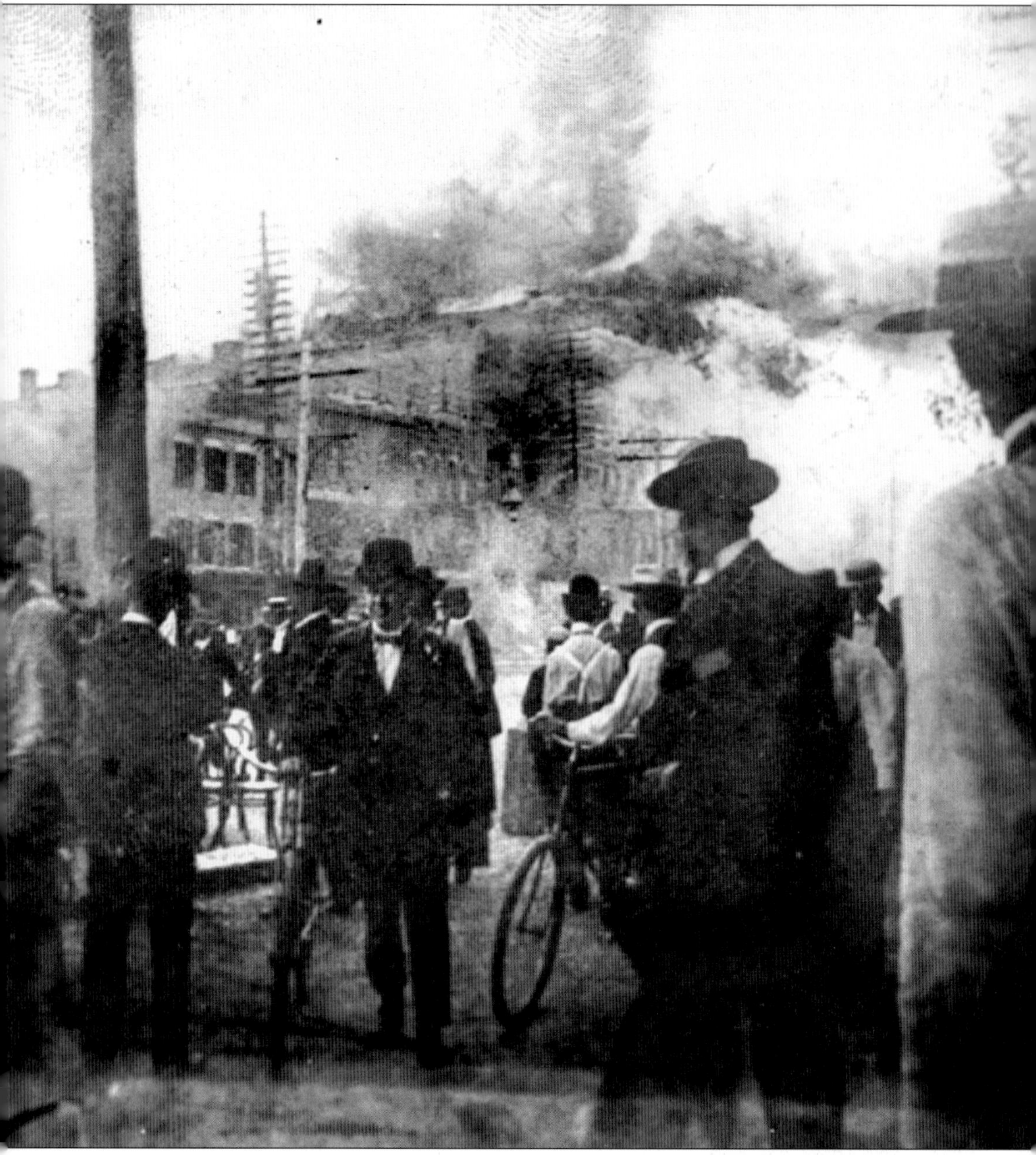

A fire ravaged the Montgomery Building in 1899. African-American men stand and watch as the inferno rages. (Courtesy of Special Collections, Reese Library, Augusta State University.)

John Wesley Gilbert was an early graduate of Paine Institute and the first African-American member of the faculty. He was a noted Greek scholar and Methodist missionary. (Courtesy of Gerald Smith Ph.D., Private Collection.)

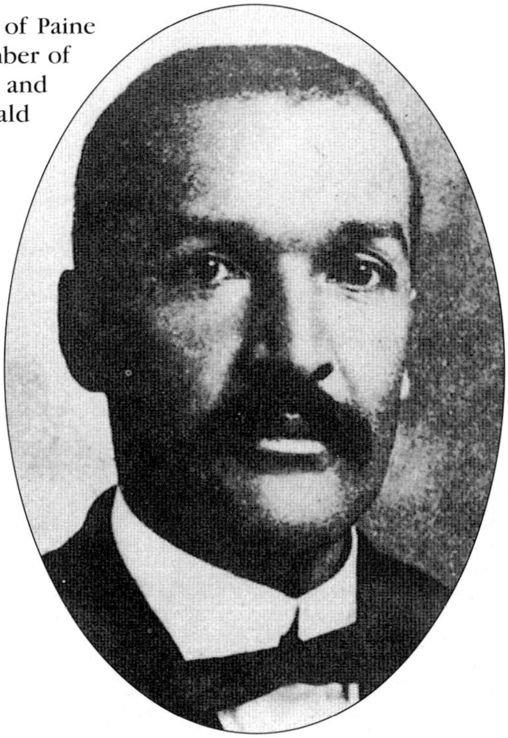

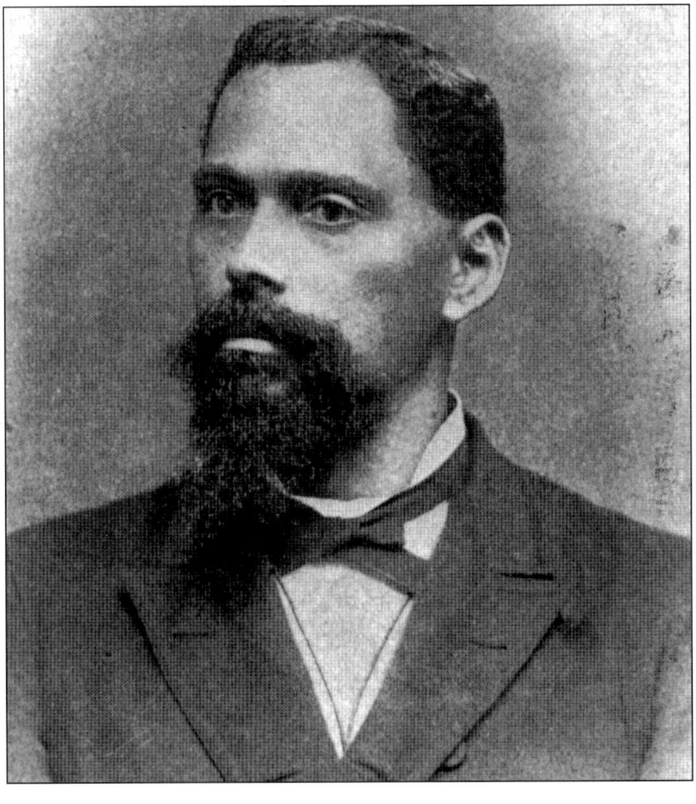

Lucius Holsey, one of the first bishops of the Colored Methodist Episcopal Church, was the primary founder of Paine Institute. Without his constant efforts, the Institute might not have survived. (Courtesy of Gerald Smith Ph.D., Private Collection.)

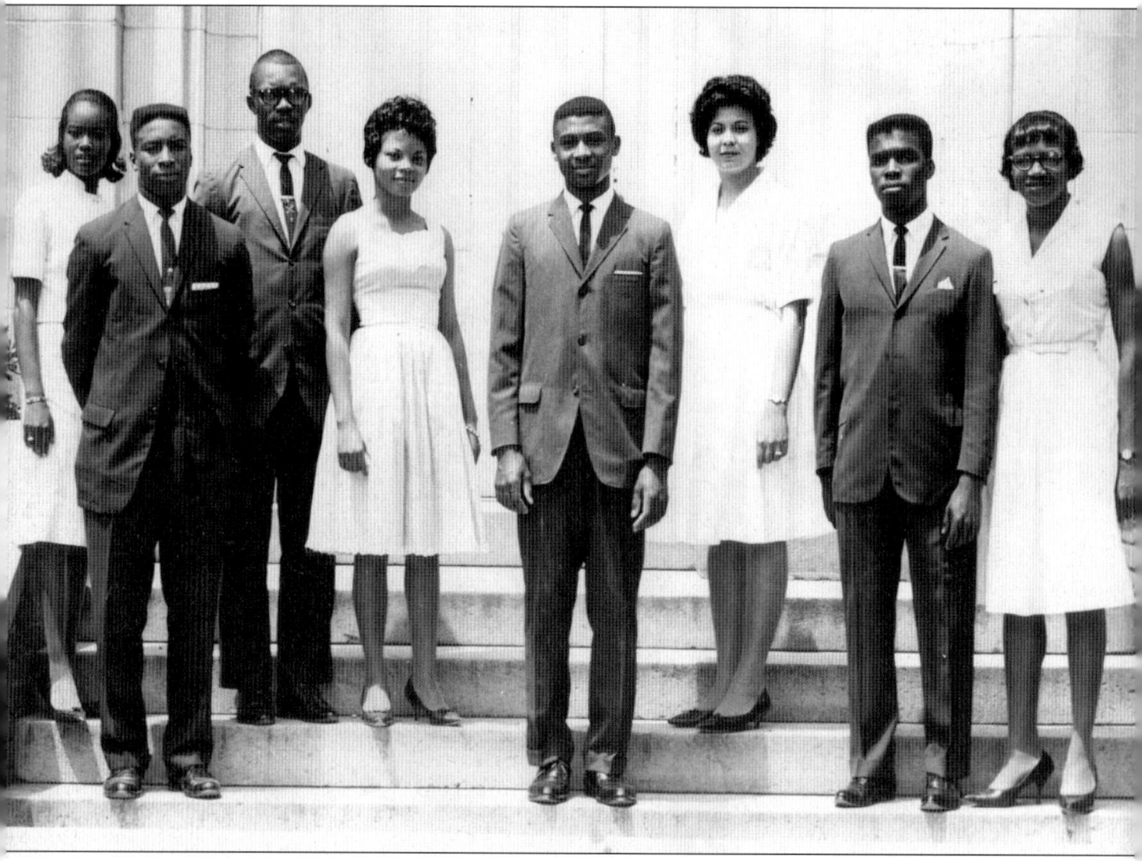

Taken during the 1950s, this is a group photograph of student alumni at Paine College. (Courtesy of Augusta Museum of History.)

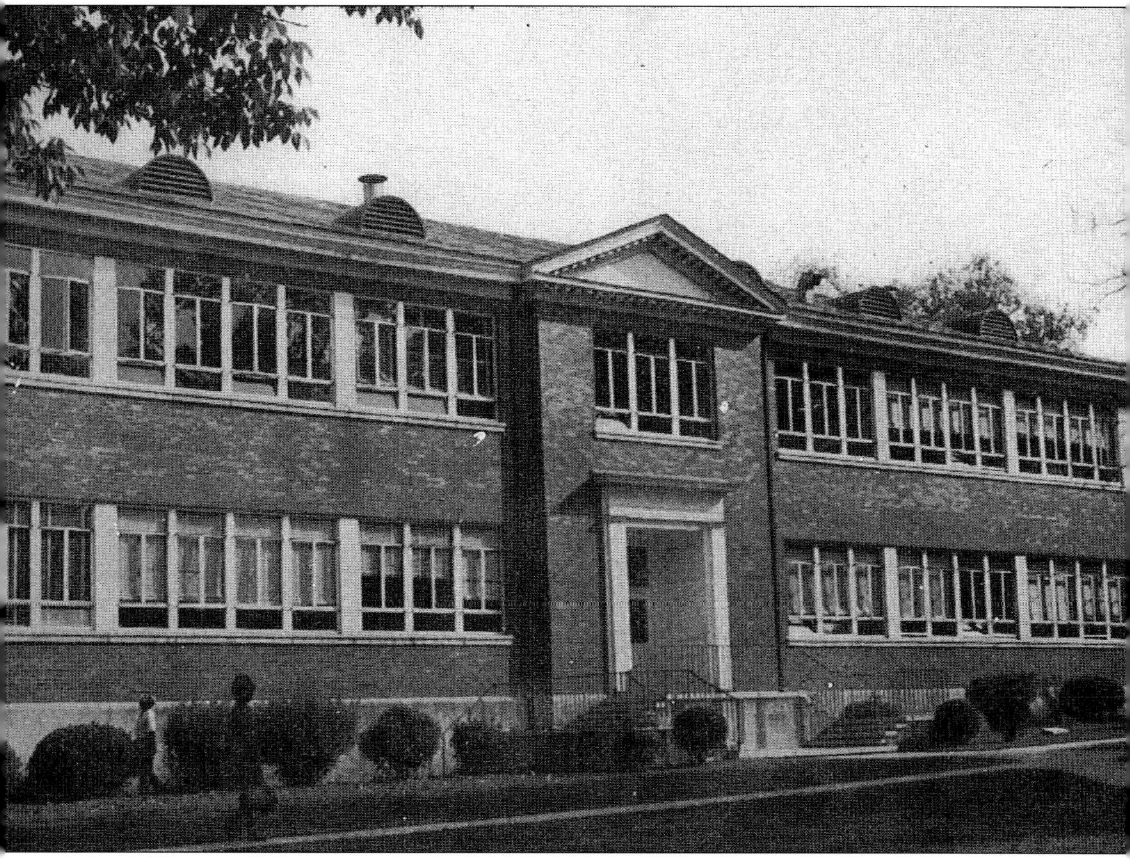

This is the Walker Science Building at Paine College. The building was constructed in the first half of the 20th century. (Courtesy of Gerald Smith Ph.D., Private Collection.)

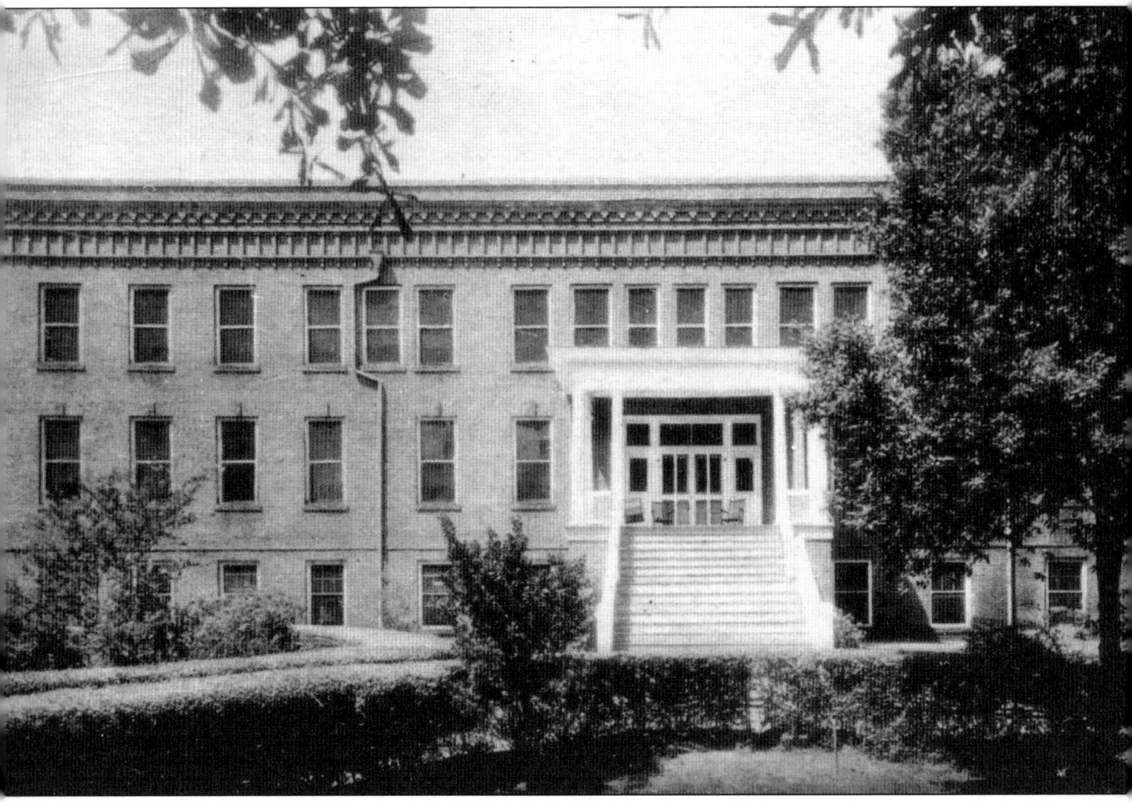

Bennett Hall at Paine College contained classrooms, offices, and the cafeteria. The building was razed in 1977. (Courtesy of Gerald Smith Ph.D., Private Collection.)

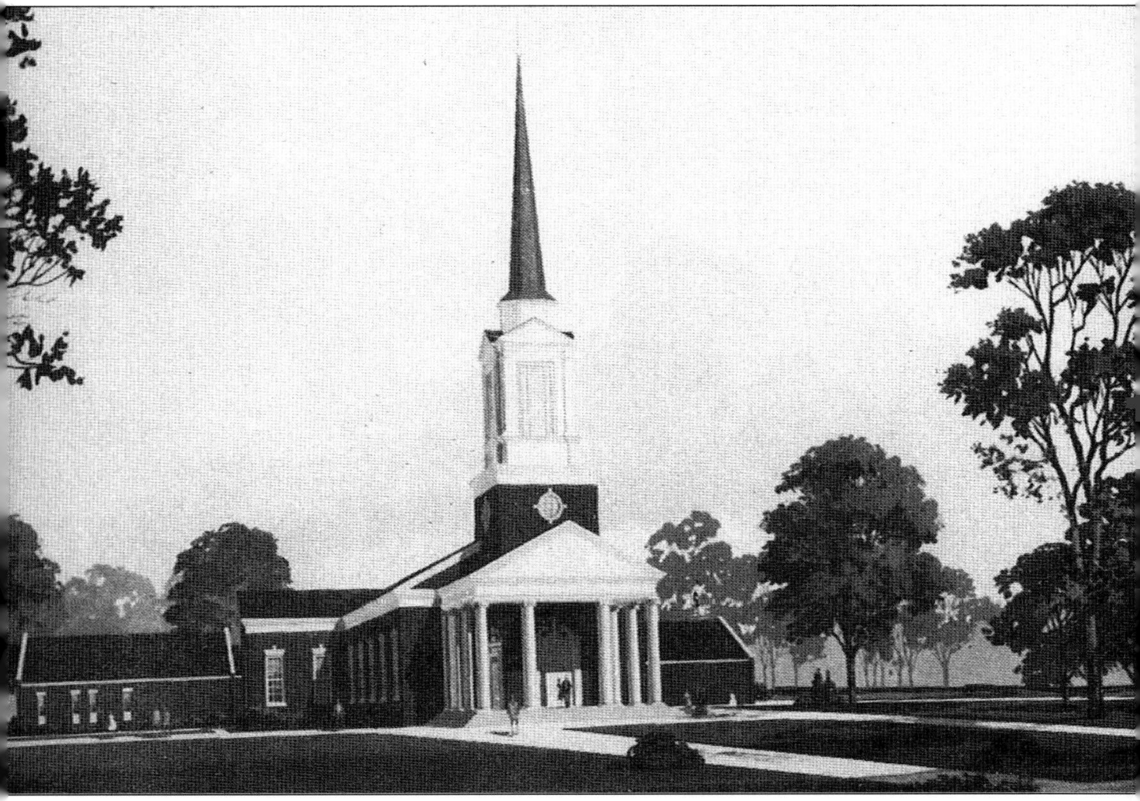

The Paine College Gilbert-Lambuth Chapel and Music Hall was named for John Wesley Gilbert and Methodist Bishop Walter Lambuth. (Courtesy of Paine College.)

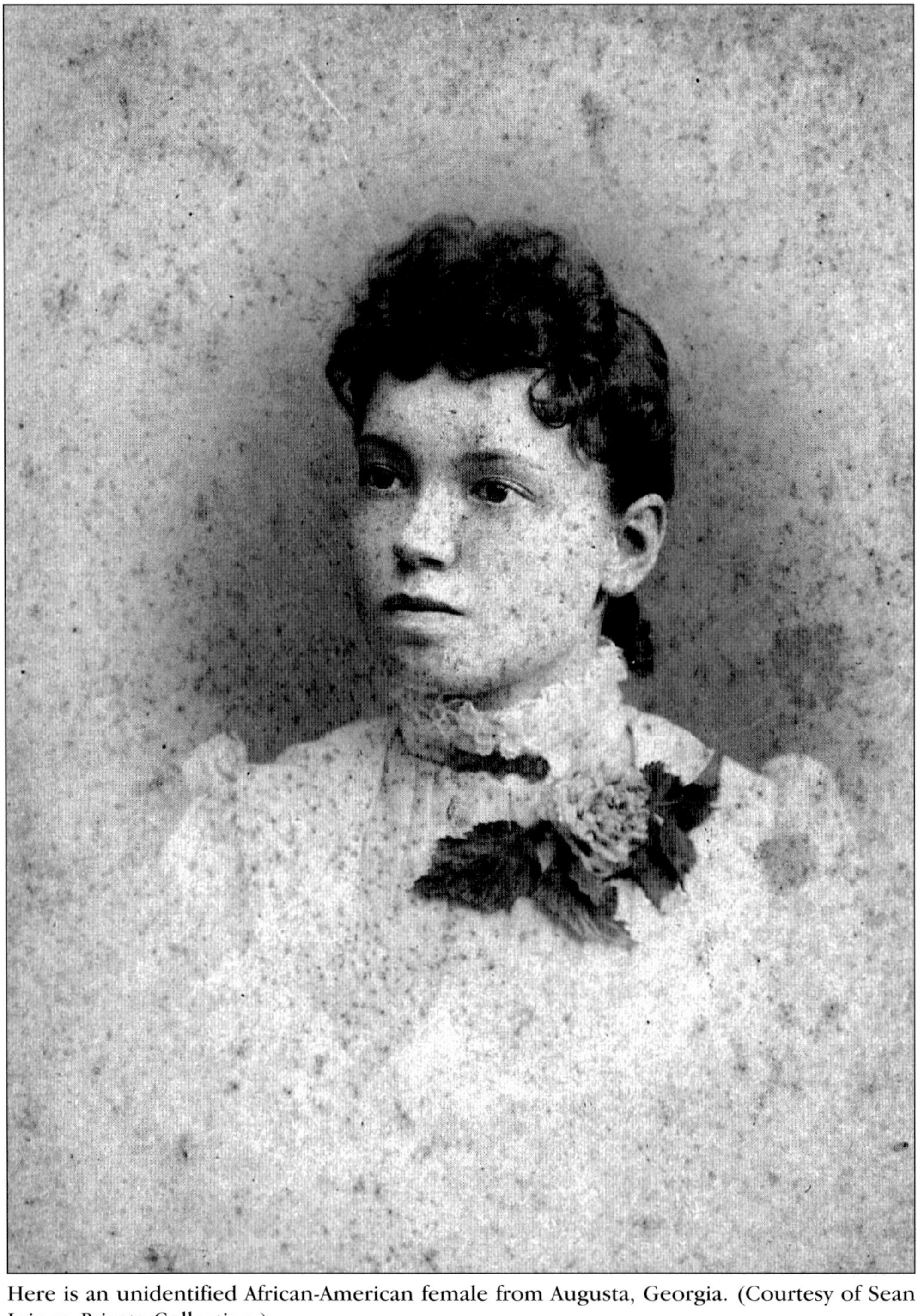

Here is an unidentified African-American female from Augusta, Georgia. (Courtesy of Sean Joiner, Private Collection.)

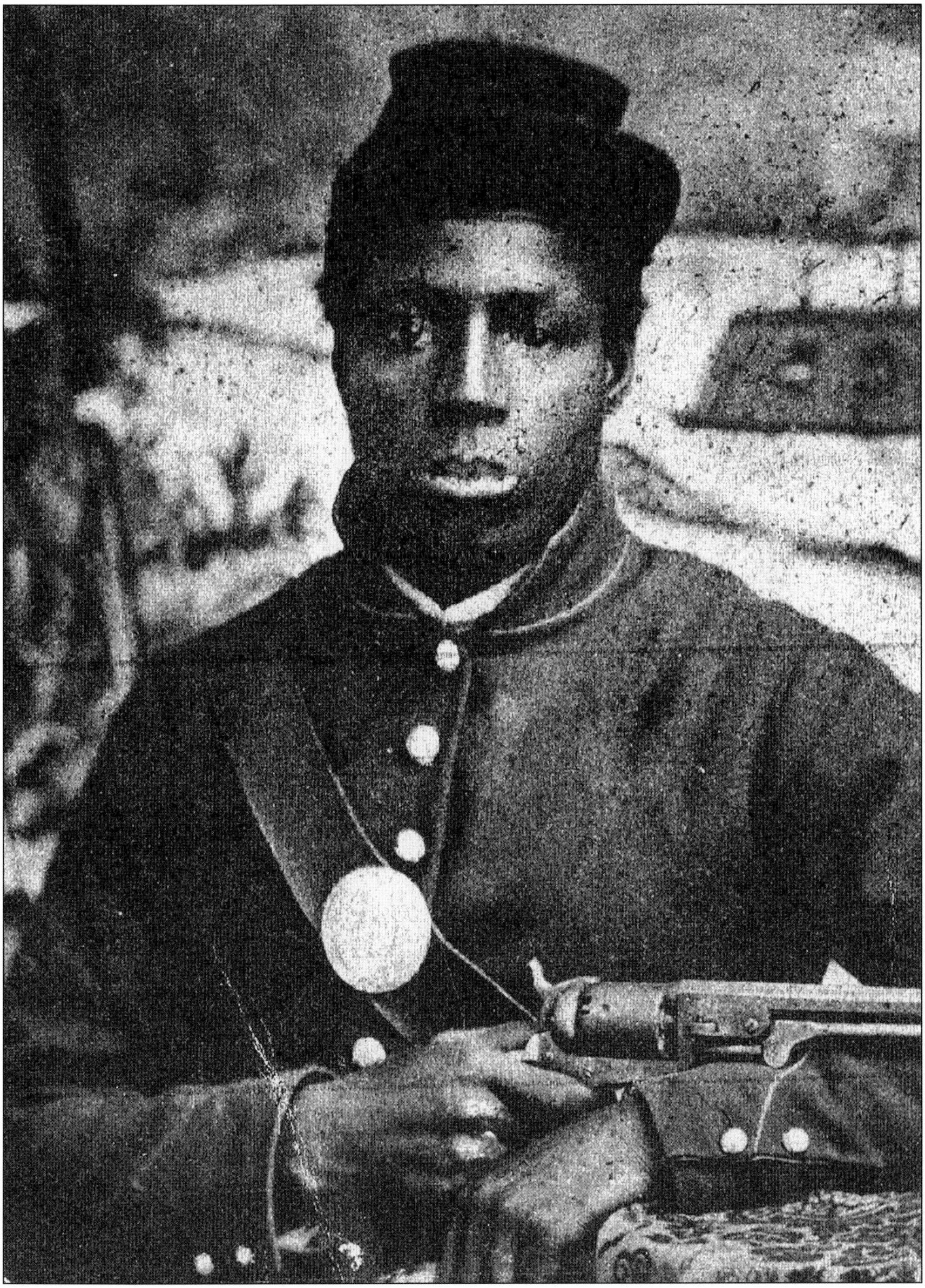

This ninth-plate tintype, *c.* 1865, shows a young African American dressed in a Union cavalryman's shell jacket with yellow piping. He was probably in the famed 10th Cavalry, which earned the name "Buffalo Soldiers" from the Indians of the Old West. He is holding an 1856 .36 Colt Navy revolver; the leather belt over his chest is his carbine sling. (Courtesy of the G.J.S. Collection.)

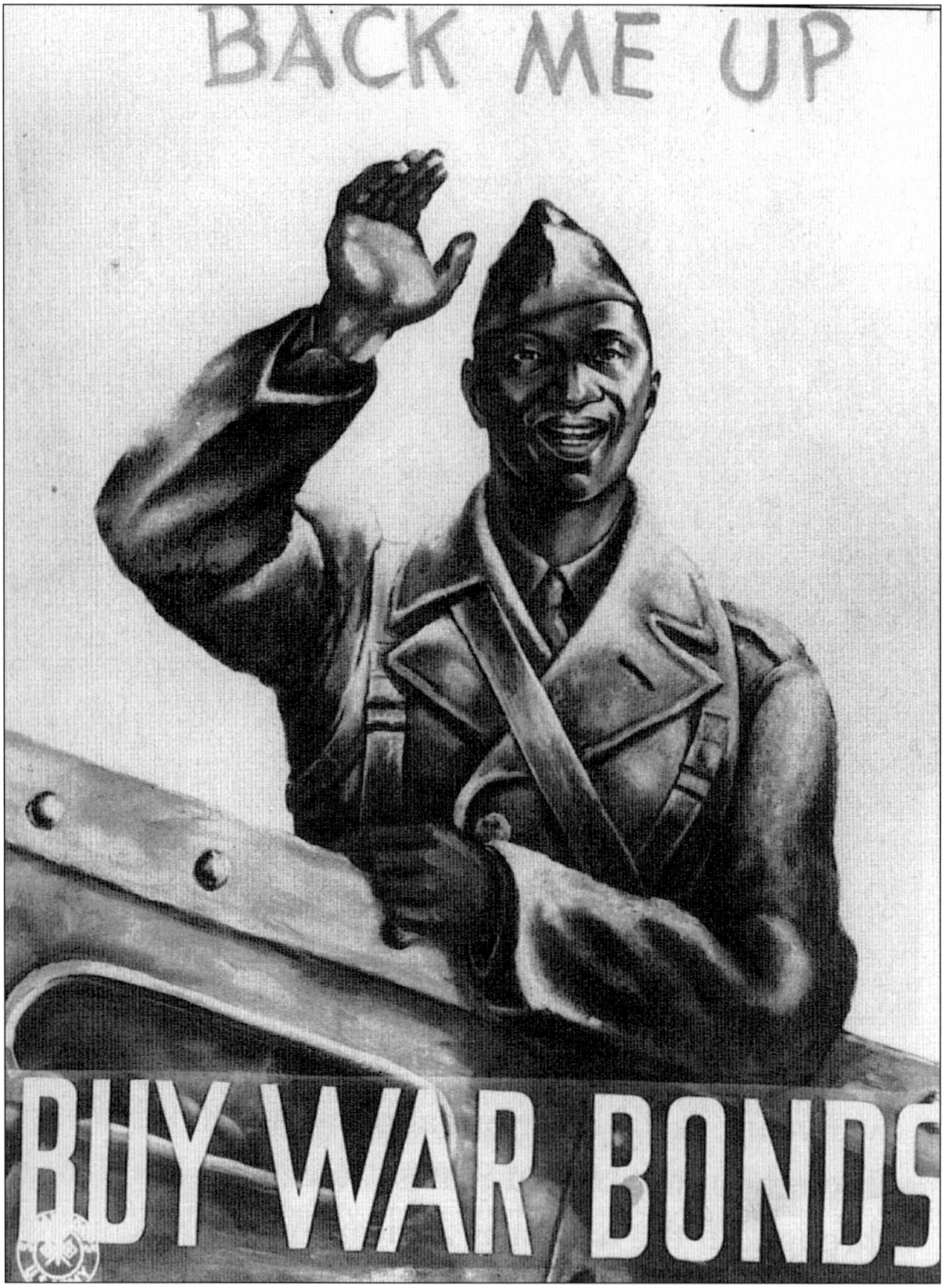

During World War II, African Americans were sought to serve in the military. Posters such as this appeared everywhere to encourage volunteers. This type of advertisement hung in the Augusta train stations. (Courtesy of Gerald Smith Ph.D., Private Collection.)

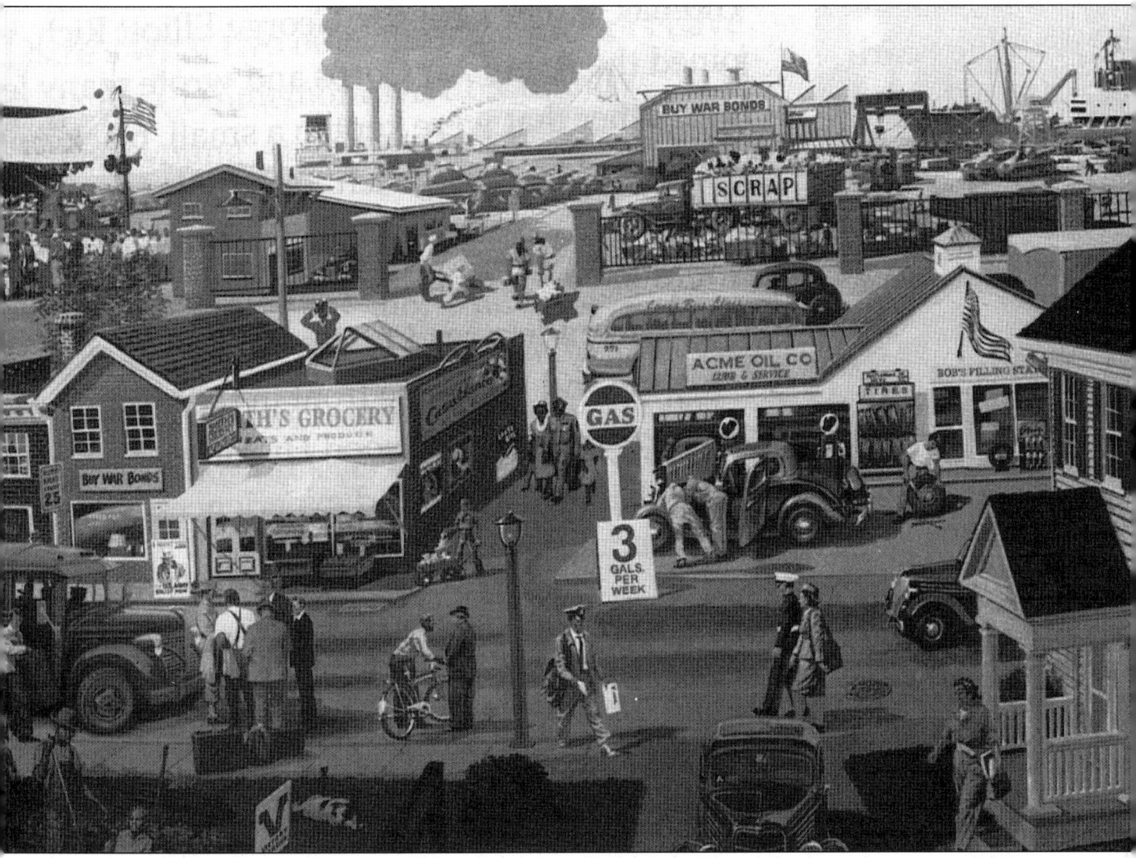

This postcard shows people during World War II and portrays the businesses of the downtown area. (Courtesy of Gerald Smith Ph.D., Private Collection.)

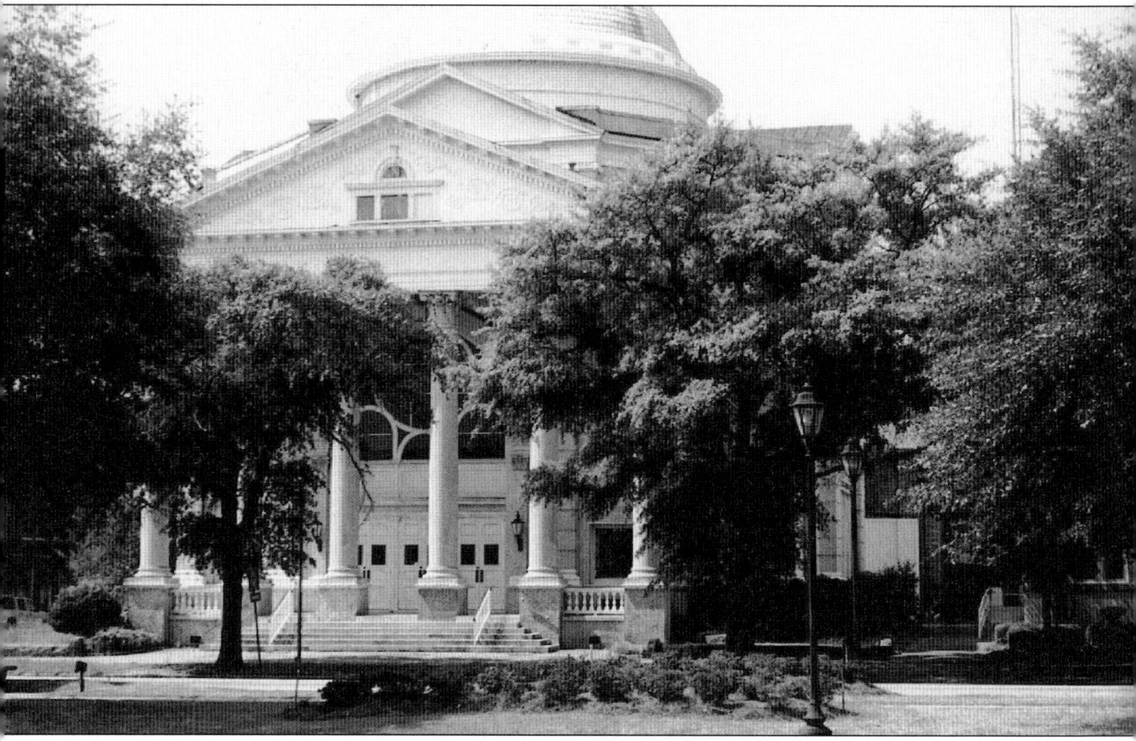

Shown here is the First Baptist Church in downtown Augusta; the new building is on Walton Way. The church has helped the African-American community over the years. (Courtesy of Sean Joiner, Private Collection.)

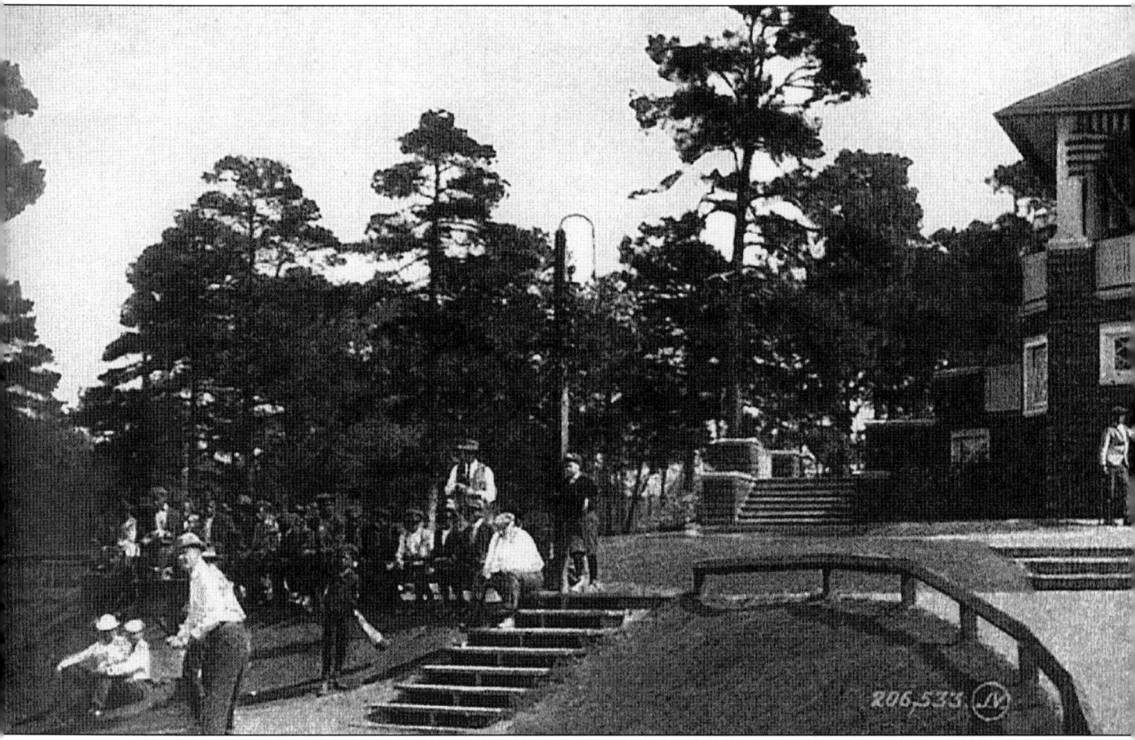

This is the Forest Hills Golf Course and Club. In the background, African-American children watch golf being played. The picture dates to the early 20th century. (Courtesy of Milledge Murray, Private Collection.)

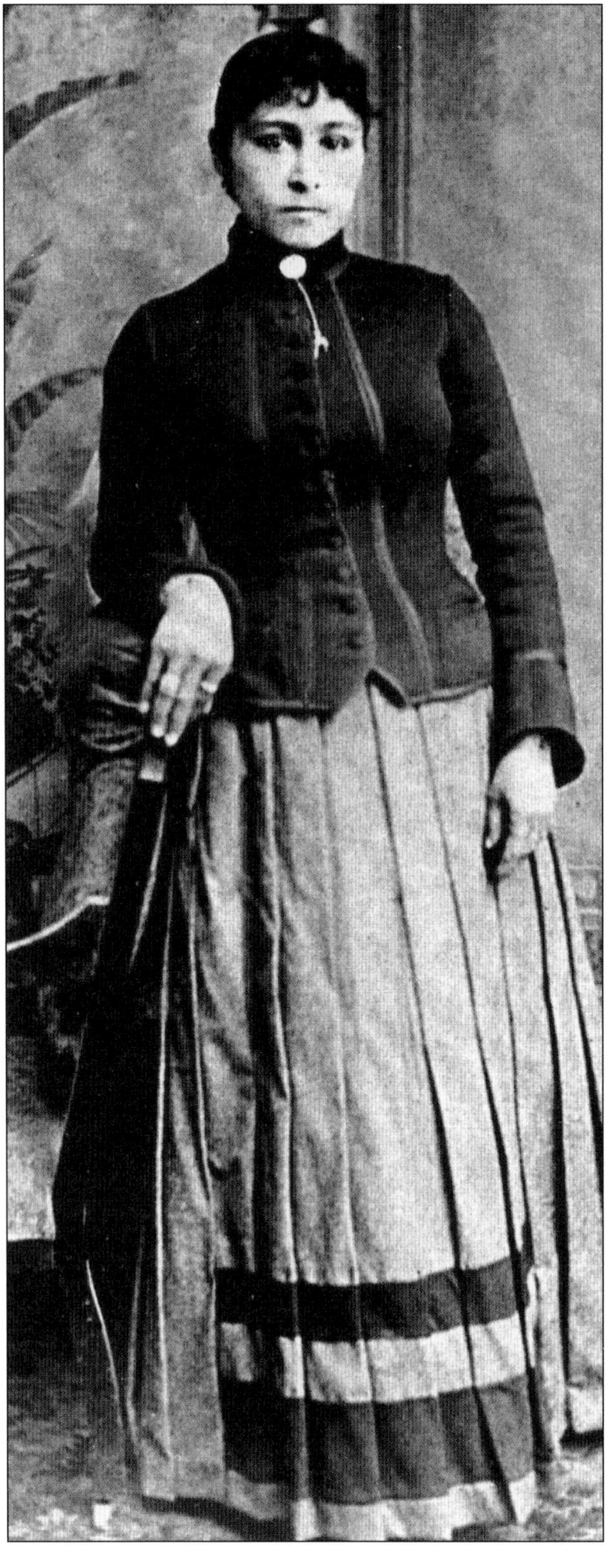

Amanda America Dickson stands in the parlor of her Augusta home. She wears a dress typical of the late 1800s. (Courtesy of Sean Joiner, Private Collection.)

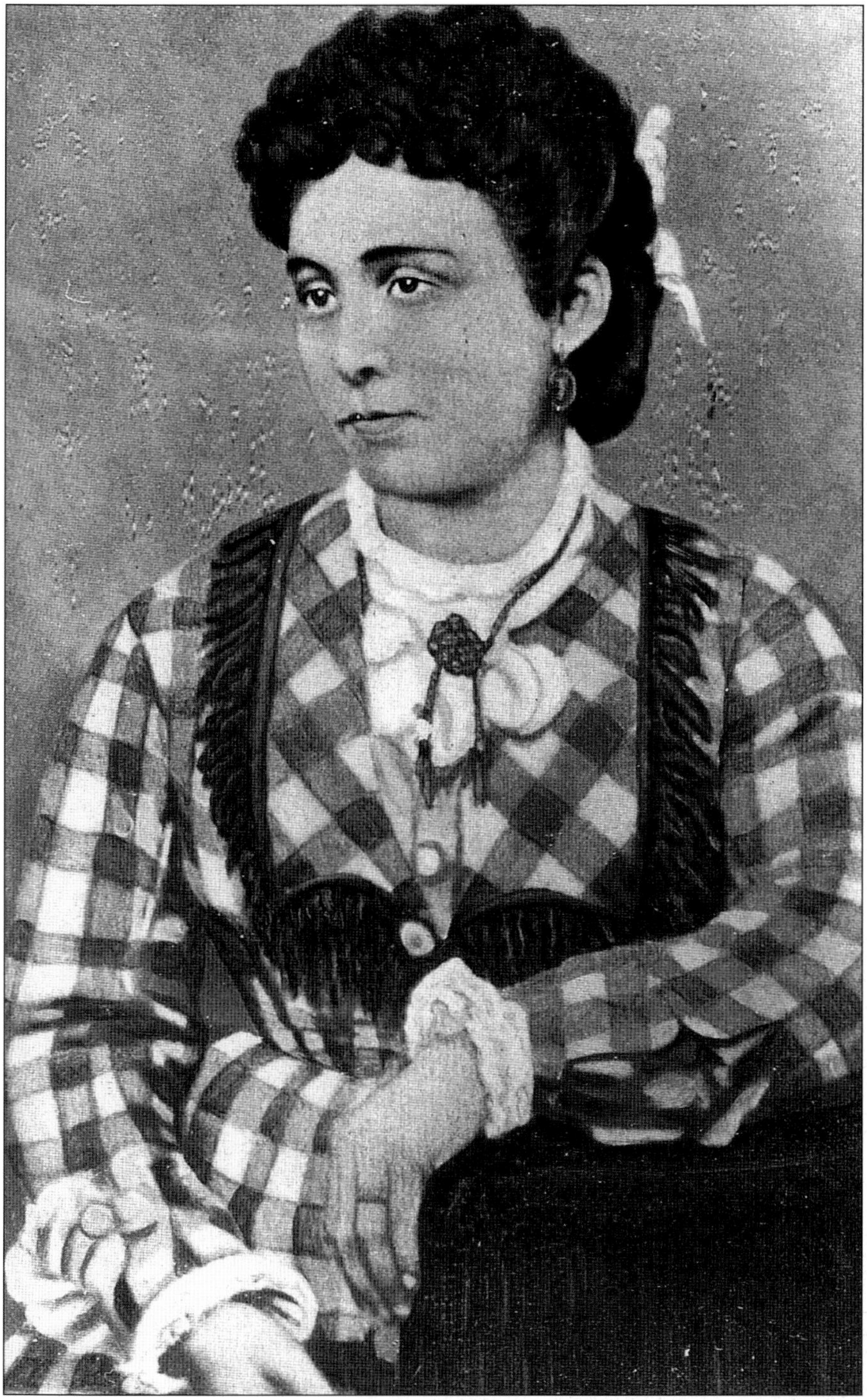

This portrait of Amanda Dickson shows her in a peaceful mood. She fought against her family for several years to receive her father's inheritance. Amanda lived next door to the first house in Augusta to be wired for electricity. (Courtesy of Sean Joiner, Private Collection.)

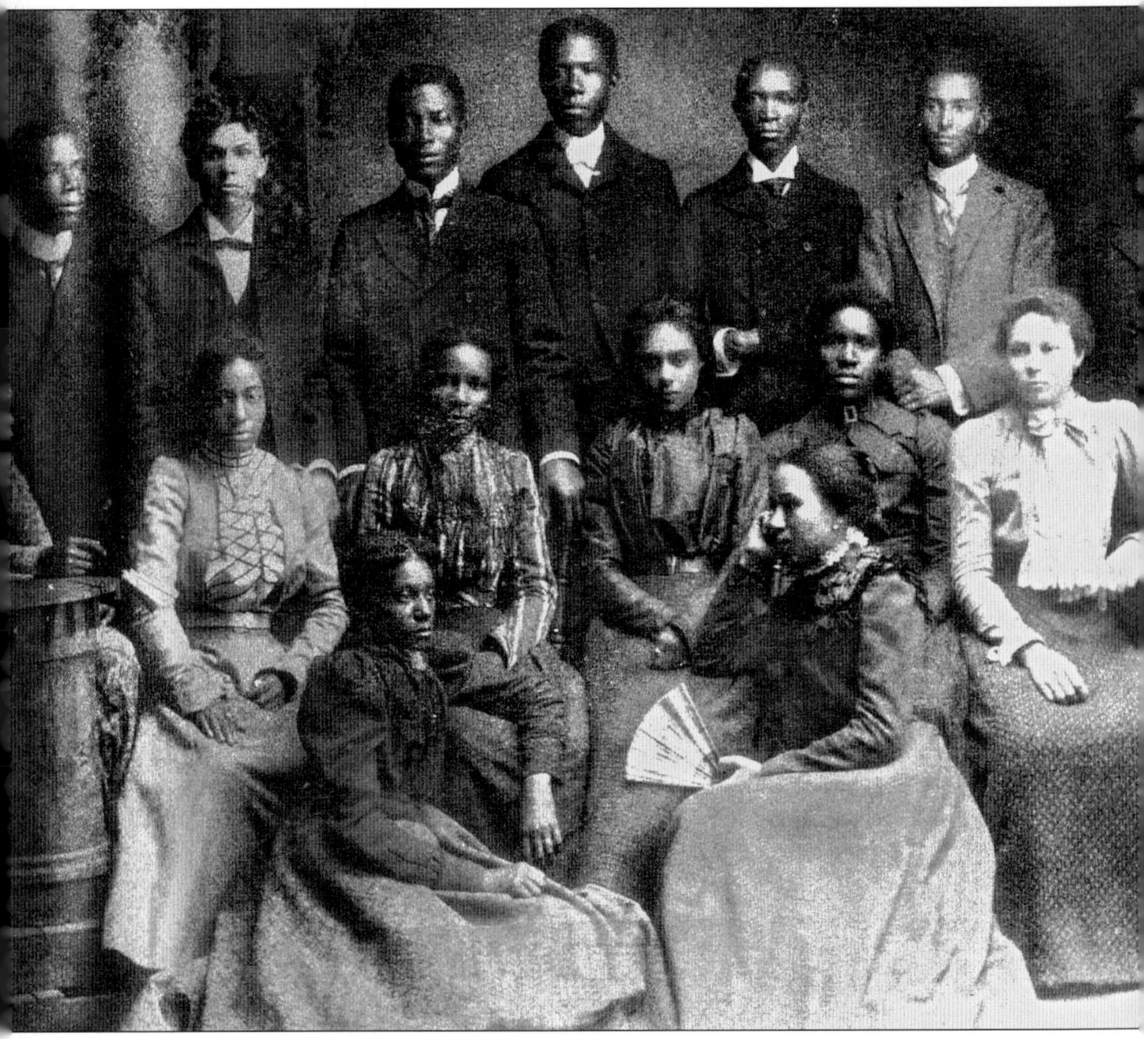

The Paine College Class of 1901 poses for its graduate photograph. These young men and women carried on the proud heritage of African-American higher education. (Courtesy of Paine College.)